THE GENDER FACTORY

The Apportionment of Work in American Households

THE GENDER FACTORY

The Apportionment of Work in American Households

Sarah Fenstermaker Berk
University of California, Santa Barbara
Santa Barbara, California

PLENUM PRESS • NEW YORK AND LONDON

Library of Congress Cataloging in Publication Data

Berk, Sarah Fenstermaker.
  The gender factory.

  Bibliography: p.
  Includes index.
  1. Housewives—United States. 2. Sexual division of labor—United
States. 3. Home economics—United States. I. Title.
HD6073.H842U62 1985   305.3   84-24861
ISBN 0-306-41795-2

©1985 Plenum Press, New York
A Division of Plenum Publishing Corporation
233 Spring Street, New York, N.Y. 10013

Printed in the United States of America

To all the Vesles—for their loving versatility

And to my mother

Acknowledgments

This book has been a long time in the making. Its role as the "second question" in a larger research project, its timing as a "post-tenure" monograph, and the demands of the analysis itself has meant a longer time from conception to fruition. It has also meant that greater numbers of people have made valuable contributions to it.

Those who lent time and encouragement to the original household labor research project have been acknowledged in an earlier monograph (Berk and Berk, 1979), but I must again thank Eliot Liebow of the Center for the Study of Metropolitan Problems at NIMH for his early and crucial support of the project. In 1976, there was no household labor research "bandwagon," but Eliot Liebow heard the drums anyway.

Since then, I have been fortunate to receive additional support through the University of California, Santa Barbara Academic Senate research funds, and through a UCSB Faculty Career Development Award. Another taken-for-granted but nonetheless critical source of support came from the facilities and staff of UCSB's Social Process Research Institute. Those who actually have a "room of one's own" know there there is no more valued possession. SPRI provided me with mine.

A number of students and staff gave time to the complicated data processing and manuscript preparation required by the project. Chris Allen, Nancy Blum, Trina Marks Miller, David Rauma, Tony Shih, and Karen Steinberg earned my gratitude many times over for the care they took with my work.

I am especially grateful to those colleagues who read portions of the manuscript in its various incarnations over a three year period. The student members of the Department of Sociology's Graduate Seminar on Gender Research provided direction in both early and later stages of the writing. The first and last chapters benefited greatly from the meticulous attentions of Phyllis Newton and Vesle Fenstermaker.

Through their own innovative work on gender, Spencer Cahill, Candace West, and Don Zimmerman provided me with just the intellectual push I needed to integrate some of my own thinking. And their unexpected enthusiasm about my work ultimately made me value my argument concerning the accomplishment of gender through the apportionment of household labor. I also thank Peter Rossi for orchestrating the final push to publication of the book. His attention to the work, his encouragement, and his sponsorship, made the transition from manuscript to publication a painless one.

Without the advice, criticism, and support given me by my husband, Richard Berk, this book would still have been written. But, undoubtedly it would have suffered in many important respects. It would surely have been less honest, more tentative, and most importantly, less "mine." His ability and willingness to influence others by encouraging *their* best— and not solely his own—makes Richard Berk my most valued colleague and friend.

Finally, I owe a continuing debt of gratitude to those project respondents, friends, and women I know only through their own writings, who have (over the last decade) patiently taught me what it is—what it must be—to practice feminist scholarship. By example and through the immediacy of their own needs, they have shown me the seductiveness of producing polemic dressed up as scholarship, or "acceptable" scholarship dressed up as service to women. In either instance, the experience of women is denied, and both feminism and scholarship lose. Thus, whatever is of value in this work owes a great deal to the experience, knowledge, and past trials of other women.

Contents

CHAPTER 1

Conceptualizing the Division of Household Labor

INTRODUCTION

It is now more than 20 years since our attention was first directed to the "problem that has no name" (Friedan, 1963). In the decades that followed, a great many people—among them a number of social scientists—embarked on a search for the "right" name for the "wrongs" of women. Along the way, we "discovered" women's growing labor force participation and its concomitant occupational sex segregation (e.g., Gross, 1968; Bowen and Finegan, 1969); male/female wage differentials and sex discrimination (e.g., Mincer, 1962; Cain, 1966); the tyranny of biological, psychological, and medical labels for women's complaints (e.g., Chesler, 1972; Ehrenreich and English, 1978; Smith and David, 1975); violence against women as more than perverted "love" (e.g., Millett, 1970; Brownmiller, 1975; Griffin, 1979; Walker, 1979); and most recently, male dominance in the everyday business of communication (e.g., Fishman, 1978; Zimmerman and West, 1975; West, 1982). The list goes on, with the manifestations of the "problem" stretching across class, culture, and social setting.

Yet, it is of more than passing interest that Friedan's awareness of the "problem" emerged from conversations with housewives:

> Each suburban wife struggled with it alone. As she made the beds, shopped for groceries, matched slipcover material, ate peanut butter sandwiches with her children, chauffeured Cub Scouts and Brownies, lay beside her husband at night. (1963, p. 15)

1

Perhaps it is in such activities—the myriad tasks marked by repetitiveness, fragmentation, and isolation—that the problem most profoundly eludes classification. It is in the household that the work women do goes unacknowledged, unresearched, and even unnamed.

The household, the family, and women have nevertheless attracted the attention of social scientists. Sociologists and economists particularly have seen the family as an ideal context for addressing a vast range of research questions. Among other things, the family has been conceptualized as a location for consumer decision-making (e.g., Foote, 1961), an arena for bargaining and exchange between spouses (e.g., Scanzoni and Szinovacz, 1980), and a battleground for both class oppression and class struggle (e.g., Humphries, 1977; Sokoloff, 1980). Yet, judging from the attention given to it, the family in the abstract, rather than in actuality, has been the only fit subject for legitimate research interest.[1] Most perspectives carry the clear message that the productive process—real work—goes on elsewhere. Activities within households are at best trivialized as mere indicators of larger, more central family phenomena.

To move beyond that particular limited vision, this book concerns itself with household *labor*—specifically, the allocation of that labor among household members.[2] From both a theoretical and an empirical standpoint, this book follows logically from a previous attempt to describe and analyze the organization of household work; its structure, characteristics, and arrangement in time (Berk and Berk, 1979). Once the questions of what constitutes household work activities and how they are organized, were addressed, an examination of how those activities are allocated to household members was made possible. Even though there are many differences between the earlier analysis and the present one, the focus in both is on the *work* of the household. Now, as then, the assumption is that households must accomplish tasks on a routine basis. And like other work organizations, they must apportion those tasks through arrangements that are relatively well understood by the members. The analysis rests on the assumption that household work fundamentally shapes the material life of household members, and from the decisions made to

---

[1]See the useful distinction by Rapp (1978) between the household as an *actual* location for living and the family as a *normative* concept of that location.

[2]For the purposes of this introductory discussion, I use the term *household labor* to denote all household and family maintenance activities undertaken by family members on a routine basis. The next chapter presents a more detailed discussion of the operationalizations of household labor employed in the analysis. For the time being, however, I will trust the reader's commonsense notions of what constitutes household labor—as long as they include child care.

manage everyday existence flow a good many consequences for the members' relations with one another.

Of course, we are not talking about just any work organization; there is a *household* in *household labor*. Within the context of everyday household labor, a great many other dramas are played out; exchanges are negotiated, power and authority are exercised, and partners come to know whether their marriages were made in heaven, hell, or somewhere in between. However, in large part, such dramas are realized through and defined by how the job of living gets done. What is to be done, and how much, how long it takes to do it, and what conditions it is done under—all affect the quality of life and determine our experience of it. Thus, the primary objective of this book is a straightforward analysis of the allocation of household work tasks and time. As a necessary part of that analysis, total household productive activity—through employment and household labor—serves as an initial focus. With that accomplished, household members' judgments about the equity of their household-labor arrangements are the basis for a reconceptualization of household production, gender, and the relationship between them.

A variation on the model of household production provided by the New Home Economics will serve as a guide to the initial specification of the equations analyzed. An appreciation of why this framework was chosen and what it brings to the study of the division of household labor requires, first, a short summary of the empirical work to date and, second, a brief discussion of two influential sociological perspectives relevant to household labor.

WHO DOES WHAT: SOME EMPIRICAL GENERALIZATIONS

A minimal interest in the allocation of household labor supports an empirical tradition with little continuity in conceptualization, method, analysis, or ultimate direction. Taken together, the prior empirical studies of the division of household labor constitute a patchwork of styles, with great variance in quality and little possibility of clear comparison.

Limits of Generalizability

To begin, one finds important substantive and methodological differences in the data employed for study of the division of domestic labor. Conclusions have been derived from estimates of family members' time allocations (e.g., Cowles and Dietz, 1956; Morgan, Sirageldin, and Baerwaldt, 1966; K. E. Walker, 1973; Chapin, 1974; Meissner, Humphreys, Meis, and Sheu, 1975; Stafford, Backman, and Dibona, 1977; Walker and Woods, 1976; Robinson, 1977a; Berk and Berk, 1979; Pleck and Rustad, 1980; Stafford and Duncan, 1980); dollar-value contributions (e.g., Gauger, 1973; Walker and Gauger, 1973); and patterns of relative participation in selected household tasks (e.g., Blood and Wolfe, 1960; Komarovsky, 1962; Lopata, 1971; Bahr, 1974; Oakley, 1974; Berheide, Berk, and Berk, 1976; Berk and Berk, 1978; Perrucci, Potter, and Rhoads, 1978; Eriksen, Yancey, and Eriksen, 1979). In the most general sense, studies that focus on members' *time* allocations (e.g., the time spent in "cleaning house") and those based on measures of the members' *task* allocations (e.g., who "cleans the house") show roughly comparable findings. Yet, very little attention has been given either to the source of disparate findings, or to the substantive implications of employing quite different units of measurement.

Second, whether measured as time or task contributions, there are genuine differences in how household labor is operationalized. In general, very little methodological attention is devoted to how these internally differentiated work activities should be defined. Somehow, everyone "knows" what activities constitute household work, and thus, empirical categorization is thought to be a relatively minor problem. Much greater attention is paid, for instance, to the ability of *respondents* to accurately estimate the time spent on specific household activities (e.g., Robinson, 1977a). Nevertheless, the ultimate classification of household activities and the application of *researcher* coding schemes to that classification are deemed problematic only in that activities should be grouped "commonsensically." The resulting estimates of either time or task allocation may be based on significantly different "job" components. (For further discussion, see Berk and Berheide, 1978.) More will be said in the next chapter about the rationale behind the definition of household work used for this analysis.

Third, what constitutes the "doing" of household labor often remains a mystery. As Oakley (1974) pointed out, for example, some measures of household labor tap normative rather than behavioral patterns of participation. More important perhaps is her distinction between "help" with household labor and "responsibility" for it. A number of studies have ignored this critical dimension, so that mere participation in a task—at any level—"counts" as full responsibility for it (e.g., Blood and Wolfe, 1960; Silverman and Hill, 1967; Eriksen *et al.*, 1979). For example, those attempting to measure husbands' household-labor contributions have typically asked wives if their husbands "help" with household labor and have (sometimes) asked how often help is forthcoming (e.g., Bott, 1957; Hoffman, 1963; Gavron, 1966; Silverman and Hill, 1967; Safilios-Rothschild, 1970; Toomey, 1971). Such methods reveal little about the division of household labor on a day-to-day basis and often obscure the real differences between taking the responsibility for and simple participation in the work of the home. Whether measured by time or task, what it means to do household labor may vary critically across the household and by individual.

Finally, there are less severe methodological problems that nonetheless limit the possibility of meaningful comparisons across studies. For example, one finds frequent reliance on the accounts of a single household member (usually the wife) to determine all members' contributions. (For discussion, see Safilios-Rothschild, 1969; Granbois and Willett, 1970; Booth and Welch, 1978; Douglas and Wind, 1978; Berk and Shih, 1980; Condran and Bode, 1982.) In addition, one might well question the nearly total neglect of children as critical contributors to household labor (for discussion, see Schnaiberg and Goldenberg, 1975; Berk and Berk, 1978; Boulding, 1979; White and Brinkerhoff, 1981), as well as the failure to treat child care as a conceptually distinct, but nevertheless crucial, activity determining the pattern of members' overall household-labor contributions. (For an exception, see Olson, 1979, 1981.) Lastly, almost all formal models are unable to address the role of reciprocal relations between the contributions of household members, or of reciprocal relations between the time spent on household work and paid work. (For discussion see Berk and Berk, 1978.)

Despite these and other shortcomings, which render most findings suspect, over the last decade empirical studies have converged on a number of questions relevant to the division of household labor. Thus, the literature can tell us where to look and even what to look for; what to make of what is found remains a bit more elusive. The following discussion emphasizes the sorts of questions asked most often about the division of household labor tasks and time and, second, the kinds of variables that have proved most promising to an explanation of it.

Empirical Questions

Regardless of the theoretical influences invoked in empirical analysis or of the types of data used, research on the division of household labor typically poses several questions under the "who does what" heading. First, a good deal of empirical effort has been spent in addressing the question of how much time (or how many tasks) women devote to household work and child care (e.g., Walker, 1969; Robinson, Converse, and Szalai, 1972; Szalai, Converse, Feldheim, Scheuch, and Stone, 1972; Meissner *et al.*, 1975; Walker and Woods, 1976; Stafford, 1980) and how the time spent varies over the life cycle (e.g., Lehrer and Nerlove, 1980). A related question is how, historically, the contribution of women to household labor has significantly changed (e.g., Vanek, 1974; Cowan, 1976a,b, 1983; Robinson, 1977a, 1980; Strasser, 1982).

Second, those factors that seem to markedly affect wives' household-labor time (or tasks) are of interest, with particular emphasis on the impact of education, small children, and employment (e.g., Epstein, 1971; Hedges and Barnett, 1972; Walker and Gauger, 1973; Farkas, 1976; Angrist, Lave, and Michelsen, 1976; Meissner, 1977; Berk and Berk, 1979).

Finally, a critical component of almost every study of the division of household labor is the analysis of husbands' household-labor contributions. In part because there is likely to be greater variation in their efforts, and in part because it is often assumed that husbands' participation has markedly increased in the last decade, the household-work participation of men often takes center stage in analyses of the division of household labor. As a result, the greatest empirical attention is typically given to what husbands do in households, and to the factors that accompany their greater or lesser participation. As in analyses of wives' contributions, particularly heavy emphasis is placed on the influence of wives' employment and income, the presence of young children, and the standard "predictors" of husbands' income, occupation, and age. These interests are salient in the growing "dual-career" literature (e.g., Scanzoni, 1970, 1978; Rapoport and Rapoport, 1971, 1976, 1978; Garland, 1972; Holmstrom, 1972; Bahr, 1974; Pleck, 1977, 1979; Perrucci *et al.*, 1978; Berk, 1979; Pleck and Rustad, 1980; Pleck, Staines, and Lang 1980; Model, 1982; Pleck and Staines, 1982). In addition, there are considerations of the differential nature of wives' and husbands' contributions to household labor and child care, as well as the likelihood of task segregation by gender (e.g., Oakley, 1974; Berk, 1979; Berk and Berk, 1979).

Largely because of the great differences in method, technical sophistication, and quality represented in the empirical literature on the division of household labor, there is disagreement surrounding both the substantive and practical significance of the findings, and even their overall validity. It is thus tempting to dismiss generalizations across studies that have often been ill conceived and laden with serious shortcomings. Yet, if one is judicious and takes a slightly longer view, it is possible to identify some relatively uniform and stable patterns of findings to answer a few simple empirical questions.

Some Tentative Answers to Who Does What

To begin, the total time spent by married women on household labor is substantial and remains so regardless of most household or biographical characteristics. Contemporary aggregate time estimates range from approximately 30 to 60 hours per week for wives' contributions to household labor. These estimates mean that, on the average, wives contribute about 70% of the total time that all members spend on household work. However, estimates can vary primarily because of the differences in wives' employment and fertility, time and task measurement, the level of aggregation of time or tasks, and the ways in which household labor is operationalized (e.g., Morgan *et al.*, 1966; Meissner *et al.*, 1975; Berheide *et al.*, 1976; Nickols, 1976; Walker and Woods, 1976; Robinson, 1977a; Hartmann, 1981b).

Important historical changes in the content of household work and in the standards applied to it are masked by aggregate estimates of time spent. The content and nature of domestic labor may have undergone profound transformation, whereas the total time spent on it remains virtually unchanged. (For examples, see Cowan, 1976a, 1983; Strasser, 1982.) Nevertheless, longitudinal time totals strongly suggest that over the last 50 years, household labor has been, and is, "woman's work." Significant variations in wives' household-labor efforts are not explained by heightened contributions from other household members. The aggregate changes that have occurred in the married woman's household-work time can be accounted for by demographic changes in employment and fertility, rather than by a reallocation of time or tasks among members. (For discussion, see Vanek, 1974, 1980; Robinson, 1980.)

Second, there is strong evidence that the two most critical determinants of wives' household-labor time are children and employment. Although the presence of children (especially young children) markedly increases the total time that *all* household members spend on household work and child care, it is *women's* employment and leisure time that are most affected by the increased time and task demands made by children (e.g., Walker and Woods, 1976; Meissner, 1977; Berk and Berk, 1979).

Further, previous research has quite clearly demonstrated that wives' employment commitments can fundamentally influence, and can be influenced by, the time spent on household labor and child care (e.g., Presser and Baldwin, 1980; Waite, 1980). Depending on the level of their employment, wives who also work *outside* the home do spend less time on household labor than their unemployed counterparts. However, the *total* number of work hours per week for employed wives (the hours spent working in and outside the home) exceeds the total for full-time housewives (e.g., Hedges and Barnett, 1972; Walker and Gauger, 1973; Walker and Woods, 1976). Moreover, the time budget diaries of employed wives show that much weekend leisure time is sacrificed to household labor (e.g., Szalai *et al.*, 1972; Meissner *et al.*, 1975; Robinson, 1977a; Meissner, 1980). Thus, the practical effects of employment on wives' household labor are limited primarily to the "shortcuts" that wives can apply to their work; a reapportionment of domestic chores among household members is very unlikely.

Given all the attention it draws, the empirical evidence surrounding the household-labor and child-care contributions of husbands is more consistent than one might imagine. In a great number of studies, using quite disparate methods, the level of husbands' contributions consistently appears to be small. Aggregate time estimates of husbands' household work hours converge on 10–15 hours per week, or an average of 15% of the total time devoted by all household members (e.g., Walker and Woods, 1976; Pleck 1977, 1979; Robinson, 1977a; Berk and Berk, 1978, 1979). And like the very different level of their wives' participation, the husbands' contributions remain relatively stable across household and background characteristics.

Although husbands of employed wives and fathers with young children seem to participate in household labor and child care at higher levels than husbands in different circumstances (e.g., Holmstrom, 1972; Bahr, 1974; Farkas, 1976; Pleck, *et al.*, 1980; Pleck and Rustad, 1980), the practical significance of that participation is certainly debatable (e.g., Meissner *et al.*, 1975; Meissner, 1977; Berk and Berk, 1978; Berk, 1979; Hartmann, 1981a). A strong case can be made for concluding that, apart from some relatively minor variations generated by background characteristics (e.g., class, race, and age), the minimal participation of husbands in household labor and child care (relative to that of wives) is virtually a constant. (For a detailed discussion of selected prior research, see Pleck,

1983.) For example, Walker and Woods (1976) found that those wives with the *longest* total work weeks (employment hours plus household labor hours) were those married to men with the *shortest* total work weeks. Thus, husbands' employment time may be responsive to wives' employment time, but husbands' household-labor time seems to remain relatively stable, regardless of the extrahousehold demands that their wives face. Thus, the general picture is one of stability, with the total amount of work to be done and the wives' work being affected by forces largely exogenous to the household.

Despite these broad generalizations, one might assume that wives and husbands would nonetheless share in the day-to-day work of the household. The evidence argues otherwise, however, as virtually all analyses of what tasks wives and husbands routinely undertake reveal profound sex-typing and gender segregation (e.g., Blood and Wolfe, 1960; Meissner *et al.*, 1975; Berheide *et al.*, 1976; Walker and Woods, 1976; Pleck, 1979). For example, Meissner (1977) noted that, within a pattern of task segregation, a male preference for "functionally specific" work characteristics operates, where the tasks in which husbands are likely to participate have clear and identifiable boundaries (e.g., mowing the lawn), greater discretion in both how and when to complete tasks (e.g., minor household repairs), and greater leisure components (e.g., playing with children).

Finally, although little attention has been given to the *reciprocal* relations between the efforts of wives and husbands, some of my own work suggests that understanding *when* husbands participate in household labor may be as revealing as knowing what tasks they undertake. Through a longitudinal analysis of the household day (Berk, 1979; Berk and Berk, 1979), we found that husbands' participation depended significantly on their wives' availability. As one might expect, employed wives and mothers with small children were often unavailable for some tasks and turned to their husbands for "help." Under these circumstances, the husbands' participation increased—until such time as the wives could resume the tasks. Thus, within the context of the wives' available time *and* their responsibility for household labor, husbands could show periodic increases in contribution (see Vanek, 1980, for review).

Although there is much still to learn about the mechanisms by which the division of household labor is realized, the overall descriptive picture is difficult to refute; wives are both responsible for and accomplish most routine household labor and child care. Husbands (and children) may be pressed into service as secondary sources of intermittent labor, but they remain the primary recipients of household services. In her conclusion to a summary of empirical studies on household labor Hartmann (1981a) wrote:

> The rather small, selective, and unresponsive contribution of the husband to housework raises the suspicion that the husband may be a net drain on the family's resources of housework time—that is, husbands may require more household work than they contribute. (p. 383)

Thus, in the study of how household work is divided among household members, one begins from work with vastly different meanings for wives and husbands, within a living environment shared by them. It is this juxtaposition of a shared work environment and quite different attachments to the work that makes the division of household labor a crucial topic for understanding the relationship of work and gender within the family.

Most of the empirical studies just reviewed have been informed by traditional sociological perspectives on women's work. In particular, two theoretical frameworks deserve discussion, as both have left some mark on the ways in which the division of household labor is posed as a research problem. More important, the argument will be made that both fall short as useful perspectives for the direct study of household labor *as* work.[3]

TRADITIONAL CONCEPTUAL FRAMEWORKS: TWO EXAMPLES

Only a minimal exposure to studies of the division of household labor is sufficient for one to conclude that the "conjugal power" school of family relations has proved crucial to the definition of the conceptual terrain on which the allocation of family work is addressed. No theoretical tradition has had more impact on the empirical study of household work than has "conjugal" or "family power." Yet, within this sociological frame of reference, an accurate rendering of the realities of household labor has never constituted a clear objective.

A second and markedly different conceptual frame is influenced by

---

[3]This short review is certainly not meant to provide an exhaustive treatment of the important theoretical strands informing the study of the division of household labor. Instead, two examples of more traditional conceptual frameworks are introduced to illustrate the general neglect of domestic labor as it is organized within households.

both a feminist and a Marxist perspective. Centering on a consideration of the status of household labor under capitalism and the functions of household work for the reproduction of labor power, this framework has affected the ways in which household labor is conceived of theoretically. It has, however, done very little to influence the empirical study of domestic labor. A discussion of these two theoretical traditions will illustrate the need for a different approach to delineating the determinants of the division of household work.

Household Labor as Family Power

Much of what is supposed to occur between wives and husbands has been studied from a perspective emphasizing power processes and outcomes. At the risk of reducing complicated academic disputes to a single issue, it can be argued that under the general rubric of *conjugal power* are also found discussions of *role and authority patterns, exchange and choice, family role typologies,* and *family decision-making.* It is beyond the scope of this chapter to provide an exhaustive summary of past or present themes in the study of family power. Fortunately, some enlightening reviews are available which illustrate that the concepts of family power derive from a variety of traditional sociological perspectives[4] and are plagued by serious problems of substance and method (e.g., Safilios-Rothschild, 1970; Cromwell and Olson, 1975b; Scanzoni, 1979; Sprey, 1979; McDonald, 1980). More important to our present purposes is some understanding of the role that the family power framework has played in the study of the division of household work. Specifically, I will briefly consider the status of household labor within the family power framework and then go on to identify a few of the implicit assumptions and the troubling features of "resource theory."

To begin, it is clear that the theoretical status of household labor has

---

[4]For example, at first blush, it might seem that the structural functionalist approach to the family would have much to say about the division of household labor. Indeed, a good deal of the work to be reviewed rests in part on the original notions of Parsons and Bales (1956) concerning role structure. Yet, a reliance on "roles" rather than on activities or behavior poses real difficulties. A case in point is the "instrumental/expressive" distinction associated with extra- and intrahousehold activities, respectively. Empirically, this distinction would suggest that "expressive" functions might include child care, dusting, mowing the lawn, and reading the newspaper. Clearly, there are important differences among these activities in any reasonable definition of expressiveness, even though all are undertaken at home. Indeed, it is easy to get the impression that household work activities do not fit anywhere within the Parsons–Bales framework.

very little to do with an interest in the work itself, or in the everyday activities of families. Instead, and in general, household labor (largely undefined) is characterized as a *domain,* a *sphere of influence,* or a *locale* for the exercise of power, decision-making, and conflict. Historically, family power has been measured as an "outcome," rather than as a "process" (for discussion, see Scanzoni, 1972, 1979), so that a few household tasks have been treated as "elements" in an array of decisions faced by spouses, with each a location for the realization of power between members. Not incidentally, within the family power tradition, household-labor task allocation is sometimes characterized as an *outcome* of differential power between the spouses (i.e., the less "powerful" spouses do more household labor) and is sometimes cast as an *indicator* of differential spousal power (i.e., if wives do more household labor, they must wield less power). Yet, regardless of the way in which household-labor allocation is conceptualized and measured (for examples, see Kenkel, 1957; Hoffman, 1963; Hallenbeck, 1966; Safilios-Rothschild, 1969; Young and Wilmott, 1973; Scanzoni, 1978), the result is the same; household labor is "about" power. That is, the perspective requires that one view the work of the household as a *mirror*—reflecting power relations—rather than as a *window,* revealing what and how everyday work is accomplished. The impression conveyed is that it is power and not the sustenance of families that is produced through household labor.

Despite this unequivocal conceptual terrain, virtually every sociologist interested in the empirical study of household labor has been influenced by the tradition of family power. Perhaps some found that, although the treatment of household labor within the family power framework did not have much to do with household work, at least it acknowledged a set of household activities worth serious consideration. In short, the family power framework first opened the door to the study of household labor—and then refused us entrance.

A collection of loose formulations referred to as *resource theory* has constituted the primary orienting framework for the empirical study of household labor and conjugal power. Following Wolfe's (1959) definition of social power as the differential control of resources that are valued by others to satisfy needs, *resources* (variously defined and operationalized) seemed ideal variables for an examination of the relative "power" between wives and husbands.

Yet it was not until Blood and Wolfe's general study of marital power (1960) that "resources" and "resource theory" were applied empirically, with the division of household tasks constituting only one locus for the exercise of family power processes. With resources typically operationalized as tangible socioeconomic characteristics of members (e.g., occupation, education, and income), a vast number of studies were undertaken to explore the efficacy of "resource theory" (e.g., Buric and Zecevic, 1967; Safilios-Rothschild, 1967; Lamouse, 1969; Scanzoni, 1972; Bahr, 1974). The findings were both promising and perplexing enough to encourage an equally large number of substantive and methodological critiques from family power researchers. The most interesting of these centered on pleas for more sensitive articulation of (1) a greater range of relevant resources and the perceived opportunity costs of alternatives (e.g., Heer, 1963; Safilios-Rothschild, 1976); (2) the relation of resources to power (e.g., Rodman, 1967; Liu, Hutchinson, and Hong, 1972; Corrales, 1975); (3) the relation of resources to normative orientations in determining power outcomes (e.g., Rodman, 1967; Burr, 1973; Johnson, 1975; Cromwell and Olson, 1975a); and (4) the importance of unequal exchanges between partners (e.g., Bernard, 1973; Safilios-Rothschild, 1976).

More recently, arguments have been made for the incorporation of resource theory into a more parsimonious framework of exchange and choice (e.g., Nye, 1978, 1979, 1980; Scanzoni, 1978, 1979). Others have called for the use of a conflict perspective as a guiding framework for the study of family processes (e.g., Sprey, 1969, 1979). These untried perspectives hold some promise for the study of family bargaining processes (e.g., Scanzoni, 1976, 1978; Scanzoni and Szinovacz, 1980). However, such frameworks may fall short in the study of the organization and allocation of household labor, as they are based on a model of the household where *scarce* resources (critical to the nature of exchanges and decision-making) are ignored.

When applied to household labor, resource theory has proved inadequate to explain the division of domestic work tasks as a complicated, multidimensional, and internally differentiated work process. In analyses typically characterized by little more than a few zero-order correlations and cross-tabulations, it is implicitly reasoned that if relative spousal power is determined by relative resources, and if particular divisions of labor reflect differential spousal power, then relative *resources* can also be conceptualized as *determinants* of the division of household tasks. It is clear that this sort of causal model may prove troublesome. More distressing are the implicit assumptions about household labor itself that lie behind the application of resource theory.

Simply put, resource theory maintains that those members with greater resources (e.g., a higher education, a higher income, and more prestigious occupations) have greater social power and thus can compel those with fewer resources (and less power) to undertake the "onerous" work of the household. Thus, the first implicit assumption is that household labor is largely, if not exclusively, a source of *disutility*. That is, it must be unpleasant and boring, and must provide very little satisfaction. Second, it follows that if household labor is a source of disutility, then surely one would need to possess greater social power, or more resources, to compel someone else to do it. That a good many people engage in household work quite willingly and derive considerable satisfaction from many of its tasks (e.g., Berheide *et al.*, 1976; Arvey and Gross, 1977; Cannon, 1978; Wright, 1978; Ferree, 1976, 1980) is completely ignored by the assumptions underlying the resource framework.

Moreover, the conceptualization and operationalization of resources has proved a hindrance to the development of empirical models to explain the division of household labor. The resource perspective itself provides no guidelines for deciding what constitutes a "resource" that might determine the allocation of household labor tasks, and no clear criteria for assuring reliable measurement of resources. Somewhat ironically, in their original study of marital power, Blood and Wolfe (1960, p. 74) stated that with respect to the division of household labor, "resources" represent (1) the available time to devote to household tasks and (2) the relative productivity (i.e., skill) of members to accomplish them. Nevertheless, socioeconomic variables typically have become reified as *direct* measures of resources (and therefore power), and as explanatory variables they take primacy over almost all other household characteristics. In short, more grounded and sensible measures of the potential determinants of work organization are lost to abstract measures of family power.

It can be argued, therefore, that the study of the division of household labor as one element of family power is plagued by the limitations of the parent framework, by the serious distortions resulting from unexamined assumptions, and by the lack of a meaningful model of the nature of the work activities themselves. Those who have studied "who does what" under the aegis of family power face the same grim state of affairs outlined by Sprey (1975) in his general comment on the power framework: "We have not yet reached agreement among ourselves on what we need to know about power in families, nor do we seem to have a clear idea of what to do with the knowledge once it is obtained" (p.

61). At the same time, Blood and Wolfe's observations (1960), although questionable on other grounds, seem to have gone unheeded in succeeding studies of household labor "as" family power:

> This is not to say that there is no connection between power and the division of labor. . . . But the two variables are related continuously to each other rather than clustering where the classical typology says they should. . . . Power and the division of labor are aspects of marriage which may coexist in almost any combination. As a result, they are best considered separately rather than welded into artificial combinations. (p. 54)

The earlier review of work on the division of household labor made it clear that despite the limitations imposed by the family power framework, considerable progress has been made, at least in describing who is likely to do what in the household. That relatively stable findings emerge, however, is testimony primarily to the stability of household-labor allocations, and not to the sensitivity of research design and method. Thus, before we conclude what *other* processes are captured by the everyday division of household tasks and time, the apportionment of work activities should be studied on its own terms. In short, at least initially, household labor could be conceptualized as being *about* household labor. A definition of what else it may be must wait for an empirical examination.

Household Labor as the Reproduction of Labor Power

From a vastly different theoretical orientation and purpose, the nature of domestic labor emerged as a critical component of a socialist-feminist analysis of the status of women. As a response to the exclusion of women from traditional Marxist treatments of social relations, feminist theorists attempted to apply existing conceptual frameworks to a theory of gender and male domination; the result was what Young (1980, 1981) termed the "dual systems theory."[5] Some compelling questions of inequality motivated this activity. For example, a successful application of Marx's theory of value to women's work held promise for addressing (1) the origins of women's subjugation; (2) the position of women as a

---

[5]According to Young's convincing critique (1980), dual systems theory asserts that "two distinct and relatively autonomous systems" interact to produce women's oppression: "the system of male domination, most often 'patriarchy,' produces the specific gender oppression of women; the system of the mode of production and class relations produces the class oppression and work alienation of most women" (p. 170).

subordinated gender class under capitalist social relations; (3) the relationship between the sexual division of labor and the division of labor under capitalism; and (4) the connection between "class" and "caste" interests with respect to the revolutionary potential of women and men. However derivative in its scope, this new theoretical tradition was most important for its formal acknowledgment of women's labors in general and for its conscious refusal to trivialize women's oppression. Indeed, this early work set the stage for later and more sophisticated efforts to delineate the interdependence of and contradictions posed by patriarchal social relations and the capitalist mode of production (e.g., Rubin, 1975; Kuhn and Wolpe, 1978b; McDonough and Harrison, 1978; Rapp, 1978; Weinbaum, 1978; Eisenstein, 1979; Hartmann, 1981a,b; Burris, 1980; Sargent, 1980). Terry Fee (1976) summarized the objectives of the early work:

> Such questions as what kind of work women do, what they produce, and what constitutes their relation to the production process are being debated not only to deal with the origin of women's oppression, but primarily to analyze women's role in the revolutionary process, and hence the most productive strategy for organizing women. (p. 1)

As critical referents for a theory of women's oppression, the family and its work took center stage in what is called the *domestic labor debate.* (For a sampling of issues, see Malos, 1980.) Yet, existing Marxist formulations set the terms of the debate from the beginning: With respect to the labor theory of value, what was being "produced" through domestic labor, and what functions did domestic labor serve for capital? It was women's relation to *capitalism,* not women's subordinate relation to men, that was deemed relevant. As Hartmann (1981b) pointed out, "the 'woman question' has never been the 'feminist question' " (p. 2). It would be an empty exercise to detail the theoretical circumlocutions that characterize this literature (Benston, 1969; Rowntree and Rowntree, 1970; Mitchell, 1971; Morton, 1971; Dalla Costa, 1972; Gough, 1972; Gerstein, 1973; Harrison, 1973; Vogel, 1973; Secombe, 1974, 1975; Coulson, Magas, and Wainwright, 1975; Gardiner, 1975; P. Smith, 1978; Weinbaum and Bridges, 1976; Molyneux, 1979).[6] For present purposes, it is the questions raised, rather than the answers given, that are important.

---

[6] I recommend this literature to those with a penchant for the theoretical puzzles posed by the labor theory of value and its relevance to the sexual division of labor. More important, perhaps, it provides a stunning example of what D. E. Smith (1979) called the "line of fault" between received theoretical doctrine and the lived experience of women.

Much of the domestic labor debate centered on the question of whether domestic labor was "productive," "unproductive," neither "productive" nor "unproductive," or something in between. It has been mentioned more than once (e.g., Himmelweit and Mohun, 1977) that Marx himself was quite clear on the definition of productive and unproductive labor. Formally, productive labor is labor that is exchanged (through wages) against capital; it produces surplus value. In contrast, unproductive labor is labor that is exchanged against *revenue*, with no surplus value sought or generated. In either case, however, labor represents the fruits of a market exchange: the selling of the commodity labor power, or the capacity to labor (Marx, 1977, p. 270). Thus, for Marx, the objects of labor and labor power itself could exhibit both use value *and* exchange value (Marx, 1977):

> A thing can be a use-value without being a value. A thing can be useful, and a product of human labour without being a commodity. He who satisfies his own need with the product of his own labour admittedly creates use-value, but not commodities. In order to produce the latter, he must not only produce use-values, but use-values for others, social use-values. (In order to become a commodity the product must be transferred to the other person, for whom it serves as a use-value, through the medium of exchange.) (p. 131)

Yet, because labor power itself is conceived to be a commodity, the activities that sustain it might well be argued to be value-producing. The often peculiar shape of the arguments surrounding the status of household labor were in part determined, then, by how much one was willing to push the old Marxist model to "fit" the everyday household labors of women. As a result, domestic labor was viewed as (1) "private" activities or services that produce directly consumable use values and/or (2) labor that produces the commodity labor power (daily and generationally), to be exchanged on the market. (For a discussion, see Himmelweit and Mohun, 1977; P. Smith, 1978; Folbre, 1982.) Within these two general positions, the specific relation of domestic labor (and by clear implication, women) to capital was developed. With considerably more succinctness than is found in the debate itself, Malos (1978) summarized its concerns:

> Did women in the home produce "use values"?, or because labor power was sold as a commodity did they also produce exchange value? Was the housewife "productive" in capitalist terms because she produced a commodity for exchange, or "unproductive" even though her work was useful, even necessary, in allowing a continuation of capitalist production at the present stage? (p. 47)

This theoretical work acknowledged that the domestic labors of women made the workings of class society possible. Such formulations helped put "work" back in the family and returned the family to capitalist society. In so doing, it made apparent the need for a more detailed consideration of women's oppression (e.g., Rubin, 1975) and a reconceptualization of the relationship between the "private" and the "public" spheres of existence (for discussion and critique, see Zaretsky, 1976; Glazer, 1980; Young, 1981). As Folbre (1982) ended her creative application of Marxist economics to the household:

> The production of commodities does not take place by means of commodities. Commodities are produced by labour, labour comes from labourers, and labourers are themselves produced. The production of commodities takes place by means of the reproduction of labour power. And the reproduction of labour power is fundamentally altered by the expansion of capitalism itself. (p. 328)

Increasingly, however, the home labors of women, as well as the workings of capital, have come to be appreciated as both separate from, and reciprocally affected by, each other (e.g., Fee, 1976; Eisenstein, 1981; Ferguson and Folbre, 1981; Hartmann, 1981b).

But even this sort of "hybrid" model does not escape criticism (see Young, 1980, for a discussion). Albeit with some ambivalence, many now maintain that the subtleties and contradictions posed by women's position in captialist society are ultimately ignored, or obscured by, a model limited to relations centering on the market workplace and wage labor. Because most arguments within the domestic labor debate sidestepped the daily and systematic subordination of women to men, some theorists advocated the abandonment of the Marxist frame. Hamilton (1978) summarized the shortcomings of past theoretical analyses:

> The marxist analysis insists that the position of women can only be properly explored through an analysis of the mode of production and therefore, through an examination of those differences among women which result from their place in the class structure. But a Marxist analysis did not generate questions about the differences between men and women, about the different ideas a society holds with respect to women and men, about how and why those ideas change; questions that deal specifically with female oppression. (pp. 93–94)

Even more critical were Kuhn and Wolpe (1978a):

> It is no coincidence that the attempt to construct analyses of the specificity of the subordination of women in capitalism in terms of orthodox approaches to the labour theory of value through an examination

> of domestic labour encountered such obstacles that attempts of this sort have now been virtually abandoned . . . in subsuming women to the general categories of that problematic—class relations, labour process, the state, and so on, it fails to confront the specificity of women's oppression. (p. 8)

We have yet to hear the last word in the domestic labor debate. Interestingly, however, its tone has changed from angry rejection to reconciliation. Feminist theorists from quite different vantage points are converging in their call for a less derivative, more autonomous feminist critique of patriarchal capitalism, at the same time retaining the metatheoretical lessons of Marx. (For some examples, see D. E. Smith, 1978; Young, 1981; Ehrenreich, 1984).

For example, Hartsock (1983) argued for a feminist materialism that draws on both the epistemological tools of Marx and the experience of women:

> An analysis which begins from the sexual division of labor—understood not as taboo, but as the real, material activity of concrete human beings—could form the basis for an analysis of the real structures of women's oppression, an analysis which would not require that one sever biology from society, nature from culture, an analysis which would expose the ways women both participate in and oppose their own subordination. (p. 304)

Although such goals are laudatory for a theory of women's subordination, a neglect of the actual work of the household—"the real material activity of concrete human beings"—poses its own serious problems for apprehending the nature of household social relations. The admirable goal of delineating "the specificity of women's oppression" or "the real structures of women's oppression" would first demand a rigorous *empirical* examination of domestic labors and their organization. Instead, past analyses have called for attention to the labors of women, but they inevitably locate their interests in the more rarefied air of theory building.

The two theoretical traditions of family power and Marxism were chosen for discussion to illustrate the shortcomings of the *strongest* sociological frameworks relevant to the study of household labor. The simple *acknowledgment* of household labor as critical to the dynamics of family interaction, or as vital to the workings of capitalism, renders these approaches "radical." At the same time, and from opposite ends of the sociological spectrum, the family power framework and Marxist theories of domestic labor converge through a shared malady: an explicit interest in "the family" has led away from an investigation of the material basis from which social relations between men and women are realized. In the former approach, household labor is subsumed under the rubric of family power and decision-making, and there is little direct concern about what prompts and shapes everyday decisions. Likewise, for the perspectives that hold promise by beginning from the point of material production, domestic labors quickly become lost within the abstract workings of capitalism. In each approach, an interest in issues quite distinct from household labor leads to an examination only of the abstracted consequences of production—not of the production itself, nor of the arrangements surrounding it.

Toward an Empirical Framework

What is required is a framework grounded in the notion of the daily production of household commodities. And to be adequate for our purposes, it should be parsimonious (rather than being simply a set of loose formulations), garnering empirical support, perhaps in contexts outside household production. Second, a useful framework should lead to clearly operationalized concepts and provide at least some signed expectations for relationships among variables. Third, a workable frame should be able to explain variance across household patterns, as well as to account for changes in individual households over time. Finally, an empirical framework for the study of household labor should allow for family members' productive activities outside the household as well as within it.

In the next section, I will briefly review three fundamental assumptions underlying such a model of household production. The discussion illustrates why this framework represents a useful starting point for the analysis of the division of household labor; at the same time, it must be viewed as only a first approximation of the social relations surrounding the allocation of household labor tasks and time. The application of this framework to the data will require some modifications if it is to take into account the unique qualities of domestic labor and its apportionment.

THE NEW HOME ECONOMICS: RELUCTANT MATERIALISM

In their recent edited collection, *Feminism and Materialism* (1978b), Kuhn and Wolpe began from Engels's now familiar statement on the production and reproduction of material life[7] to outline the "materialist problematic":

> The materialist problematic is based on a conceptualization of human society as defined specifically by its productivity: primarily of the means of subsistence and of value by the transformation of nature through work. United with this is a conceptualization of history as the site of the transformation of the social relations of production and reproduction. As far as an analysis of the position of women is concerned, materialism would locate that position in terms of the relations of production and reproduction at various moments in history. In doing this, one of its central concerns would be with the determinate character of the sexual division of labour and the implications of this for power relations between men and women at different conjunctures. (p. 7)

When taken as a guide to the ways in which daily household labors would constitute a research agenda, the materialist problematic departs fundamentally from the mainstream treatments previously reviewed. As Young (1980) wrote:

> A feminist historical materialism must be a truly *materialist* theory. This does not mean it must "reduce" all social phenomena to economic phenomena narrowly understood as processes of the production and distribution of material goods. . . . This requirement mainly calls for a methodological priority to concrete social institutions and practices, along with the material conditions in which they take place. (p. 185; emphasis in original)

Historically, neoclassical microeconomic theory has been wedded to a bifurcation of the "productive" market workings of firms and "consumption" by the household. According to this view, through income, households simply "receive" market goods from which utility (i.e., satisfaction) is directly derived. The link between market goods and utility, and thus the inner workings of households themselves, goes unexamined. (For discussion, see Hawrylyshyn, 1976.)

---

[7]Engels (1972) wrote: "According to the materialist conception, the determining factor in history is, in the last resort, the production and reproduction of human life. But this itself is of a twofold character. On the one hand, the production of the means of subsistence, of food, of clothing and shelter and the tools requisite therefore; on the other, the production of human beings themselves, the propagation of the species. The social institutions under which men of a definite historical epoch and of a definite country live are conditioned by both kinds of production: by the stage of development of labour, on the one hand, and of the family, on the other" (pp. 25–26).

More recently, however, this characteristic bifurcation has been challenged through a reconceptualization of the household and of its functions and activities. Largely through the pioneering contributions of Reid (1934) and the work of Becker (1976b, 1981) and others (e.g., Lancaster, 1966), households have become newly conceived of as sites for productive activities. Becker (1976b) wrote:

> The integration of production and consumption is at odds with the tendency of economists to separate them sharply, production occurring in firms and consumption in households. It should be pointed out, however, that in recent years economists increasingly recognize that a household is truly a "small factory": it combines capital goods, raw materials and labour to clean, feed, procreate and otherwise produce useful commodities. (p. 92)

Once the household was reconceptualized as a "small factory," its productive or work activities were rendered "researchable," and the integration of the historically distinct interests of market and home economists was made possible. (For discussion, see Lloyd, 1975.) Although hardly an example of a full-blown model for a materialist analysis of the household, the New Home Economics, and within it Becker's model of household production, does identify household relations as *productive* relations. This identification alone would argue for serious attention to the potential for applying the New Home Economics to the work of the household.

Becker's Model of Household Production[8]

Sociologists unaccustomed to the economist's approach to the study of the empirical world will be struck initially by the simplicity of Gary Becker's household production model. Rather than beginning from a conceptual framework that allows for all *possible* determinants of a social phenomenon, his model begins with a utilitarian perspective from which is formally derived a relatively small set of signed relations that are presumed to reflect some fundamental social processes. Similarly, for

---

[8]There are now a good many discussions and extensions of Becker's original model of household production (e.g., Becker, 1974, 1976a, 1981; Gronau, 1974, 1977; Willis, 1974; Michael and Becker, 1976; Rosenweig, 1977; Wales and Woodland, 1977; Berk, 1980; Berk and Berk, 1983). For our purposes, however, the general outline of the model is the most instructive, and thus the primary source for discussion and application of it is Michael and Becker (1976).

meaningful applications to data, most sociological models require extensive simplification, whereas economic models move from the simple to
the complicated via empirical application. Thus, Becker's model is "economic" in much more than disciplinary orientation.

For present purposes, Becker's model of household production seeks
to address one critical question: How do households allocate their
resources to achieve the greatest possible well-being? More specifically,
the model initially poses a parsimonious framework to account for why
households allocate their resources in particular ways, and to explain
what promotes change in members' allocation of time to the production
of household commodities. As we shall see, the model shares with every other the inability to incorporate all the forces that determine individual members' household labor efforts. Nevertheless, with some
modifications, it can be usefully applied to data and can address some
of the more perplexing questions surrounding the division of household
labor tasks and time.[9]

To begin, Pollack and Wachter (1975) described the household
productive process:

> The household purchases "goods" on the market and combines them
> with time in a "household production function" to produce "com-
> modities." These "commodities," rather than goods are the arguments
> of the household's utility function; market goods and time are not
> desired for their own sake, but only as inputs into the production of
> "commodities." (p. 255)

The household production function rests on the premise that the
sources of household utility (i.e., well-being and satisfaction) are *household* commodities, not market goods, as traditionally conceived. (For discussion, see Hawrylyshyn, 1976.) Given the available resources (including the members' abilities), households will seek to enhance their quality
of life (to maximize utility) through the *combined* optimal allocations of
(1) market goods and services and (2) household members' efforts. With
the goal of utility maximization, households seek the "best" configura-

---

[9]It is necessary to point out that the model of household production does not go on to ask
about the relative *distribution* of the utilities (or the disutilities) generated from household
production. The model is one not of distribution, but of production. Distributional questions are addressed through a complementary theory of marriage (Becker, 1974, 1981, Chapters 3 and 4). For another approach to the distribution of the fruits of household labor, see
Manser and Brown (1980).

tion of inputs, given opportunity costs and productivity. This process of combining the inputs of goods and effort is, not surprisingly, always subject to the dual constraints of income and time.[10]

An "optimal" allocation of resources, under the two constraints of available time and household income, requires that (1) the ratio of the members' marginal productivity within the household equal the ratio of the members' real or foregone wages in the market, and (2) the ratio of the marginal productivity of goods and services to the marginal productivity of given individuals equal the ratio of the price of the goods and services to the wages of household members. (For discussion, see Becker, 1974.) As it was phrased more simply in earlier work (Berk and Berk, 1978):

> In other words, the ratio of the "worth" of household productivity equals the ratio of the "worth" of market productivity. These results are analogous to the maximization processes of consumers or firms and are therefore consistent with more general microeconomic theory. (p. 434)

As a theoretical matter, such relationships hold only for households "at the margin," where resources are optimally allocated within the household, and between home and market, in order to maximize productive output and overall well-being. That it would be difficult (if not impossible) to *find* a household actually "at the margin" does not necessarily do violence to the theoretical power of the model. The world is not stable enough, nor are families responsive enough, to achieve economic equilibrium. Rather, optimization at the margin can be viewed as a target at which households "aim," and as a theoretical baseline from which to discover empirical consistencies and departures. (For a general discussion, see Schultz, 1974; Blaug, 1980.)

More important, the model carries a number of implications for explaining variation in the household production process. For example, it hypothesizes a set of relationships for predicting how changes in the level of available resources (e.g., wealth), price changes in members' time (e.g.,

---

[10]In order to move more swiftly to the empirical analysis, I exclude from this discussion equations illustrating the formal derivations of the model. Also excluded are extensions that allow for time to be allocated to enhance human capital (Becker, 1981, pp. 9–13), as well as its allocation to household and market activities. For those interested in more detailed treatments of the household production function, a number of accessible expositions exist elsewhere (e.g., Michael and Becker, 1976; Berk, 1980; Becker, 1981; Berk and Berk, 1983).

a raise at work), and price changes in other inputs (e.g., the price of electricity) lead to alterations in the efforts contributed to household production by individual members. Addressing such implications, Michael and Becker (1976) commented:

> By incorporating production concepts into the theory of consumption, the household production function approach implies that households respond to the changes in the prices and productivities of factors, to changes in the relative shadow prices of commodities and to changes in their full real income as they attempt to minimize their costs of production and to maximize their utility. A reduction in the price of some factor of production will shift the production process toward techniques that are more intensive in the use of that factor and toward commodities that use the factor relatively intensely. (p. 139)

On its face, this model suggests the possibility of understanding how material production in the household determines the allocation of the members' efforts. And as a conceptual framework, the model of household production represents an important advance over past work that either ignored household activities altogether or simply constructed a world where families made decisions under few constraints and without consideration for the opportunity costs of those decisions. Notwithstanding the model's apparent promise, however, a few fundamental underlying assumptions must be addressed before it can be meaningfully applied to data. These assumptions are the source of some controversy among sociologists and economists alike.

Some Problematic Assumptions[11]

Three closely related assumptions underlie Becker's model of household production. Together, they have shaped both past formulations and past critiques of the New Home Economics. To begin, as the model is concerned with *household* production—the combination of household goods and time to produce utility-generating commodities—it assumes a single utility function for the household. That is, *households,* not individuals, maximize. Interestingly, this assumption is not found in Becker's theory of marriage (1974, 1981, Chapters 3 and 4). There, it is

---

[11]This brief discussion is in no way exhaustive of the first premises and assumptions relevant to the application of the New Home Economics to household production. The reader is directed to the more didactic discussions recommended above.

argued that marriage decisions are based on the self-interested assessments of individuals with respect to the best marriage "bargain" that they can achieve. Yet, once the bargain is struck, and household production begins, a unitary utility function prevails (e.g., Becker, 1976b, 1981). For example, Mahoney (1961) discussed the housewife's choice to enter the labor market as a decision in which *household* utilities are maximized:

> We start with the concept of the spending unit defined as a household of persons who pool their resources to make joint decisions concerning the expenditure of those resources.... The welfare of the entire spending unit is assumed to be the criterion for decision-making. (pp. 12–13)

Of course, this implies that the welfare of *all* members is subsumed within the utility function of *each* member. How such a convenient simplification occurs is unclear, although Becker's analysis of altruism (1981, Chapter 8) provides one perspective. In brief, Becker postulated a head of the household who incorporates the well-being of the other members into his or her own utility function and thus takes all the members into account when decisions are made. It can then be proved that, under certain circumstances, it is in each members' self-interest to cooperate fully. A kind of benevolent autocracy unfolds, with cooperative behavior from all.[12]

The assumption of a single utility function for the household has been roundly criticized over the years, and there is little resolution in sight (e.g., Griliches, 1974; Sawhill, 1980; Ben-Porath, 1982; Berk and Berk, 1983). For example, Nerlove (1974, p. 532) referred to the "John Donne effect" implied by the assumption that the head "incorporates" the welfare of others into decision-making. More generally, he characterized the model as a "condensation of a sequential dynamic set of decisions into a theory of choice based on the maximization of a single, static, timeless

---

[12]In a recent effort to draw some similarities between sociology and the New Home Economics, Geerken and Gove (1983) instead misrepresented both. Simplifying the assumption of a single utility function nearly beyond recognition, they wrote: "Though economists are not generally aware of it, such an assumption is substantially equivalent to the approach in sociology that attempts to explain family structures in terms of their contribution to the life of the *family unit itself*" (p. 16; emphasis added). Not so. Through a host of assumptions, the economic model is one of utility maximization for a *single* decision-maker who can speak for all family members. There is no entity called a family beyond a single utility function that all happen to share. As the following discussion illustrates, this troubles many, even Becker himself (for discussion, see also Berk and Berk, 1983).

utility function." Similarly, Schultz (1974) called for a very different model of the household as a set of *individual* utility functions rather than a single manifestation of a unitary maximizing process requiring full and unbiased knowledge of all members' welfare.

In contrast, others have maintained that this simplifying assumption is necessary to generate *a priori* signed expectations in empirical application. For example, Reid (1977) argued that insofar as households pool their resources for particular productive purposes, they may well be considered a *maximizing* unit.[13] Even some Marxist economists (e.g., Folbre, 1982) have argued from a "household maximization" point of view, apparently without doing violence to the Marxist logic of exploitation. Recent work (Manser and Brown, 1980) retains the traditional perspective of the New Home Economics, but it appears promising for the specification of a model allowing for members' individual utility functions. Yet, this work concerns only the process by which household utility is distributed to members through consumption; it ignores the decision-making surrounding household production.

This brings us to the second assumption: the exclusion of the joint production of commodities in a single household productive process. On its face, the assumption that "one thing gets done at a time" may not seem particularly troubling. And judging from the more vitriolic critiques of the New Home Economics and the household production function (e.g., Ferber and Birnbaum, 1977; Amsden, 1980), it is not of primary concern. After all, one "produces" a "made bed" or a "dinner," and so on. Of course, a question may be raised about the status of *intermediate* products, such as a "fluffed pillow" or "a dish of vegetables." But a more serious result of this assumption is the exclusion of *psychic* (or "process") outcomes linked to productive activities. Satisfaction, pleasure, frustration, boredom, and the like are precluded from the maximizing household's calculus if they result from activities where *in addition* something

[13]Such arguments are vaguely reminiscent of Hartmann's discussion (1981b) of the historically dual nature of families. From a perspective seemingly far removed from the New Home Economics, she wrote: "Yet tensions between households and the world outside them have been documented by family historians and others, and these suggest that households do act as entities with unified interests, set in opposition to other entities. This seeming paradox comes about because, although family members have distinct interests arising out of their relations to production and redistribution, those same relations also ensure their mutual dependence. Both the wife who does not work for wages and the husband who does, for example, have a joint interest in the size of his paycheck, the efficiency of her cooking facilities, or the quality of their children's education" (p. 369).

else is produced. Even a moment's reflection on household work reminds one how pervasive joint production really is. Yet, it is ruled out as fatal to a model that seeks to generate unique signed expressions for estimated parameters under linear budget constraints. (For discussion, see Gronau, 1974, 1977; Reid, 1974; Ryder, 1974; Pollack and Wachter, 1975; Berk, 1980.)

The status of joint production holds very serious implications for the way in which the model formulates the relation between production and consumption. Becker (1976b) was one of the first to point out the flaw in the traditional bifurcation of work and leisure; every "work" activity carries leisure components, and likewise, there is "work" embedded in leisure. For Becker (1976b), *anything* produced by households that results in utility can constitute a commodity (though not in the Marxist sense), with the presence of utility in consumption being the sole criterion for identifying earlier commodity production. Others (Hawrylyshyn, 1976; Gronau, 1977; Wales and Woodland, 1977) are uneasy with this broad definition. For instance, Gronau (1977) has returned to a more traditional distinction between "home production" and "leisure":

> An intuitive distinction between work at home (i.e., home production time) and leisure (i.e., home consumption time) is that work at home (like work in the market) is something one would rather have somebody else do for one (if the cost were low enough), while it would be almost impossible to enjoy leisure through a surrogate. Thus, one regards work at home as time use that generates services which have a close substitute in the market, while leisure has only poor market substitutes. (p. 264)

Although this separation seems empirically sensible, it, too, has been criticized for reintroducing the problem of joint production, as virtually all human activities have some features that fit the "surrogate-impossibility" criterion. (For discussion, see Berk, 1980, p. 127.)

In the next chapter, much more will be said about the development of an operational definition for household labor. At present, the problem is not whether the categories of consumption and production should be separated or combined. On the contrary, in the household production model that excludes joint production, consumption as an activity simply has no place in the formal model, except insofar as it is implied within the process of utility maximization. Households organize the production of commodities *in light of* the maximization of utility through consumption, but the model itself does not acknowledge consumption as part of production, or as occurring simultaneously with it. As Pollack and Wachter (1975) concluded:

> In the household, time spent in various activities is often a direct source of satisfaction or dissatisfaction as well as an input into a production activity. This is a case of joint production, and the household production function is not a suitable framework for analyzing joint production. (p. 271)

Consequently, the act of consuming has theoretical status only as an "end point" in the production process, and as a necessary condition for the generation of utility. It has no formal role in an empirical translation of the model. Yet, in this analysis, consumption operates through some rough measures of psychic rewards and costs.

This brings us to one final assumption that is particularly troubling to sociologists. "Tastes" (preferences not determined by price) are precluded from any real consideration and are usually consigned to the status of a *ceteris paribus* condition. Preferences are treated as being given, as not being subject to theoretical analysis, and as being held constant in empirical models (for discussion, see Becker, 1976a, 1981). The assumption of stable preferences results in a view of the world that many sociologists find untenable. Namely, "preferences are assumed not to change substantially over time, nor to be very different between wealthy and poor persons, or even between persons in different societies and cultures" (Becker, 1974, p. 5). This view has prompted some critics (see, for example, Hannan, 1982) to question the theoretical viability of the household production function.

Although one might justify the neglect of preferences on the grounds that they are not directly "economic," preferences may nevertheless influence household decision-making. Tastes may, in fact, vary across households and thus should be included if specification errors are to be avoided. One feature of the analysis to come will be a consideration of the relative importance of "tastes" in the division of household labor.

It is quite clear that the household production function may fall far short of portraying a complete picture of family relations. The last three assumptions in particular have been the source of long debate and some consternation (e.g., Duncan, 1974; Lloyd, 1975; Pollack and Wachter, 1975; Ferber and Birnbaum, 1977; Berk and Berk, 1978, 1983; Amsden, 1980; Sawhill, 1980; Brown, 1982). As yet, no fundamental transformation of the model has been offered that counters these problematical features and that, at the same time, salvages the model's theoretical power and elegance. More important perhaps, much greater attention to the empirical worth of the model is needed to specify the degree to which it is indeed sensitive to critical processes in household production and the allocation of family work.

In addition to genuine concern about the primary assumptions of the New Home Economics and Becker's model of household production, there have been significant questions raised by the prospect of an empirical application and interpretation of the model.

Additional Problems in the Use of Becker's Model

First, the necessary estimation of the "shadow price" of members' time and their marginal productivities within household production poses both conceptual and empirical problems for the application of Becker's model (e.g., Gronau, 1977; Berk and Berk, 1978; Chiswick, 1982). Often, the price of adult members' time is operationalized as the wage that they command in market activity. Some wage level is usually imputed to those household members who are not employed and for whom there is no observed wage. As one might imagine, this is a rather common procedure necessitated by the occupational position of women; housewives (as well as other women and men not employed) must be "assigned" a wage equivalent to their occupational level *were they to be employed*. Thus, the shadow price of adult members' time is operationalized as the wage that they could command in market activity. Alternatively, the shadow price of time for unemployed household members can be defined as "equal to the marginal product of time in the household sector" (Becker, 1981, p. 7). How such a price could be operationalized, however, is unclear.

An additional quandary attached to the shadow price of time is one posed by the incorporation of children's household productivity into Becker's model. For example, one might estimate a shadow wage for unemployed women by estimating what they could earn were they to enter the labor market. The comparable estimation process for children is perplexing. Indeed, what do children "forgo" that is comparable to the forgone earnings of adults? In principle, one might argue that it is leisure and time spent in human capital enhancement (e.g., time in school and time at homework) that are forgone. Apart from these conceptual issues, the empirical problems of estimating the monetary equivalents of time forgone are overwhelming.[14] No satisfactory solutions have emerged, and thus, any incorporation of children's contributions into empirical models must be undertaken with caution.

Second, and of great importance to those interested in mapping the varied terrain of gender inequality, is the absence of normative and institutional constraints on members' activities within and outside the household. Both those sympathetic to and critical of the New Home Economics have identified this shortcoming in the model of household production (e.g., Hannan, 1982; Berk and Berk, 1983). For example, Nerlove (1974) has pointed to the need to examine institutional constraints that may differentially affect the labor market decisions of men and women. Moreover, with respect to sex-linked norms within the household, Ryder (1974) argued "that it is necessary to specify...those ways in which the decision by the wife to divide her time between the world inside and the world outside the home is a peculiarly constrained choice" (pp. 76–77). In the absence of institutional constraints, structural forces that may lead members to particular household time allocations are ignored.

Although no empirically viable solution has been developed to incorporate institutional and normative constraints into the household production function, some theoretically based suggestions have been made (e.g., Lesourne, 1977). Somewhat naively, Ferber and Birnbaum (1977) concluded that "tradition" accounts for the division of household labor between spouses. Treating "tradition" as a constant, and as not subject to the rationality assumed by microeconomic models of choice, they argued that the process of maximization and the workings of "tradition" are mutually exclusive. In a rejoinder to Ferber and Birnbaum, Robinson (1977b) took issue with the unitary conception of tradition and maintained that decisions informed by traditional normative concerns represent a rational process of choice like any other.

---

[14]An estimate of the opportunity costs of time spent in household work would require estimating the *future* losses that result. Suppose, for example, that a teenaged daughter were to spend two hours per day in household work that might otherwise be spent on homework. Presumably, her performance in school would suffer, and presumably, she would forgo the learning of relevant labor-market skills. However, in order for the forgone costs to be calculated, these "lost" hours must be aggregated, given some monetary value in terms of future forgone wages, and properly discounted to establish the present discounted value of wages forgone (cf. Becker, 1981, pp. 9–13).

In fact, one might easily combine economic models with normative perspectives by allowing norms to affect the preferences that household members bring to the allocation process. Normative preferences between putting children in day-care centers versus caring for them at home, for instance, are implicit in the household utility-maximization process but, to date, have been taken as given. Yet, there is no reason that (at least in empirical work) preferences cannot be allowed to vary. In other words, there is nothing in the household production function that precludes the operation of norms in the determination of household members' preferences among different household commodities. These preferences, in turn, can affect the allocation of the household's efforts. For example, in a more formal exposition, Richard Berk (1980) developed a theoretical alternative where norms are allowed to place additional constraints on the division of work. Thus, the maximization process would proceed only within certain normative boundaries (e.g., if the wife invests at least six hours per day in household labor.) Although the empirical viability of such suggestions has yet to be demonstrated, such new models would, as Hannan (1982) argued,

> recognize that individuals can rebel against norms and coercion and, acting collectively, can change institutional structures. They would also recognize that institutional structures have lives of their own, that they impart inertia to social systems, slowing the speed of response to changed conditions. (p. 71)

Taken together, the assumptions of household utility maximization, of no joint production, and of stable preferences, as well as the problem of shadow price estimation and the neglect of normative and institutional constraints, lead to a more general indictment of the New Home Economics and its models of household production.

Because the model of household production rests on a framework of maximization, it presumes that members will optimally allocate their time and resources in response to members' market and household productivities—their human capital. The question of the "real" worth of members' time often develops into *substantive* explanations heavily laden with normative assumptions. This is especially common in accounts of why the market value of women's time is generally lower than that of men's, and of why women invest more time in household labor and child care than do men. The lower wages that women command in the market are a likely result of discrimination and sex-stratified occupational opportunities, but they are nonetheless accurate representations of the price of women's time as it is defined in the here and now. It is often the case, however, that if one forgets the exogenous and institutional forces that determine wage differentials between men and women, the lower "value" of women's time can "justify" a one-sided division of household labor. That is, *because* women earn lower wages, it is argued, their greater time spent in household labor is "appropriate." Conveniently, this circular argument also "explains" women's lower market wages: because women spend more time in household labor and child care, their commitment to employment is lower, and thus it is "understandable" that their wages will also be lower. Gender roles are influenced by market forces, and market forces are influenced by gender roles. The result, as Ben-Porath (1982, p. 53) pointed out, is the familiar puzzle of distinguishing head from tail.

Ultimately, however, Becker must account for why patterns of market and household specialization and differences in human capital investments take their gender-specific forms. After all, there is nothing inherent in the theory of household production that requires women to be the ones to invest in household-specific human capital and men in market-specific human capital. In reaction, Becker (1981) went far afield from the household production function:

> Although the sharp sexual division of labor in all societies between the market and household sectors is partly due to the gain from specialized investments, it is also partly due to intrinsic differences between the sexes. (p. 21)

That is, some undefined *biological* differences associated with bearing *and* rearing children provide women an initial comparative advantage in household production, relative to men; maximizing households build on this advantage, generating familiar patterns of household and market specialization. Thus, wage differentials between men and women become another rational response to biology. Kipling himself could not give us a better "just so" story.

One can rightly wonder whether the model of household production as developed thus far is the one best suited to description or to prescription. Some have argued that the model is prescriptive in its functionalist implications of an optimal allocation of members' resources and time to the "neutral" worlds of market and household production (e.g., Sawhill, 1980). Others (e.g., Robinson, 1977b; Reid, 1977) have argued that the model is descriptive, but only as an "ideal type" for modeling household production. Like the economist's "free market" model, such ideal abstractions may tap fundamental social processes and provide a foundation (or at least a context) for understanding inevitable departures generated through other processes (e.g., normative and institutional constraints). Nevertheless, there is no doubt that what may strike some as a useful simplifying abstraction is to others a dangerous distortion of reality. As Ben-Porath (1982) noted in his review of Becker's (1981) recent work, "it is but a short step from the productive to the ridiculous, and every application has to stand on its own merits" (p. 62).

A clear constraint on constructive criticism of the New Home Economics is the dearth of empirical work surrounding it. And it is an application of the model of household production that is of interest here. When contemplating the development of a workable model, one can anticipate that, at the very least, it must be made more inclusive of factors with potentially crucial causal importance. Perhaps the most obvious of these are the psychological and normative influences on production.

Finally, no matter what advanced billing it receives, no theory can "explain" everything, and the model of household production derived from the New Home Economics is no exception. Despite its limitations, the model can be broadened to cover an exploration of the empirical patterns that emerge and to provide real insights into its own viability. Taking this approach does not mean that theory has been *abandoned*, only that it has been complemented through exposure to the real world. This eclectic approach is further justified by the purpose of the analysis undertaken here and by its more modest goals. A meaningful causal model is of primary concern, whereas anticipating the comparative static results (i.e., giving signed relationships) is a task better left to those more reckless. Indeed, with fewer constraints placed on the model itself, the specification of the equations for household and market production can be informed by insights from past empirical work, other theoretical traditions, educated hunches, and just plain curiosity.

The analysis will rest on a framework for household production that can be sensibly elaborated to include the role of causal factors not normally associated with those of traditional economics. It may be possible to compare the influence of economic variables (e.g., wages) with that of other sorts of variables (e.g., psychic rewards) to uncover where the greater explanatory power lies. For example, a measure of psychic rewards (i.e., pleasure) reaped through household labor tasks and time is incorporated as a regressor in some of the equations. In addition, measures of the orientations of wives to household labor, as well as a measure of the perceived importance of household tasks, are included as exogenous variables. It is my hope that these modifications of the formal model will result in its greater explanatory power and will reflect the unique combination of work and gender found in the division of household labor.

AN OVERVIEW OF THE ANALYSIS

Chapters 2 and 3 focus on the methods used for the analysis and sample characteristics, respectively. Among other concerns, Chapter 2 describes the methods of data collection and the development of the operational measures of household labor and market time. Chapter 3 presents the relevant characteristics of the sample of husbands and wives in 335 households and examines the descriptive statistics for the household labor efforts of wives, husbands, sons, and daughters, as well as the market hours of wives and husbands.

Chapters 4–6 represent the major portion of the analysis of members' allocation of efforts to household and market spheres. There, it is argued that at least three questions must be addressed if we are to understand the division of household labor; each is posed in turn in the three chapters. The first question, addressed in Chapter 4, requires that one explain the *total level* of household labor and market time investments of household members, regardless of those members' individual contributions. This chapter posits a structural model with two equations to be estimated; one explains total household market investment, and the other explains the total commitment to household labor. Throughout the analysis, the reciprocal relations between household and market labor are presumed to be critical and are addressed explicitly.

Chapter 4 serves as the context for a consideration of the second question in Chapter 5: How are household tasks and market time allocated to members, *given* the total productive output of the household? Chapter 5 presents a nonrecursive structural model of five equations for the primary determinants of, and the reciprocal relations among, the household *task* contributions of wives, husbands, sons, and daughters, and the market contributions of wives.

In Chapter 6, the final analytic chapter, a third and complementary question is posed: Given total household commodity and market production, how is household labor *time* and market time allocated to members? This question is addressed through a more limited analysis, but one comparable to the one presented in Chapter 5. The chapter explores the differences in results when household time, rather than task, becomes the relevant metric of apportionment. In Chapter 6, however, only wives' market and household time are the focus.

The analyses are motivated in part by the expectation that the impact of exogenous variables and the relationships among endogenous variables may vary not only in kind, but also in effect, depending on whether one is explaining (1) the total amount of work undertaken; (2) the apportionment of tasks to members; or (3) the allocation of household and market time to members. Each of the three analytic chapters shares, at least roughly, the specification of predetermined variables, informed in large measure by expectations derived from Becker's model of household production. However, in each chapter, some important variations on the formal theoretical model—those centering on affective and normative orientations—are obvious.

The formulations of the New Home Economics are helpful in modeling the causal determinants of household labor and market time allocations to members. But those models do not represent the full story of household labor and the mechanisms by which it is divided. Thus, Chapter 7 raises more general issues relevant to the ways in which such work arrangements are understood by household members themselves. Specifically, a look at wives' and husbands' assessments of the equity of their work arrangements provides an empirical basis for a reconceptualization of household work and gender—how they may combine, and how they are actively accomplished by family members. Through the explanatory models presented in Chapters 4–6, as well as the theoretical reformulations of Chapter 7, a picture of household members' productive activities will emerge more clearly than it has in the past. It is a multidimensional, complex, and compelling picture—not only worthy of study, but integral to our understanding of the social world.

CHAPTER 2

Measuring Household and Market Labors

INTRODUCTION AND BACKGROUND

The data that describe the allocation of household tasks and time are drawn from a larger research effort launched in 1976. For that study, the data allowed for an analysis of the apportionment of household and market labors, the content and organization of the household day (Berk and Berk, 1979), and the reactions of women to the "job" of household work (e.g., Berheide *et al.*, 1976; Cannon, 1978; Berk, 1983). Because it was a first attempt to comprehensively portray the domestic work life of women and their families, only intact American households were included in the original sample. Moreover, given that the literature to date had devoted only scant attention to the organization of domestic work, and to avoid the complications posed by agricultural labor (see Hacker, 1977), only urban areas with populations greater than 50,000 were sampled.

In the next chapter, much more will be said about the sample of 335 households employed for this anaysis. However, it should be made clear that for the larger study, both the variety of the survey instruments and the time demanded of the respondents limited the response rate and the size of the sample ultimately achieved. Our initial hope was to achieve a random probability sample of 800 wives and 400 of their husbands. In fact, only 748 wives and 353 of their husbands completed all or part of the survey instruments administered. Thus, depending on the method of calculation, the response rate for wives was between 50% and 70%, and that for husbands was much higher, at 94%. As will become clear in this chapter, wives were asked to provide a great deal more information than were their husbands, and thus, the burdens of being a respondent fell primarily to them.

For the study as a whole, a number of different data-collection methods were used. Each has some place in the analysis to come, and each will be described in detail. Briefly, however, for households where all the data-collection instruments were completed, wives participated in two face-to-face interviews spaced about a week apart and lasting about one hour per interview. After completion of the first interview, wives were given a diary form or "log," in which to record all their household activities for one randomly assigned weekday covering a 24-hour period. The interviewer returned a week later to collect the diaries and to conduct the final interview with wives. All interviews were conducted separately for wives and husbands. For the random sample of husbands, a single interview was undertaken. More will be said below about some of its characteristics. If households participated in all three phases of the study, they were given the opportunity to choose a "premium" from a list that included cookware, garden tools, transistor radios, and the like.

At the risk of anticipating a more detailed discussion in the next chapter, it should be pointed out that, although the achieved sample for the larger study was 748 wives and 353 husbands, this analysis rests on the *paired* sample of wives and husbands who completed *all* the survey instruments. Thus, for the present book, the relevant sample is 335 wives and their husbands, or 335 intact households.

In this chapter, I describe the survey instruments in order to clarify the construction of the *endogenous* variables: the number of household work tasks undertaken, the amount of time spent on household work, and the time spent on employment. In addition, however, discussion centers primarily on the measurement and the operationalization of household labor. How household work is defined and measured poses thorny questions about work and leisure and about the nature of household production. It is the measurement of household labor that is, on the one hand, most innovative and, on the other hand, most fraught with methodological pitfalls.

The chapter begins with a descriptive treatment of the data-collection methods used to construct the measures of household-labor task and time apportionment. After an initial discussion of the metrics of task and time, and of their relevance to the division of household labor, the measurement of *task* contribution through respondent card sorts is considered.

Next, I describe the allocation of *time*, through the use of the wives' household diaries and the husbands' retrospective accounts of their household days. In addition to the description of the methods used to measure household labor and of the construction of the variables drawn from those measures, a number of methodological questions are raised. For instance, as this analysis centers only on household and market *work* activities (and not on all household activities), what is a reasonable rationale by which to define what is and is not domestic labor? Once the data and methods are fully described, these and other issues are considered.

The third major section of the chapter focuses on the measurement of husbands' and wives' market time contributions. There, measurement problems are slightly less troubling, as some precedents exist for reasonable (if not perfect) ways of proceeding. The final section of the chapter serves as an outline for the application of the endogenous variables to the analytic models.

THE MEASUREMENT OF HOUSEHOLD LABOR

The Metric of Task versus Time

How household production has been operationalized in the past has surely influenced our understanding of how domestic work is doled out to household members. Those who have studied "who does what" in households have typically chosen to operationalize the apportionment of household members' efforts through their respondents' estimates of the time devoted to broadly defined categories of household activities (e.g., "child care," "cleaning," and "marketing"). (For examples of such studies, see Szalai *et al.*, 1972; Meissner *et al.*, 1975; Walker and Woods, 1976; Robinson, 1977a.) Others have operationalized domestic labor contributions through the task (e.g., Blood and Wolfe, 1960; Bahr, 1974; Oakley, 1974; Berk and Berk, 1978). Each method presents its own methodological costs and benefits, but depending on the method chosen, good arguments are invariably offered for why one or the other approach is better (for examples of such discussions, see Robinson, 1977a; Berk and Berk, 1978). Yet, because they are in part *post hoc* methodological rationalizations, such arguments typically skirt the more fundamental question: How do *members* experience the "job" of household labor and its apportionment? With respect to the decision-making surrounding household production and the allocation of members' efforts, this question becomes critical. Do household members "make sense" of their own and others' efforts through the unit of the task or through time? And when members consider the ways in which work should be apportioned, is it the task that counts, or is how much time is spent of greater concern?

Such questions are rarely posed, let alone systematically addressed. With them in mind, however, this analysis begins from the premise that *both* task and time represent relevant "units" to household members, depending on the particular dimension of household production that is of concern to them. Prior research (e.g., Berk and Berk, 1978), as well as sheer common sense, suggests that through the metric of the *task*, households may first establish the degree to which they will invest in household labor and then may exercise the mechanisms by which they ordinarily apportion that labor. In other words, through the unit of the task, household members determine what has to be done and who will do it. However, when the mix of household tasks is "added up" to reflect overall effort, the implications that tasks carry for expenditures of *time* may become crucial. Based on a sense of time costs, for example, some members of a household may decide to avoid especially labor-intensive tasks or may decide to undertake some tasks less frequently because they simply take "too much time." Moreover, household members may allocate tasks to one another, but some members may never undertake particular tasks requiring time that they are unable or unwilling to give. And as we shall soon see, some members' time is clearly "worth" more than that of others. Thus, the metric of *time* becomes one input into household production, even though the *task* may remain the conceptual unit through which the work is originally defined and allocated. Clearly, there is more complexity here than might first appear. For example, time is purely an input, perhaps roughly analogous to "labor power" in the Marxist argot. Tasks, however, reflect a combination of input and output. They combine the "clean" input of labor power, along with the somewhat abstracted notion of output, or the resulting commodity itself. And, just as it is true of "realized" labor power, in practice the two are hopelessly confounded. Related subtleties are considered at greater length in Chapter 4.

Household Task Allocation: Wives' and Husbands' Card Sorts

To establish a measure of the differential allocation of tasks among wives, husbands, and children, couples were asked to undertake a card-sorting procedure. Task card-sorting was part of the first interview with wives and was part of the single interview with husbands. Wives and husbands were given an identical stack of 48 cards, each card representing one household activity.[1] Table 2.1 lists the activities sorted by the respondents, which constitute the basis for constructing a measure of household task apportionment.[2] Respondents made an initial pass through the tasks by sorting each card on the frequency with which the task was accomplished within the household, *regardless* of which member did the work.[3] Those tasks that were sorted as "never accomplished" were removed from the stack, and the respondents were then asked to designate who "generally" accomplished the remaining tasks.[4] Interviewers explained to the respondents beforehand that "generally" was conceived to be accomplishment greater than half the time the task was undertaken. And as multiple responses were permitted, the respondents were told that a shared or joint contribution could be reflected in their answers. From this method, it was possible to establish (1) a list of relevant tasks for each household and (2) routine household labor contributions by the individual household members.[5] As a final chore, the respondents were asked to resort the cards along two 9-point scales representing each task's degree of pleasantness in its accomplishment, as well as each task's degree of importance in maintaining the household. Eventually, the variables drawn from these two measures were used as explanatory variables and will be discussed more fully in Chapter 5.

As a result of the card-sorting procedure, it was possible to construct

[1]The 48 tasks sorted by husbands and wives actually represent a randomly selected "half" of an intital 97 tasks, and all wives sorted all 97. This additional sorting by the wives provided important reliability checks on the card-sort method. But as the paired sample of wives *and* husbands sorted only the randomly selected set of tasks listed in Table 2.1, *only those tasks will be analyzed.*

[2]Three tasks were excluded from all analyses as primarily "leisure" activities: "talking with husband/wife"; "telephoning friends or neighbors"; and "telephoning relatives." This left to be analyzed 45 tasks sorted by the paired sample of 335 wives and husbands.

[3]Response categories for task frequency were "never"; "less than once a month"; "once a month"; "several times a month"; "once a week"; "several times a week"; "once a day"; and "several times a day."

[4]Response categories for task contribution were "myself"; "spouse"; "daughter"; "son"; "relative"; 'friend'; "neighbor"; "servant"; and "other."

[5]One should note that the popular 5-point scale of task participation was rejected as a method by which to measure task allocation (e.g., Blood and Wolfe, 1960; Douglas and Wind, 1978). Although the "wife always" to "husband always" scale encourages the documentation of shared and joint participation, it nevertheless rests on the problematic assumption that the scale units are of equal intervals.

TABLE 2.1
Household Activities Sorted by Wives and Husbands

1 Cleaning bathroom	26 Putting ironed clothes away
2 Cleaning kitchen sink	27 Putting washed clothes away
3 Cleaning oven	28 Serving meal
4 Clearing food or dishes from table	29 Setting table
5 Cooking	30 Sewing or mending to repair clothes
6 Cutting grass	and household items
7 Diapering children	31 Shopping by mail or catalog
8 Disciplining children	32 Shoveling snow
9 Disposing of garbage or trash	33 Sorting or folding clean clothes after
10 Dressing children	drying
11 Dusting	34 Sweeping floors
12 Gathering clothes for washing	35 Taking children to school or day
13 Going to gas station	care
14 Going to grocery or supermarket	36 Talking with children
15 Household repair	37 Talking with door-to-door sales-
16 Ironing	people
17 Keeping an eye on children	38 Telephoning local merchants, stores,
18 Making beds	or shops
19 Paying bills	39 Telephoning repair or service
20 Pet care	40 Vacuuming
21 Picking up or putting away toys,	41 Washing dishes or loading dish-
books, clothes, etc.	washer
22 Plant care	42 Washing floors
23 Playing with children while doing	43 Weeding
nothing else	44 Wiping kitchen counters or ap-
24 Putting children to bed	pliances
25 Putting clothes in washer or dryer	45 Wiping kitchen or dining table
and taking them out	

variables for the total number of household tasks routinely accomplished by each member.[6] However, a variable that reflects only the *number* of household tasks undertaken, regardless of how often tasks are done, is hardly adequate. In order to incorporate the dimension of task *frequency* into the variable, the number of tasks attributed to each individual household member was multiplied by a number corresponding to the frequency with which each task was accomplished per month. Thus, task frequency and task contribution operate together in a single measure as the "number" of tasks that each member routinely undertook. That is,

[6]As the number and frequency of tasks routinely accomplished by household members other than wives, husbands, sons, and daughters were so low, all other categories were dropped from the analysis. However, in the presentation of descriptive statistics in Chapter 3, the overall contribution of others will be briefly resurrected.

the tasks are weighted by their frequency of accomplishment, where each time a task was done, it "counted" as a unique task. For example, if washing the dishes was reported as a thrice-daily task, the member or members who were reported to "generally" wash dishes were credited with not 1 but 90 "tasks" (task × frequency per month). One obvious drawback of this method of portraying task contribution is that it is impossible to distinguish between the infrequent accomplishment of many tasks and the frequent accomplishment of only a few tasks. Indeed, if a household member routinely does a task that is accomplished daily, her or his contribution will appear to be greater than that of a member who takes on more tasks less often. Yet, if one is interested in the *routines* of household labor, it might well be argued that the first member's contribution *is* greater. This somewhat unorthodox way of measuring task contribution does incorporate the characteristic of repetition as an important feature of household labor as it is experienced by the members. (For discussion, see Berheide *et al.*, 1976.) Particularly in analyses where the contributions of individual members are examined, this method of weighting by task frequency reflects the routine, ordinary, and day-to-day efforts of household members. And when accompanied by measures of the *time* contributed to household labor, it reveals a good deal about work relations within the household.

Household Time Allocation: Wives' and Husbands' Diaries

Measures of the total *time* that wives and husbands spent on household labor tasks were drawn from two different sources. In earlier work (Berk, 1979; Berk and Berk, 1979), the "diaries" elicited from the respondents were used in an analysis of the organization of household activities over time. In that research, the diaries enabled us to render observable the shape of household life—its work and leisure—as it was determined by the ongoing relations among activities, the external constraints imposed on their organization, and the dynamic relation between the activities of husbands and wives. In the present book, however, the use of diary data follows a more traditional, and considerably less complicated, course. Consistent with past research (e.g., Morgan *et al.*, 1966; Szalai *et al.*, 1972; Robinson, 1977a), diary data are used to generate *cross-sectional* estimates of the time that members allocated to *household work* activities only. There are surely costs in portraying longitudinal processes as cross-sectional contrasts, and in excluding all but "work" activities (however broadly defined). But this way of handling the diaries provides measures of time contribution that complement those in the task metric, allows for useful cross-household comparisons, and makes possible comparisons with prior research. An understanding of the diary data analysis first requires a description of the diary instruments and the development of endogenous variables from them.

To begin, wives who agreed to keep the 24-hour log, or diary, of a random weekday[7] were told to record in detail all their household activities as they occurred, and to note the starting and ending times of those activities.[8] In addition, if the diary respondents left the house, they were instructed to record their destination and the time they left and returned. To supplement the verbal instructions, a set of written guidelines was left behind, along with a blank diary form. (See Appendix A for the written diary instructions and Appendix B for a blank diary form.) An example of a partially completed diary was left with the respondents to illustrate the detail to which respondents should aspire, the allowance for simultaneity in the recording of activities, and the range of activities that might well appear in a diary.

The wives' diary form also allowed for the collection of a good deal of information about *each* activity noted. Not only were starting and ending times elicited, but in addition, for every activity the respondents were asked to note (1) whether they saw the activity as "work," "leisure," "both," or "neither"; (2) who else was present during the activity; (3) who, if anyone, was "helping" with that activity, (4) who, if anyone, was "just keeping them company"; (5) whether they were listening to TV, the radio, or the like during the activity; and (6) what their immediate feelings were about the activity (e.g., whether it was pleasant, satisfying, tiring, or boring; see Appendix B). Most of the data from these items do not figure in the present analysis of the division of household labor; they have been analyzed elsewhere (see, for examples, Cannon, 1978; Berk and Berk, 1979).

---

[7]Ideally, one would wish to sample from all seven days of the week. However, without a larger sample of diarists, we could not have done justice to the separate analyses that would be required for the presumably different dynamics of weekend housework and child care. (For examples of how data on weekend days are handled, see Pleck and Rustad, 1980.)

[8]Unlike some researchers employing diary data, we decided to *sum* the time devoted to discrete activities undertaken simultaneously. For example, if a diarist spent 90 minutes on child care and 25 of those minutes fixing dinner, her household work time would equal 115 minutes. This procedure more accurately reflects household life and does not require the artificial classification of activities as either "primary" or "secondary." (For a markedly different approach to simultaneity, see Robinson, 1977a.)

As one might imagine, both the number and the range of activities resulting from the wives' diaries posed a challenge to develop reasonable data reduction and coding schemes. The total number of diary entries exceeded 41,000, and the mean was 60 entries per diary. However, a considerable number of respondents recorded well over 100 activities in their diaries. To reduce this vast number of data, a diary-coding scheme developed earlier for a pilot study of 300 diaries was employed. (For further discussion, see Berheide *et al.*, 1976; Berk and Berheide, 1977.) With approximately 650 categories of household activities, this coding scheme was arranged so that highly specific activities (e.g., "put presoak in washing machine") could be collapsed "upward" into more broadly recorded activities (e.g., "do laundry"), or even into the most general categorization of that type of activity (e.g., "care of clothes"). (See Appendix C for the full diary-task coding scheme.) Thus, the coding scheme applied in the pilot work and to the national sample of diaries seemed to exhaust all but the rarest of household activities, and the coders easily managed the job of assigning specific task codes to the recorded activities. Moreover, this coding scheme allowed for diary data analyses at very different levels of specificity, ranging from the relatively general (e.g., Cannon, 1978) to the nearly overwhelming in detail (e.g., Berk and Berk, 1979).

The present analysis adds a new wrinkle to the way in which the original diary-task codes must be employed. Recall that the earlier study (Berk and Berk, 1979) was consciously designed to elicit information about all kinds of household activities, including those activities with large leisure components. Here, however, the concern is exclusively with the diary tasks of household labor, specifically the total time devoted to them by household members. As a consequence, for the diary data drawn from the wives and husbands, it was necessary to define a subset of diary activities that would be treated as "household labor." For example, for the wives' diaries, the orginal set of task codes (Appendix C) was refined to reflect household "work" tasks only. Table 2.2 lists the task codes for the household work activities included in the wives' diary analysis. One will note that a vast range of activities is incorporated into a measure of the time devoted to household labor tasks. (In the interests of brevity, Table 2.2 lists only two levels of specificity for tasks; the codes in parentheses indicate those highly specific activities also included as "household work.")

Even though one may employ clear and reasonable criteria by which to distinguish household work tasks from "non"-household work tasks,

TABLE 2.2
Wives' Diary: General Task Codes for Household Work-activity Categories

Clean house

Whole process (1000–1006)
Furniture (1010–1015)
Windows, mirrors, pictures, lights
(1020–1029)
Floors, rugs, ceiling, baseboards, surfaces, woodwork (1031–1039)
Toys (1040)
Books, papers, magazines (1051–1054)
Glasses, dishes (1060)
Odds and ends (1070–1075)
Other's damage (1080)
Handling tools (1090–1092)
Kitchen—While process (1100–1102)
Kitchen—Oven (1111–1114)
Kitchen—Refrigerator (1120–1127)
Kitchen—Other appliances (1130)
Kitchen—Floors, woodwork (1141–1144)
Kitchen—Furniture (1150–1151)
Kitchen—Sinks (1160)
Kitchen—Counters, cabinets, shelves
(1171–1173)
Kitchen—Curtains, windows (1180)
Kitchen—Other's damage (1190)
Bathroom—Whole process (1200)
Bathroom—Floors, walls, doors
(1211–1213)
Bathroom—Sink (1220)
Bathroom—Toilet (1230)
Bathroom—Bowl (1240)
Bathroom—Showers, tubs (1251–1252)
Bathroom—Towels and other changeable
items (1261–1262)
Bathroom—Clean specific items (1270)
Bathroom—Windows, glass (1280)
Bathroom—Tile (1290)
Bedroom—Whole process (1300–1301)

Bedroom—Furniture (1310–1312)
Bedroom—Beds (1321–1326)
Bedroom—Floor (1330–1332)
Bedroom—Clothes (1340)
Bedroom—Toys (1350)
Bedroom—Dishes (1360)
Bedroom—Other's damage (1370)
Living room—Whole process
(1400–1401)
Living room—Floors (1411–1412)
Living room—Furniture (1420–1421)
Living room—Objects (1431–1434)
Living room—Windows (1440)
Dining room—Whole process
(1450–1451)
Dining room—Floors (1460–1462)
Dining room—Furniture (1470)
Dining room—Pictures (1480)
Breakfast room—Floors (1490–1491)
Family, TV, recreation room, and den
(1500–1590)
Hall, foyer—Whole process (1600)
Hall, foyer—Floors (1610–1612)
Porch—Floors (1620)
Porch—Dishes (1630)
Closets—Whole process (1640)
Closets—Floors (1650–1651)
Closets—Clothes (1660)
Basement—Whole process (1670)
Basement—Floors (1680–1681)
Basement—Objects (1690–1691)
Home and vehicle maintenance
(1710–1790)
Garbage (1810–1870)
Yardwork (1900–1990)

Meal preparation

Plan menus (2000–2040)
Make meal (2100–2109)
Make breakfast (2110–2112)
Make dinner (2120–2141)
Make lunch (2150–2155)
Make snack (2160–2161)
Outdoor cooking (2200)
Baking (2300–2310)
Set table (2400–2440)
Serve meal (2500–2580)

Clean up after meals—Whole process
(2700)
Clean up after meals—Put away food
(2710)
Clean up after meals—Clear table (2720)
Clean up after meals—Wiping (2730)
Clean up after meals—Other's damage
(2740)
Clean up after meals—Breakfast
(2750–2752)

Continued

TABLE 2.2 *(continued)*

Clean up after meals—Dinner (2760-2762)	Wash dishes—After-washing tasks (2931-2932)
Clean up after meals—Lunch (2770-2772)	Wash dishes—Polish silver (2940)
Wipe table (2800-2810)	Wash dishes—Wash appliances (2950)
Wash dishes—Whole process (2900-2905)	Wash dishes—Breakfast (2960-2966)
Wash dishes—Dishwasher (2911-2914)	Wash dishes—Dinner (2970-2971)
Wash dishes—Before-washing tasks (2921-2926)	Wash dishes—Lunch (2980-2983)
	Wash dishes—Snack (2990-2992)

Care of clothes

Sewing (3000-3060)	Hanging clothes (3700)
Laundry (3100-3400)	Pack/unpack (3800)
Hand laundry (3500-3510)	Shoe care (3900)
Ironing (3600-3620)	

Shopping

Groceries (4100-4160)	Errands (4200-4340)

Care of family

Wake family (5010)	Baby-sitter (5380-5390)
Family medical (5021-5022)	Taking children places (5410-5490)
Gathering (5031-5032)	Instructional aid for children (5500-5508)
Ready to go (5040)	Instructional aid for children—Outings (5510)
Husband—Wake (5110)	
Husband—Chauffeur (5120-5123)	Instructional aid for children—Walks (5520)
Husband—Help (5130)	
Husband/wife relations (5171)	Instructional aid for children—TV (5530)
Feed children (5210-5219)	Instructional aid for children—Managing (5540)
Dress children (5220-5228)	
Diapers (5230)	Interaction with children (5610-5680)
Wake children (5240)	Clean children—Hygiene (5711-5719)
Putting children to bed (5250-5253)	Clean children—Bathe (5721-5725)
Children's naps (5251-5262)	
Supervise children (5300-5370)	

Care of plants and pets

Pets (6100-6210)	Plants (6300-6340)

Interaction with others

Neighboring (7210; 7230-7260)	Entertaining (7710-7720)
Talk (7460-7470)	Answering door (7800)
Phone calls (7500; 7520; 7550-7570)	

Household papers

Paperwork (8100)	Mail (8310; 8330-8350; 8370)
Finances (8210-8260)	Get newspaper (8400)

Going to and from places

Driving (9300)	

such a procedure nevertheless represents the imposition of a dichotomy ("work" vs. "leisure") on what is more likely a continuum, where typically, activities possess qualities of both "work" and "leisure." The question becomes one of assessing the degree to which an activity is "mostly" work or "mostly" leisure. And in the end, one is wise to remain dissatisfied with the whole business. Despite the compromises implied, the need for an endogenous variable representing the *total* time that the wives devote to household *labor* required that a subset of household activities from the wives' diary-coding scheme be designated "work." Once work activities were distinguished from the others, it was possible to construct a variable for the wives' summed elapsed time devoted to domestic labor activities. This variable complements the endogenous variable of the wives' total task contribution to the household. In the next section, much more is said about the methodological implications of this decision.

For the husbands' "diary," a comparable, but somewhat different, instrument was employed. Unlike the wives' log of household activities, the instrument used to chronicle the domestic activities of husbands can only loosely be called a diary. Because a larger proportion of husbands than wives were employed during the day, we sought an instrument that would accurately reflect the household activities of husbands without incurring the costs of administering a diary to a large sample of (perhaps uncooperative) respondents. The result was a card-sorting operation unique to the husbands' interview, requiring a *retrospective* accounting of domestic activities for two time periods in the previous 24 hours.

The two relevant time periods were described to husbands as "yesterday evening after the time you would normally return from work" and "today after waking up but before the time you would normally go to work." For the unemployed husbands, the time periods remained the same: the early morning and the early evening. For the employed husbands, the time periods varied, depending on husbands' particular work schedules. For each of the two time periods, husbands sorted a list of 81 household activities and indicated those activities that they had undertaken.[9] Throughout this first phase of the card sorting, the respondents were reminded that "blank" cards were available, so that they could include any tasks that were done, but that were not found on the interviewer's list. (See Appendix D for the full list of 81 house-

---

[9]The establishment of this list was informed by insights gained from a pilot study of household labor (Berheide *et al.*, 1976; Berk and Berheide, 1977), and by the need to include a wide variety of household activities.

hold activities.) With this initial sorting completed, the cards with the activities not accomplished for the respective time periods were removed. Respondents were then asked to sort the remaining cards in their order of accomplishment for each time period.[10] This chronological rank-ordering procedure seemed to be the most accurate way of getting a sense of when each activity occurred in relation to others.

As a final task, husbands answered a set of questions on the back of each of the sorted cards: (1) how long each activity took; (2) whether TV, radio, or the like was "on" during the activity; and (3) what adjectives husbands would use to describe the activity (e.g., *boring, pleasant, satisfying,* or *frustrating*)—the same adjectives offered to wives for their diary activities. For the purposes of this analysis, the most critical piece of information about the husbands' sorted activities is the time spent on them, as these estimates formed the basis for a variable describing the total time that husbands devoted to household labor.

Not surprisingly, we faced the same problem with the list of activities sorted by husbands that we faced with the full range of wives' diary activities. Although the list of 81 activities for the husbands was not nearly as various nor as exhaustive of domestic chores as the task codes developed for wives, it still contained a number of activities that could not easily be considered household "labor." Thus, for this analysis, only those activities judged to be largely "work" on the "work/leisure" continuum were considered. Table 2.3 lists the 51 activities that remained once the "leisure" activities were culled from the original list. The final list of 51 household work activities and the time that husbands devoted to them constitute the second endogenous variable describing the time spent on household labor.

Taken together, the wives' and the husbands' task-card sorts and the construction of the wives' and husbands' "diaries" provide a glimpse of the apportionment of household labor on more than a single dimension. From the task-card sorts, the endogenous variables capturing the couples' assessments of their own and others' (including their children's) task con-

---

[10]Husbands were also encouraged to rank-order an activity as often as it occurred during the time period in question. If, for example, they reported that they "talked to children" two, three, or more times during the evening, duplicate cards were provided. More important, husbands were also encouraged to "write in" activities that they had undertaken but which were not included as activities in the prepared set of task cards. Blank cards were provided for these additional tasks. It should be pointed out, however, that there was so little demand for blank cards that the "other" task category had to be dropped from the analysis.

TABLE 2.3

Husbands' Retrospective Diary: Household Work Activities

1 Bathed children	28 Put dishes in sink
2 Called (specify who)	29 Rinsed dishes
3 Cleaned kitchen	30 Ran errand (where?)
4 Cleaned up after breakfast	31 Served dinner
5 Cleared dinner table	32 Set table
6 Dressed children	33 Straightened house
7 Dried dishes	34 Talked with children
8 Drove children to school or bus stop	35 Washed dishes
9 Emptied garbage	36 Wiped dinner table
10 Fed pet	37 Wiped stove top or kitchen counters
11 Went to bank	38 Woke children
12 Went to gas station	39 Woke wife
13 Did household repair or remodeling	40 Did yard work
14 Let pet out or in	41 Handled banking (checking, savings, loans)
15 Loaded dishwasher	
16 Made beds	42 Did household budgeting
17 Made breakfast	43 Planned change in or around house
18 Made coffee or tea	44 Planned family activities
19 Made dinner	45 Prepared household records or paperwork
20 Made part of dinner	
21 Made sack lunch	46 Went to store
22 Made snack	47 Did arithmetic
23 Paid bills/handled finances	48 Wrote a list
24 Played with children	49 Copied a document
25 Put away dinner leftovers	50 Filed household records or paperwork
26 Put children to bed	
27 Put dishes away	51 Helped children with schoolwork

tributions were constructed. From the "diaries," two endogenous variables were developed for the total time spent by wives and husbands on household labor.

Several issues surrounding the measurement of household labor contribution deserve further discussion. The next section first addresses the necessary evil of distilling the wives' and the husbands' diary tasks so that they represent only "work" activities. Second, a brief consideration of the comparability of the wives' and the husbands' diaries is crucial to a later evaluation of the findings. Third, the role of the children is described, as not every measure of household labor contribution employed in this analysis reflects their productive efforts. In this study (as in almost all others), children are often "seen but not heard" as potentially important providers of household labor. Finally, the problem of employing *both* wives' and husbands' versions of "who does what" demands some attention. Obtaining accounts of the relative contributions of both spouses is certainly an advantage when studying the division of household labor. Yet, the issue of differential perception raises interesting epistemologial questions and analytic choices.

Some Methodological Compromises

To begin, the methodological decision with the most far-reaching implications is one where "household work" is distinguished from "non-household work" and the latter is excluded from analysis. Recall that, for the task cards sorted by wives and husbands, the presence of leisure activities did not pose a problem; household-work-like tasks were selected *a priori* for administration to the respondents. However, in the case of both the wives' self-administered diary and the husbands' retrospective diary, the activities list had to be refined *ex post facto* so that only household labor remained.

This decision to cull from a larger list of household activities only those tasks that appear to constitute "work" raises the very problems confronted in discussions of the household production function. Recall that the household production model cannot really tolerate a formal distinction between "productive" and "leisure" activities because, as Becker (1976b) originally maintained, work and leisure are inextricably connected in all human activities. Nevertheless, it is also the case that others (e.g., Gronau, 1977) have become uneasy about this position and have argued for a distinction between those household activities for which market substitutes can be found and those for which there are no substitutes (or "surrogates"). With this new distinction, however, one inherits all the problems of incorporating the existence of joint production into models that, at least formally, are not equipped to handle it.

There is certainly a strong precedent for distinguishing between "work" and "non-work" activities in the household, and most researchers have arrived at some version of the "surrogate-impossibility" criterion favored by Gronau (1977, p. 264). For example, in their large-scale survey of the economic behavior of individuals, Morgan *et al.* (1966) distinguished between "regular housework" and "home production." They offered little theoretical justification for these categories other than a brief comment that "home production" is largely a substitute for marketable goods and services.

John Robinson's work (1977a) devotes less attention to the theoretical definition of household labor and more attention to the problems of reliable and rigorous measurement of it. Unlike many other researchers, however, he does seem mindful of the pitfalls associated with the classification of household activities as household *labor*. Contemplating the categorization of activities emerging from his general study of time use, Robinson noted that

> There are complex definitional problems given the richness of the data—should "housework" include child care, shopping for durables or related travel; should playing with children or organizational activity be considered part of "free time"? (p. 8)

Robinson clearly appreciated the problems that plague (or should plague) the researcher who is concerned with the appropriate classification of data. He voiced the confusion that results when one tries to classify household labor according to whether it is "work," "leisure," "obligatory," "pleasant," or "unpleasant," and he tried to consider both the social context in which activities are undertaken, and the intrapsychic states of those who engage in them:

> Very little of it [unpaid housework] is obligatory in the sense that the individual's life is threatened if it were not performed. Being defined as work that is "never finished" only adds to its nonobligatory character. . . . Moreover, certain parts of what we include under homemaking are found to be extremely pleasurable and rewarding. . . . Much the same highlights occur in the world of work, however, and few jobs carry with them the "lows" of housework, such as making beds, washing dishes, and doing the general cleaning along with the simple, if often boring necessity of being at home. Since these ultimately represent activities "that have to be done" there is little doubt that their classification as obligatory is appropriate. (p. 45)

Thus, Robinson organized his classification of respondent diary activities according to whether they seem "obligatory." These necessary *a priori* assumptions concerning the psychic rewards and costs of household labor, as well as Robinson's distinction between work and leisure, leave little question that either Becker's (1976b) failure to distinguish household work and nonwork activities or Gronau's (1977) much simpler distinction between market and nonmarket substitutability carries less methodological risk.

In a much earlier treatment that foreshadowed the New Home Economics, Reid (1934) offered a definition of household labor fully consistent with the one proposed by Gronau over 40 years later:

Those unpaid activities which are carried on by and for the members, which activities might be replaced by market goods, or paid services, if circumstances such as income, market conditions and personal inclinations permit the service being delegated to someone outside the household group. (p. 11)

Again, the market-substitute criterion becomes the primary way by which "work" and "nonwork," or productive and unproductive household activities, are distinguished by researchers.

Clearly, there is at least empirical precedent for the use of the market-substitute criterion for the definition of household labor tasks. In our study, it was this criterion that was applied to both the self-reported diary activities of the wives, and to the list of tasks presented to the husbands, through which they reconstructed their household days (see Tables 2.2 and 2.3).

Yet, this is obviously not an ideal methodological state of affairs. Indeed, the problem could be avoided altogether by simply analyzing *all* household activities, and by assuming (along with Becker) that each activity combines some qualities of "work" *and* "leisure."[11] Thus, excluding leisure activities from the analysis represents a departure from the formal requirements of the household production model, and it means that a set of household activities (i.e., "leisure") that may critically determine members' allocation of tasks and time is ignored.[12] At the same time, however, the discussion of the household production model in the last chapter made clear that this analysis will not be bound by all the usual formal requirements. Further, if one is *reasonably* comfortable with the market-substitute criterion for the definition of household labor, it is possible to speak in terms of the productive activities of households with much greater clarity than if the definitional question is skirted altogether.

Second, brief mention should be made of another potential drawback of the use of wives' and husbands' diaries in the construction of the

[11]In earlier work, where all kinds of household activities were analyzed (Berk and Berk, 1979), we could apply *respondent* designated categories of work and leisure to tasks and then explore variation around those designations.

[12]Even more perplexing are the problems presented by nonsubstitutable components in *work* activities. That is, apart from the exclusion of leisure, also ignored are the "surrogate-impossiblity" characteristics of activities that can in theory be replaced by market goods or paid services. For example, although Sara Lee may bake a very good cake, it may still lack the extra value accruing to one that is "homemade." (For discussion see Berk, 1980, pp. 133–135.)

summed variables describing couples' total household-labor time. Recall that coding categories for the wives' diaries were drawn directly from self-reported diary data; through their diaries, wives *told* us what they did, and the activity categories were developed accordingly. In contrast, the husbands' diaries were based on categories of household labor activities *presented to the respondents;* from these were drawn the relative order of task accomplishment and the estimates of time spent on them. As a result, we presented husbands with what they *might* have done during the two time periods, and they had to match their household days to the activity categories presented to them.

This difference in method raises some very real questions concerning the comparability of the results. Obviously, the ideal situation would be one in which husbands had been pressed to complete a 24-hour diary in the same fashion as their wives. Had this been the procedure, the resulting calculations of the total time spent on household labor would be as comparable as those of the two task-contribution variables. There is some consolation in the fact that the analysis does not depend on a task-by-task comparison of the wives' and the husbands' time; it requires only *aggregate* estimates of time devoted to household work and child care. Moreover, one should not assume that because the wives' diaries allowed for a great deal more specificity in task description than the husbands' retrospective accounts, the wives' household labor time was necessarily greater. In fact, a reasonable case can be made for the opposite effect: *because* wives were asked to provide starting and ending times for each specific activity as it occurred, the resulting calculation of task duration might constitute an underestimation of time spent. In contrast, asked to estimate the duration of more broadly defined household activities *after the fact,* husbands might well have exaggerated the time that they spent. Obviously, it is impossible to know for certain how these and other sources of measurement error operate. Luckily, the task analysis provides another measure of household labor contribution, so that the patterns of task and time can be compared.

Third, one strength of the task contribution analysis is that wives and husbands were asked to report on their children's household labor. Such a report was not possible for the analysis of time spent on household work. As a consequence, although one could argue that the analysis as a whole looks at the members' household labor from the perspective of the dual dimensions of task and time, this is, in fact, true only for husbands and wives. In a very real sense, the primary analysis of household

labor apportionment must rest on the number of *tasks* routinely undertaken by household members. The analysis of the time spent on tasks will
remain a secondary, albeit important, feature of the analysis.

Finally, the literature on the division of household labor has made
a great deal of the difference in the reports of wives and husbands about
their own and others' household contributions (e.g., Brown and Rutter,
1966; Granbois and Willett, 1970; Larson, 1974; Booth and Welch, 1978;
Douglas and Wind, 1978). Ordinarily, the potential for discrepancies in
reports are viewed as serious methodological problems. A few other
researchers have treated such discrepancies as valuable data on the
differential perceptions of family relations and the organization of work
within the home (e.g., Safilios-Rothschild, 1969; Larson, 1974). Earlier
work using much the same data as the present analysis (Berk and Shih,
1980) found high agreement overall between wives and husbands about
who generally accomplished tasks, although agreement surrounding the
wives' household labor was greater than that for husbands. However, the
degree of disagreement was found to vary significantly by the sex-
stereotypic "loadings" of the tasks. That is, wives and husbands were less
likely to disagree on their contributions to stereotypic "female" and
"male" tasks. Lastly, and in general, based on what wives and husbands
reported about their own contributions, the partners systematically *underestimated* each others' household labor efforts.

With these findings in mind, some decisions had to be made concerning whose "account" would be used for the analysis of task contribution.
It seemed useless to spend time wondering whose version represented
the "true" report of who did what and how often. Thus, it was decided
that when *total* household tasks and time (without respect to individual
members' contributions) were analyzed, the wives' reports would be employed. However, when the task contributions of *individual* members
were at issue, the wives' reports would be used to determine their own
and their children's efforts, and the husbands' reports to describe only
their own contributions. This decision should not be misconstrued as resting on the notion that wives were somehow more *honest* than their husbands. Rather, because the household is more likely to be a site of wives'
work and (more important) of wives' *responsibility,* it is to them that one
should turn for estimates of total household labor, their own labor, and
the labor of their children. Husbands will speak for themselves.

With these methodological quandaries at least temporarily resolved,
the more straightforward measurement of employment time can be

described. Market labor hours and minutes, respectively, form the basis for the two remaining endogenous variables used in the analysis.

The Measurement of Market Labor Time

Market Hours Per Month

Wives' and husbands' monthly hours of employment were measured somewhat differently. Unfortunately, husbands were not asked how many hours they *actually* worked per week or month. If husbands were employed, they were presumed to be employed full time at 40 hours per week, and their hours worked per month were simply designated as 160. A more detailed examination of the data revealed that only a small number of the employed husbands worked part time, part year, or a great deal more than 160 hours per month.

If wives were employed, they were asked how many hours per week they actually worked, and this figure was multiplied by 4 so as to be translated into a convenient monthly metric. The monthly metric was chosen for these variables because it is used in the models that analyze the reciprocal relation between market hours per month and household tasks accomplished per month.

Market Minutes per Day

An alternative construction was used to generate a measure of the total number of minutes per day that wives and husbands spent in market activity. Respondents were asked to estimate the duration of their working day through the interview question "What time do you usually leave for work and return from work?" Elapsed times for market activity were calculated from these estimates. These alternative measures of market time are employed in the models that examine the reciprocal relation between market minutes per day and household work minutes per day.

In chapters to come, the effects of these two market time measures are compared, and their substantive differences are explored more fully. And one should expect differences because the two measures of market activity really tap separate dimensions of market work. Standard estimates of how "much" one works per month or week obviously ignore the actual duration of the employment day. Time devoted to commuting, time spent at the place of employment while not actually on the job, and time spent on other activities after work, but before returning home, all contribute to estimates reflected in the market "minutes per day" variables—variables describing total employment-related time taken away from the household.

HOUSEHOLD AND MARKET WORK: ENDOGENOUS VARIABLES

Now that the measures of household and market work have been described, the endogenous variables developed from them can be introduced. They figure prominently in Chapters 4–6, which together constitute the bulk of the analysis of the apportionment of household labor.

Chapter 4: Total Household Tasks and Time, Total Market Time

Chapter 4 begins the analysis of the division of household labor tasks and time by examining the total number of tasks that households undertake, the total amount of time given to household labor, and the total time devoted to market work by the adult household members. This analysis is designed to provide a basis from which to consider the allocation of household work and market time for the *individual* members, but the analysis in Chapter 4 combines all individual efforts into the single unit of the household.

Thus, the measures of household tasks, household time, and market time are represented in Chapter 4 as *summed* measures of individual efforts. That is, the endogenous variable for the total number of tasks that households undertook per month is drawn from the wives' reports on their households' monthly tasks. The alternative endogenous variable for the total amount of time spent on household labor is represented in Chapter 4 by the summed totals of wives' and husbands' household labor minutes per day. Similarly, the two market time measures, hours employed per month and duration of the employment day, are also translated into variables reflecting the summed market time of husbands and wives.[13]

[13]A measure of the *total* time spent by wives and husbands on household labor was a necessary variable for all subsequent analyses (Chapters 4–6). However, that variable was constructed from a linear combination of the two summed household-labor diary-time totals. Thus, when the analysis of *individual* members' time becomes relevant (Chapters 5 and 6), only *one* member's time can serve as the dependent variable. This decision will be discussed at greater length in Chapters 5 and 6.

Chapter 5: The Apportionment of Household Tasks and Market Hours

With total household productive capabilities addressed in Chapter 4, Chapter 5 turns its attention to the allocation of household labor tasks and market time among *individual* family members. In Chapter 5, the individual household-labor efforts of wives, sons, and daughters are each represented by endogenous variables, reciprocally related to one another. Likewise, in Chapter 5, the individual labor-market efforts of wives (directly) and husbands (indirectly) are introduced into the model as wives' hours of employment per month.

Chapter 6: The Apportionment of Household and Market Time

For a last look at the division of household and market labors, the supplementary analysis of time spent is presented in Chapter 6. There, the endogenous variables are constructed from the diary measures of the wives' household labor activities, represented by household labor "minutes per day," and a measure of the wives' market time based on estimates of the duration of the wives' employment day. Thus, in Chapter 6, it will be possible to note the potential differences resulting from the measures of task versus time and formal employment hours versus the time spent in employment-related activities.

With the general discussion of methods behind us, Chapter 3 presents some characteristics of the sample of 335 households and the descriptive statistics for the endogenous variables.

Sample Characteristics and Initial Description

INTRODUCTION

This chapter includes a brief discussion of the sample of 335 households, as well as a first glimpse of the measures of household labor and market time. The short discussion of some selected characteristics of the sample gives a broad overview of the households under study and provides some basis from which to later judge the external validity of the findings. One could argue that simply because the data were collected in 1976, the patterns that emerged (particularly for the division of household labor) depart from those that might be found today. Those who believe that the social relations of the household have been radically transformed since the 1970s will find the descriptive statistics presented in this chapter useful for comparison with future studies of the division of household labor.

This chapter also examines the simple descriptive statistics for the endogenous variables analyzed later, and it presents some supplemental measures of the division of household labor. In this study, more than one measure was employed to address the "who does what" question. Although only two are later translated into endogenous variables, they provide a view of household labor apportionment from more than a single vantage point.

THE SAMPLE

To reiterate a bit from the last chapter, the analysis rests on a sample of 335 wives and their husbands who completed both the survey and diary instruments. When a sample must be defined by the two criteria that all survey instruments were completed and that wives' and husbands' responses were paired by household, its characteristics may depart significantly from those of the general population. Although the demands made of respondents may have limited the ultimate representativeness of the sample, the range of measures and reports from both spouses seemed well worth the costs. In this case, some external validity has been traded away for enhanced construct and internal validity.

Table 3.1 presents the relevant descriptive statistics for the sample households, including features of the physical residence, family composition, and some characteristics of wives and husbands. Turning first to some characteristics of the household work environment, we see that the average family had lived for a little more than seven years in a single-family dwelling that they owned. Although there was some variance, the mean number of rooms within the home was about $7^{1}/_{2}$. Most of the households had some property they called a yard, had facilities for doing laundry within their home (as opposed to a laundromat or shared building facilities), and had an average of almost four "household work" appliances.[1]

It appears that about one third of all the sample households were childless. However, this is somewhat misleading because, for purposes of the study, a household was defined as childless if no children were currently living at home. Thus, one cannot know what proportion of the one third of "childless" households actually represented families with no living children. Table 3.1 also shows the distribution of the households for each of the age categories of children 0–20 years of age. Of the households with children, 13% had at least one child under the age of 2. For households with children between the ages of 2 and 16, about a third had at least one child within that age range. Much older children living in the sample households represented a smaller proportion: only 16% of the sample households had children between the ages of 16 and 20 living at home.

There is nothing particularly startling about the characteristics of the wives' sample, with the exception of the modest proportion (36%) who were employed. Of this group, 16% were employed part time, and 20% were employed full time. This somewhat lower proportion of full-time workers was a likely function of the quite demanding interview proce-

---

[1]The household work-appliance index was constructed from responses to whether or not the respondents owned the following appliances: dishwasher, clothes washer, clothes dryer, garbage disposal, blender, no-frost refrigerator, or self-cleaning oven.

TABLE 3.1
Selected Household Characteristics[a]

Variable	Mean or proportion	Standard deviation	Minimum	Maximum
Residence characteristics				
Years at current address	7.37	7.94	0	36
Own home	0.67	0.47	0	1
Single-family home	0.74	0.44	0	1
Number of rooms	7.54	2.51	2	20
Yard	0.95	0.23	0	1
Laundry done at home	0.87	0.33	0	1
Number of appliances	3.87	1.74	0	7
Household composition				
No children	0.33	0.47	0	1
Child 0–2 years	0.13	0.34	0	1
Child 2–5 years	0.29	0.45	0	1
Child 6–10 years	0.30	0.46	0	1
Child 11–15 years	0.26	0.44	0	1
Child 16–20 years	0.16	0.37	0	1
Wives' characteristics				
Currently employed	0.36	0.48	0	1
Part time	0.16			
Full time	0.20			
(If employed; $N = 121$)				
Professional/managerial	0.34	0.48	0	1
Clerical/sales	0.40	0.49	0	1
Craft/operative	0.08	0.28	0	1
Service	0.16	0.37	0	1
Job length (no. of years)	5.06	5.47	0.5	26
Earnings	$4,891	$4,905	$60	$32,000
(All wives; $N = 335$)				
Age	38.74	14.33	18	76
Race: white	0.79	0.41	0	1
Prior marriage	0.13	0.33	0	1
High-school diploma	0.62	0.49	0	1
College degree	0.12	0.32	0	1
Advanced degree	0.03	0.18	0	1
Hours/day household labor—All wives	4.58	3.32	1	20
Hours/day household labor—Employed wives	3.64	2.67	1	14
Husbands' characteristics				
Currently employed	0.83	0.38	0	1
Professional/technical	0.19	0.39	0	1
Manager/proprietor	0.12	0.32	0	1

Continued

TABLE 3.1 (continued)

Variable	Mean or proportion	Standard deviation	Minimum	Maximum
Sales/clerical	0.12	0.33	0	1
Craft	0.13	0.34	0	1
Operative	0.15	0.36	0	1
Service	0.10	0.29	0	1
Earnings (if employed: N = 278)	$14,765	$7,143	0	$50,000
Age	41.74	14.76	20	78
Race: white	0.83	0.38	0	1
High-school diploma	0.51	0.50	0	1
College degree	0.14	0.34	0	1
Advanced degree	0.10	0.30	0	1

[a]N = 335.

dures. Women employed full-time were simply less likely to participate in a study that required two separate interview sessions and a diary covering a 24-hour period. Indeed, this was found to be true not only of the group of 335 households, but also for the full sample of 748 wives. (For discussion, see Berk and Berk, 1979.)

Apart from the number employed full time, the wives' sample seems straightforward enough; if employed, sample wives had been at the same job an average of five years, most were employed in clerical or low-level professional or managerial jobs, and they earned an average of about $5,000 (although their 1976 incomes ranged from $60 to $32,000 per year). The sample wives had a mean age of 39 years, and 79% were white; 62% had a high-school diploma, and another 15% had earned college degrees or postgraduate degrees. More than 10% had been married at least once before. Finally, the sample wives spent an average of 4½ hours per day on household labor. When they were employed outside the home, this figure dropped by about 1 hour to 3.64 hours per day. to 3.64 hours per day.

Turning to the characteristics of the sample husbands, we can see from Table 3.1 that, at a mean of 42 years, husbands were slightly older than their wives. Eighty-three percent were employed, in the full range of occupational categories. If employed, the sample husbands earned a mean of almost $15,000 (1976 dollars). Seventy-five percent had earned at least a high-school diploma, but they surpassed their wives only in the slightly greater number who had postgraduate degrees. Eighty-three percent of sample husbands were white.

HOUSEHOLD MEMBERS' MARKET TIME
AND HOUSEHOLD LABOR

Table 3.2 presents the means and the standard deviations for the variables describing wives' and husbands' market time and all the members' household-labor contributions. These data constitute the endogenous variables in the formal models to come. Even in the next chapter, where the sole concern is the *total* of the productive efforts of households, the variables seen here are combined for that analysis. Moreover, Table 3.2 suggests differences in the two measures of market time, as well as some potential differences between the measurement of household labor by task and by time. The justification for using more than a single measurement strategy was presented in the last chapter. However, the analysis to come illustrates how such strategies can generate somewhat different substantive findings.

Wives' and Husbands' Market Time

For the dual measures of wives' and husbands' market time, Table 3.2 indicates that wives devoted a mean of 36.07 hours per month to employment. Recall that this variable was constructed from a question put to employed wives about the number of hours they worked per week and is a likely estimate of the "formal" hours devoted to employment. Of course, the relatively small mean figure of 36.07 hours results because the labor force participation of all 335 wives is reflected in it. To provide a more accurate description of the wives' employment time, Table 3.2 also presents (in parentheses) the means and the standard deviations for the market hours per month for the 121 employed wives. Thus, we see that employed wives worked an average of about 100 hours per month (this number includes the market hours of those working both part time and full time).

The mean number of minutes per day spent by all wives on employment was 138, or about 2 hours, but for employed wives, the mean becomes more realistic at 382.35 minutes per day, or about $6^{1}/_{2}$ hours. In either case, the standard deviations are large, suggesting that the wives' market time was subject to great variation, even among the employed.

The comparable figures for husbands' market time are also presented in Table 3.2, but they must be interpreted with caution. Recall that for the variable that reflects "formal" market hours, husbands were not

TABLE 3.2
Means and Standard Deviations for Endogenous Variables[a]

Variable	Mean		SD	
Wife's market time				
Hours/month	36.07	(99.88)	63.79	(70.02)
Minutes/day	138.10	(382.35)	221.49	(205.85)
Husband's market time				
Hours/month	130.87		61.84	
Minutes/day	475.92	(575.48)	255.61	(147.43)
Wife's household tasks (times frequency/month)	1,126.97	(1031.82)	472.72	(437.46)
Wife's household work time (minutes/day)	504.27	(429.36)	261.25	(290.91)
Husband's household tasks (times frequency/month)	361.52	(385.88)	321.24	(355.75)
Husband's household work time (minutes/day)	189.69	(194.06)	188.33	(179.35)
Daughter's household tasks (mother's report)	132.83		261.50	
Son's household tasks (mother's report)	63.30		138.84	

[a]$N = 335$.

asked to make specific estimates of their hours at work. Instead, we made the assumption, however inaccurate, that if a husband was employed, he worked 160 hours per month. Therefore, the mean figure for the husbands' hours per month is an artifact of this procedure. We see that for all households, the mean number of hours husbands spent in employment was about 130; for those employed, the presumed mean was 160 hours. Much more accurate is the mean minutes per day husbands spent in employment-related activity. For all 335 households, the mean duration (in minutes) of the husbands' employment day was 475.92, or about 8 hours per day. And for only those husbands who were employed, the figure was somewhat larger, at 575.61 minutes, or about 10$^1/_2$ hours. Again, however, one will notice the particularly large standard deviations; for those variables that include all employment-related time (e.g., commuting, socializing after work, and errands), the variance is pronounced.

A comparison of husbands' and wives' market hours and daily employment-related minutes reveals a pattern familiar to those who study men's and women's labor-force participation. Table 3.2 certainly does not contain new information about the relative participation of wives and husbands in the labor market. In our sample, the husbands' attachment to the labor force was more consistent than the wives' and at a higher level, and, it showed considerably less variance across households. However, when viewed in tandem with the mean figures for the members' attachment to *household* labor, one can certainly see where wives spent the remainder of their work time.

Wives' and Husbands' Household Labor

Table 3.2 next presents the five endogenous variables that figure importantly in the analysis of household labor tasks and time. For both wives and husbands, household-labor contribution was measured through the numbers of tasks and through the time measured in the household diaries. For sons and daughters, household contribution was captured through the *mothers'* reports of their children's task contributions.

If we turn first to the wives' efforts, Table 3.2 indicates that sample wives took on approximately 1,126 tasks per month, calculated through the weighting of tasks by their frequency of accomplishment. The corresponding measure shows that the mean number of minutes per day spent by wives on household labor was 504.27, or about $8^1/_2$ hours per day.[2] It should be noted here that this mean represents time spent by the full sample of wives and thus reflects both employed and unemployed wives' household-labor time. The figures in parentheses indicate that the mean for the employed wives' household tasks and time dropped by 95 monthly tasks and 75 minutes per day, respectively.

For the husbands' household tasks and household work time, the mean figures are considerably smaller but may still represent a significant *practical* effect on the household. For the measure of the husbands' household tasks per month, Table 3.2 indicates that husbands took on approximately 361 monthly tasks, or about 33% of what their wives con-

---

[2]Somewhat surprisingly, this total for the wives' household labor time is approximately double that of the mean for the question "How many hours per day do you spend on household work?" Judging from past interviews and participant observation in households (for discussion, see Berheide *et al.*, 1976; Berk and Berheide, 1977), the difference most probably results from varying definitions of household labor. The operational definition that I applied to the diary entries is no doubt much more inclusive than the definition used by the respondents. Those engaged in the actual work of a household generally apply a much more limited definition of what does and does not constitute household work. In part, this more stringent definition results from the normative understanding that much of what women do in their homes simply doesn't count as "real" work. Moreover, those household tasks that carry large leisure components (e.g., some tasks of child care) are likely to be systematically excluded from respondent estimates of the time spent on household labor, but for us, they "count" in all calculations from diaries.

tributed. In households with employed wives, that figure rose to 386 tasks, or about 37% of the wives' contribution. The mean for the husbands' household labor *time* was also considerably less than the comparable figure for their wives, but it was larger than one might expect.[3] Table 3.2 shows that husbands spend roughly 190 minutes per day (about 3¹/₄ hours) on household labor, again slightly more than 33% of the wives' contribution. Husbands with employed wives spent, on the average, about 5 minutes more per day on household labor than those husbands with unemployed wives. Yet, because their employed wives also spent less time, the husbands' relative contribution rose to about 45% of their wives'. It remains to be seen, however, whether these differences did, in fact, result from the wives' employment, and whether they mattered statistically and/or practically.

It should also be remembered that these figures are based on the husbands' retrospective diaries and, in contrast to the measure used for the wives' time, is based on the respondents' *estimation* of the time spent. Recall that the wives were able to note the starting and ending times of each activity as they progressed through the tasks of the day. The variable of the wives' household work time is simply the summed minutes reported. In contrast, the nature of the husbands' retrospective diary allowed only for a report of the average duration of each activity sorted. Thus, the result may be an overestimation of the actual time spent.

For daughters and sons only reports of task contributions were used; the children provided no diaries of their own. Table 3.2 shows that, according to their mothers, the daughters took on approximately 133 tasks per month, and the sons undertook about 63 tasks.

Solely from this broadly descriptive view, one can already see a clear division of attention to the work worlds of home and market, with husbands attending primarily to the market and wives to the household, and children providing household labor commensurate with traditional gender expectations. Such findings are obviously not news to anyone who has studied market labor patterns or household labor patterns, or, one

---

[3]Here, it is easy to forget that for both wives and husbands, there was a wide range of household activities defined as "household work." Therefore, one should not assume that all the time spent by wives or husbands on household work necessarily means that they were engaged in laborious or unpleasant tasks. Moreover, it should be kept in mind that time spent on individual tasks undertaken simultaneously (e.g., making coffee and feeding the baby) was added together, a process necessarily inflating the totals reported. (For a reminder of the range of activities defined as household work, see Chapter 2, Tables 2.2 and 2.3.)

might argue, who has lived in a family. However, this analysis will move beyond the simple observation that wives represent primarily household workers and, when employed, provide "supplementary" market labor, or that husbands are primarily "breadwinners" and, when they perform household labor, usually supplement the more intensive labors of their wives. Instead, the analytic models to come draw from both microeconomics and sociology and seek to explain, first, some of the likely mechanisms behind the *amount* of labor faced by households and, second, variation around the allocation of that labor. It is variation around this familiar pattern that the analysis takes as problematic.

Despite these more ambitious goals for the remainder of the analysis, the rest of this chapter is devoted to very brief descriptions of the division of household labor from a few different vantage points. For this study, a number of measures of "who does what" were employed, and each provides its own version of the patterns revealed in Table 3.2. More important, this glance at more detailed data on everyday household tasks may mean that the later models will not seem so far removed from the very real efforts of those who labor in their homes.

ADDITIONAL MEASURES OF THE DIVISION OF LABOR

Three additional measures of contribution to household labor are presented here: (1) a measure of the overall proportion of the whole contributed by each household member; (2) the wives' listing of those tasks for which their husbands and their children routinely took "responsibility"; and (3) providing a last look at household labor allocation in disaggregated form, the percentage distribution of the tasks sorted by wives and husbands. It is these 45 tasks that formed the basis for the endogenous variables of mean household tasks accomplished per month, which are reported in Table 3.2.

Members' Proportional Contributions to Household Labor

Whereas the total number of tasks done by each member (weighted by their frequency of accomplishment) provides a general description of the amount of routine household labor undertaken by households, the *proportion* provides a standardized measure of work apportionment. Table 3.3 presents the summary statistics resulting from the calculation of

TABLE 3.3
*Weighted Proportions of Total Household Labor
Contributed by Members*

I. Wives' version (N=331)	
	Proportion
Wives	.92
Husbands	.24
Daughters	.10
Sons	.05

II. Husbands' version (N=331)	
	Proportion
Wives	.80
Husbands	.42
Daughters	.08
Sons	.05

the card-sort data as a series of proportional contributions. Here, both the husbands' and the wives' "versions" of who did what are presented. The proportions can be thought of as each member's "share" of the total productive output of the household. Recall that wives and husbands first reported what tasks were accomplished in their households and how often these tasks were accomplished. They then resorted those tasks according to which members "generally" accomplished each. This procedure allows for the division of each member's weighted contribution by the *total* undertaken in that household. The result is an average proportion for each household member.

It is immediately clear from Table 3.3 that, regardless of which adult member was reporting, the proportions do not add up to 100%. Both the measurement procedures and the nature of household labor itself require this. Household members not only substitute for one another's labor but also complement each other's efforts. Indeed, by adding the proportions that appear in Table 3.3, one can conclude that roughly one third of the household labor was at least *shared,* if not substituted for, by husbands and wives. In addition, the husbands placed this "overlap" between their own and their wives' labor at a much higher level than did their wives.

Responsibility for Tasks

As Oakley (1974) and others (e.g., Berk and Berk, 1978) have pointed out, there is considerably more to household labor than the simple "doing" of a task. The accomplishment of household labor involves thinking about or planning for the task, as well as the actual work demanded by the task itself. As a consequence, our early research involving participant observation and open-ended interviews revealed a clear distinction between "help" with and "responsibility" for household labor.[4] We will return to this distinction later on. To begin, however, two items from the wives' interview captured the level of their husbands' and their childrens' *responsibility* for tasks. Wives were first asked to provide a list of tasks for which their husbands took "the responsibility most of the time." This question was open-ended, requiring the respondent to name the particular tasks herself. Similarly, an identical question was asked of wives with respect to their children's responsibility for household tasks. Husbands and children were mentioned as routinely taking responsibility for a mean of over two tasks (2.53 and 2.80, respectively), and Tables 3.4 and 3.5 indicate the particular tasks mentioned most often by wives. In both tables, the tasks were listed if they garnered mention from at least 5% of the wives. As one can see, there were a number of wives who mentioned additional tasks for which their husbands (.36) and their children (.23) took responsibility, but no one task was mentioned with enough frequency to warrant a separate listing. Second, wives are noted as mentioning whether their husbands or children took no responsiblity for any tasks (i.e., "nothing"). Inclusion in this category meant that wives made such an unsolicited comment, not that they simply refused to answer the question or claimed that they didn't know.

A look at those tasks listed most often for husbands makes it clear that the patterns of their responsibility for specific tasks reiterate the aggregate patterns found in Table 3.2. Table 3.4 suggests that the rigid sex-typing and the relative infrequency of these tasks combine to lower the overall contribution of husbands to household labor. For example, apart from the tasks that require relatively infrequent attention (e.g., household repair and painting) and/or are invariably associated with the more "masculine" side of domesticity (e.g., taking out the garbage or trash, yard

---

[4]The initial interviews with the women confirmed their working distinction between having the responsibility for household labor and providing "help" with it. Here are only two examples of how the distinction figured in the wives' discussion of their husbands' household labor contributions: "Now that I'm home most of the time, I do most of the work. When I was working, he helped sort and fold the laundry"; "He doesn't help them [the children] get dressed. He takes them hiking sometimes when I visit my mother. He reads to them and goes into their rooms to talk to them. *It's not actual work*, like helping them lay out their clothes. I would call it *occasional help*" (emphasis added).

TABLE 3.4
Tasks for which the Husbands Took "Responsibility": Wives' Report[a]

Task	Percent of wives mentioning task
Household repairs	38
Takes out garbage/trash	36
Yard work	31
Mows lawn	20
Paints	13
Car maintenance	13
Cleans floor	11
Washes dishes	8
Washes windows/installs storm windows	7
Shovels snow	6
Child care	6
Prepares meals/cooks/bakes	6
Pet care	5
Pays bills	5
Runs errands	5
Nothing	9
All other tasks	36

[a]$N = 326$.

work, and mowing the lawn), there were very few tasks for which husbands took routine responsibility. This does not mean that husbands did *nothing but* these tasks, only that they took the primary responsibility for relatively few. In contrast, any aggregate measures of *routine* household labor (such as our endogenous variables) inevitably reflect this difference. Moreover, 9% of wives responded to the question by saying that there were no tasks for which their husbands took routine responsibility.

The tasks that wives mentioned for which their children took responsibility suggest a wider range of household labor chores than those listed for husbands. Where husbands' chores seemed to follow clear sex-stereotypic patterns, the tasks for children would be expected to combine those tasks deemed gender-appropriate for sons and daughters; hence, the combination of "masculine" chores like "yard work," with "feminine" chores, such as "does laundry," and more "neutral" activities, such as "cleans bedroom." And 6% of the wives responded to the question about their children's responsibility by saying that their children took no routine responsibility for any tasks.

Of course, with responsibility can come the task of supervising others. With this in mind, we asked wives to tell us what their usual role was when (1) their children and (2) their husbands did household work. Although these results are not reported in tabular form, brief mention of them may be instructive. Of the 173 mothers to whom this question applied (i.e., mothers with children who did some household work), 33% reported that they "told them what to do" and the children did the work unassisted; 12% said that their children needed no supervision in their household work, and 7% said that they had to supervise their children "every step of the way." Because questions of age (and presumably competence) do not enter in when the work of husbands is considered, the figures for the wives' supervision of their husbands are more interesting than those for their children. To begin, in answer to this question, almost 16% of wives said that their husbands never did any household work; 5% reported supervising their husbands "every step of the way"; and 22% said that they simply "told them what to do." Finally, about 50% of the sample wives reported that their husbands required no supervision in their household work.

Even at this stage of simple description, there is a clear suggestion that the "gendering" of household labor tasks may affect both the kind of work that may be expected of individual family members and the degree of responsibility taken for them. In short, normative constraints on

TABLE 3.5
Tasks for which the Children Took "Responsibility": Wives' Report[a]

Task	Percent of wives mentioning task
Cleans bedroom	44
Takes out garbage/trash	32
Washes dishes	27
Makes bed	24
Helps with "Table"	19
Picks up toys/games/books	18
Does laundry	16
Cleans floor	11
Dusts	11
Cleans bathroom	10
Mows lawn	9
Pet care	9
Prepares meals/cooks/bakes	8
Yard work	5
Picks up clothes	5
Nothing	6
All other tasks	23

[a]$N = 173$.

who *should* do what may well affect who *does* do what. Thus, for example, husbands may exempt themselves from a variety of responsibilities, even as children may be uniquely *subject* to certain household labor tasks, with chores not only constituting labor, but also providing occasions for gender-related *socialization*.[5] (For discussion of this point in another context, see Wittner, 1980, and, more generally, White and Brinkerhoff, 1981.) Lastly, wives may find themselves engaging in chores *regardless* of the nature of the task, in part because of the stronger expectation that all household labor is ultimately a wife's *responsibility*. We return to such issues and a more lengthy development of their implications when the mechanisms behind, and variations surrounding, the division of household labor are explored.

The Apportionment of Labor by Task

Tables 3.6 and 3.7 show the percentage distributions of reported accomplishment for the 45 household tasks sorted by the wives and husbands. Table 3.6 summarizes the wives' responses to the card-sorting procedure, and Table 3.7 summarizes the husbands' responses.

A great deal of information is contained in these tables, and it is easy to become overwhelmed by them. However, only a few points bear mention in anticipation of the analysis that incorporates these data into a single set of endogenous variables. First, with 335 wives and husbands sorting 45 tasks, the total number of card sorts possible was 15,075. However, not every respondent sorted every task presented to him or her. Some tasks were never accomplished in the households and were therefore not sorted for who generally did them. Other tasks were not sorted by some respondents because of interviewer error or respondent refusal. The actual number of respondents who said that each task was accomplished at some level of frequency in their households is listed in parentheses after each task.[6]

[5]Compare, for example, the very different ways in which wives describe the contributions of their husbands—"It used to be that I'd clear the table and get the kids to watch TV. Now they stay in the kitchen. My husband reads them a story while I do the dishes. We'll do that, or if he's tired he'll watch me. If not, he'll help."—and their children: "We have a daily schedule to stick to. My kids are expected to help. I'm a tremendous disciplinarian, and I'm proud of my children. They live by my rules. I tell them if they don't like my rules, they can have their own when they have their own homes."

[6]There were instances in which tasks were sorted by the respondents, but no one was identified as "generally" accomplishing the task. This occurred for 292 tasks in the wives' data,

As one might expect, these numbers fluctuated by task frequency or the characteristics of particular households. For example, the tasks that involved children (especially very young children) were sorted by far fewer households than were tasks that one would find relevant to the demands of most households. Similarly, tasks that allowed for greater discretion (e.g., plant care, pet care, and shopping by mail) invariably were sorted by fewer households. Last (but unfortunately not least), one can compare Tables 3.6 and 3.7 and notice that, in general, the number of tasks sorted by husbands was considerably smaller than those sorted by the wives (i.e., 11,197 vs. 12,124, respectively). One can only guess at why husbands and wives might differ so markedly in the number of tasks that they reported accomplished in their households. Perhaps the best guess is that husbands may simply not have known as much as their wives about the routine tasks undertaken and thus may have significantly underestimated the total. Whatever the reason for the difference, it does lend indirect support to the decision to use the wives' accounts exclusively for an analysis of the *total* number of tasks undertaken by households.

Second, in the analysis to come, only the allocation of household time and tasks among wives, husbands, sons, and daughters is examined. Although provided for in the card-sorting procedures, there were too few household chores done on a routine basis by relatives, servants, friends, neighbors, and others to justify separate equations for them. However, simply to provide a complete picture of household contribution, the efforts of these "others" are reported in Tables 3.6 and 3.7 ("Other").

Third, Tables 3.6 and 3.7 recapitulate, albeit in much greater detail, the substantive message of Tables 3.2-3.5. The individual task allocations summarized in Tables 3.6 and 3.7 illustrate why the aggregate measures of Table 3.2 appear as they do. Because the wives took on a greater *number* of tasks and seemed to do those tasks that occurred more *frequently*, the incorporation of both task number and task frequency into the construction of the endogenous variables would result in a significantly

---

and for 616 tasks in the husbands' data. In this initial presentation of the card-sort data, these tasks are included in the calculation of the total number of tasks undertaken in the households, even though we don't know who did the tasks. In the chapters to come, where "who does what" is the most important question, these tasks are dropped from the analysis. Although these missing data are troubling, they represent an "error" rate of less than 2% for the wives and 4% for the husbands. Moreover, these errors do not cluster around certain tasks, and they appear to be randomly distributed in all respects throughout the card-sort data.

TABLE 3.6

Percentage Distribution of Household Task Contribution for 45 Sorted Tasks: Wives' Version[a]

Task[b]	Wife	Husband	Daughter	Son	Other
1. Cleaning bathroom (327)	91.44	9.17	7.34	0.61	4.28
2. Cleaning kitchen sink (326)	96.32	9.20	6.44	0.92	1.84
3. Cleaning oven (312)	91.03	7.37	0.64	0.64	3.21
4. Clearing food or dishes from table (323)	90.09	21.67	20.12	8.36	2.48
5. Cooking (321)	96.26	13.08	4.98	2.18	2.49
6. Cutting grass (218)	19.72	73.85	2.75	16.97	5.05
7. Diapering children (88)	94.32	25.00	5.68	0	4.54
8. Disciplining children (216)	92.13	58.80	3.70	1.39	1.85
9. Disposing of garbage or trash (316)	58.23	56.96	8.23	16.46	0.95
10. Dressing children (155)	92.90	19.35	10.97	7.10	2.58
11. Dusting (328)	91.77	4.88	11.28	1.52	3.96
12. Gathering clothes for washing (324)	95.99	9.26	7.72	4.01	2.78
13. Going to gas station (278)	62.23	79.14	3.96	3.60	0.72
14. Going to grocery or supermarket (326)	91.10	39.57	4.29	2.45	1.23
15. Household repair (266)	27.07	83.08	1.50	1.88	5.64
16. Ironing (287)	91.64	4.53	6.62	1.04	2.79
17. Keeping an eye on children (218)	96.79	36.70	6.42	2.75	5.96
18. Making beds (326)	94.17	12.57	15.03	7.67	2.15
19. Paying bills (309)	77.02	44.66	0.97	0	0.97
20. Pet care (194)	70.10	53.09	20.62	19.59	3.60
21. Picking up or putting away toys, books, clothes, etc. (279)	92.47	21.51	23.66	18.64	2.51
22. Plant care (293)	89.42	14.33	7.51	3.41	1.02
23. Playing with children while doing nothing else (209)	93.78	57.42	6.22	5.26	5.26
24. Putting children to bed (177)	93.79	45.20	2.82	2.82	3.95
25. Putting clothes in washer or dryer and taking them out (321)	94.39	10.28	6.85	1.87	2.18
26. Putting ironed clothes away (284)	92.96	4.58	9.51	2.46	3.17
27. Putting washed clothes away (322)	94.10	6.52	10.56	4.04	2.48
28. Serving meal (319)	96.24	12.85	6.58	1.88	2.19
29. Setting table (319)	86.83	15.05	22.84	8.15	1.88
30. Sewing or mending to					

Continued

TABLE 3.6 *(continued)*

Task[b]	Wife	Husband	Daughter	Son	Other
repair clothes and household items (313)	96.49	5.43	3.51	1.60	1.92
31. Shopping by mail or catalog (169)	89.94	20.71	4.14	1.78	0.59
32. Shoveling snow (145)	35.86	75.17	8.97	19.31	2.76
33. Sorting or folding clean clothes after drying (323)	95.36	6.50	7.74	2.48	1.55
34. Sweeping floors (293)	94.20	8.87	7.51	3.41	2.73
35. Taking children to school or day care (118)	86.44	23.73	2.54	1.69	4.24
36. Talking with children (257)	96.11	55.25	3.50	3.11	7.39
37. Talking with door-to-door salespeople (254)	94.49	23.62	1.97	0.79	1.18
38. Telephoning local merchants, stores, or shops (234)	88.46	29.06	2.99	1.28	0.85
39. Telephoning repair or service (246)	79.27	33.33	0.41	0	1.22
40. Vacuuming (305)	90.49	16.07	10.16	4.59	5.25
41. Washing dishes or loading dishwasher (311)	92.28	21.54	16.72	6.75	3.54
42. Washing floors (310)	89.68	9.35	2.58	0.97	4.52
43. Weeding (222)	61.71	53.60	5.86	6.76	4.05
44. Wiping kitchen counters or appliances (324)	94.44	11.73	7.41	1.23	1.85
45. Wiping kitchen or dining table (319)	95.92	13.79	12.85	3.45	2.51

[a]N = 335.
[b]The sample size for each task is in parentheses.

higher average contribution for wives. In contrast to the work of wives, the work of husbands and children seems more subject to the gender "loadings" of tasks. More important, the level of the husbands' and the children's participation exhibits greater variance across task. Perhaps this variance holds across households as well.

Finally, in anticipation of the analysis to come, it is worth remembering that some hard choices had to be made concerning who would speak for whom, with respect to who did what. Recall that, for the analysis in the next chapter of the *total* productive output of households, we will depend exclusively on the wives' reports of what tasks were accomplished. When task allocation is explored in Chapter 5, the wives' reports are used for their own contributions and for the contributions of their

TABLE 3.7
Percentage Distribution of Household Task Contribution for 45 Sorted Tasks: Husbands' Version[a]

Task[b]	Wife	Husband	Daughter	Son	Other
1. Cleaning bathroom (270)	84.07	20.74	10.00	1.48	2.96
2. Cleaning kitchen sink (291)	89.69	24.40	10.30	2.41	0.69
3. Cleaning oven (260)	82.69	16.15	1.15	0.38	2.31
4. Clearing food or dishes from table (312)	84.29	36.54	17.31	8.97	0.96
5. Cooking (298)	90.60	22.82	6.71	1.01	0.67
6. Cutting grass (261)	14.56	75.48	2.68	13.03	6.60
7. Diapering children (70)	94.29	45.71	5.71	2.86	1.43
8. Disciplining children (219)	83.11	80.37	1.83	0.91	0.91
9. Disposing of garbage or trash (321)	38.63	74.45	4.36	11.84	1.25
10. Dressing children (140)	90.00	40.00	5.00	3.57	0.71
11. Dusting (273)	86.45	16.48	10.62	1.47	2.56
12. Gathering clothes for washing (274)	91.97	18.61	5.84	3.28	1.09
13. Going to gas station (310)	38.06	88.06	2.26	2.26	0.65
14. Going to grocery or supermarket (322)	83.23	57.14	3.11	4.04	0.93
15. Household repair (298)	14.09	86.24	0.34	2.68	3.36
16. Ironing (230)	89.13	10.00	7.39	0.87	1.74
17. Keeping an eye on children (206)	87.38	64.08	4.37	1.94	1.94
18. Making beds (279)	92.11	19.00	12.54	8.60	0.36
19. Paying bills (313)	56.55	59.43	0.64	0	0.32
20. Pet care (197)	57.36	58.37	13.71	17.77	2.54
21. Picking up or putting away toys, books, clothes, etc. (263)	87.07	41.06	19.77	15.59	1.14
22. Plant care (252)	84.92	30.56	3.57	1.59	0.79
23. Playing with children while doing nothing else (211)	77.25	80.57	5.21	3.79	1.42
24. Putting children to bed (165)	83.03	54.55	3.03	2.42	0.61
25. Putting clothes in washer or dryer and taking them out (271)	90.77	20.30	6.27	2.58	1.85
26. Putting ironed clothes away (237)	89.87	13.50	10.55	3.80	0
27. Putting washed clothes away (277)	88.81	21.30	12.27	5.42	1.08
28. Serving meal (290)	90.00	17.59	7.59	1.72	1.03
29. Setting table (301)	79.07	27.24	17.94	5.98	1.33
30. Sewing or mending to					

Continued

TABLE 3.7 (*continued*)

Task[b]	Wife	Husband	Daughter	Son	Other
repair clothes and household items (244)	89.75	12.70	2.87	0	1.64
31. Shopping by mail or catalog (146)	77.40	37.67	1.37	1.37	0
32. Shoveling snow (176)	20.45	77.84	4.55	15.91	3.98
33. Sorting or folding clean clothes after drying (266)	92.48	18.05	8.65	1.50	1.13
34. Sweeping floors (272)	82.35	25.00	8.82	3.68	1.84
35. Taking children to school or day care (103)	77.67	32.04	0.97	0.97	2.91
36. Talking with children (240)	83.33	78.75	2.50	0.83	2.08
37. Talking with door-to-door salespeople (229)	79.91	51.97	1.31	0.44	0.44
38. Telephoning local merchants, stores, or shops (217)	71.43	52.07	0.92	1.84	0
39. Telephoning repair or service (243)	55.97	63.37	0	0.82	0
40. Vacuuming (285)	82.46	29.47	10.88	2.81	2.81
41. Washing dishes or loading dishwasher (277)	89.17	28.52	14.80	5.05	2.53
42. Washing floors (261)	81.23	18.77	3.83	1.53	3.83
43. Weeding (236)	41.52	72.03	2.97	8.47	3.39
44. Wiping kitchen counters or appliances (292)	87.67	27.40	12.67	4.11	0.68
45. Wiping kitchen or dining table (299)	86.62	30.43	14.05	5.35	1.34

[a]N = 335.
[b]The sample size for each task is in parentheses.

children. The husbands' reports are used solely with respect to their own household task contributions. It is pertinent to mention this here, as a comparison of Tables 3.6 and 3.7 indicates that there was some disagreement between wives and husbands, particularly with respect to the level of the *husbands'* contributions to household labor. Indeed, in *every* instance, wives reported a smaller level of contribution for husbands than husbands reported for themselves. Thus, the decision to use the husbands' version of what they did is probably a conservative one with respect to the actual difference between the household labor efforts of wives and husbands. (For a consideration of this as a "Rashomon" problem, see Berk and Shih, 1980.)

CONCLUSIONS

It is important to stress that three different dimensions of household work have already been described; the *amount* of work done, the *allocation* of that work among family members, and the *responsibility* for the work accomplished. In this light, there is little doubt that this sample of households invested enormous energy in domestic labor. On the average, all household members contributed, and the efforts of husbands and children were sometimes substantial. Yet, there seems little doubt that wives bore the heaviest burdens. In other words, there is nothing contradictory in the claim that husbands and children can make significant contributions to the household, while also asserting that most of the work and the responsibility for it falls to wives.

The data presented in this chapter describe what household work was done and who did it in our sample. However, it contains only hints about underlying causal mechanisms. These mechanisms are explored in the chapters ahead, with a clear distinction made between *what* work households accomplish and *who* does it. The former question is addressed before the latter; household needs are determined before the work is apportioned.

CHAPTER 4

The Household "Pie"
Market Time, Household Tasks, and Household Time

INTRODUCTION

The discussion of theoretical, conceptual, and methodological concerns in the last three chapters has set the stage for an examination of the total effort that households devote to domestic and market activities. In the introductory chapter, I argued that a study of the apportionment of household and market labors must rest fundamentally on an understanding of what households need to accomplish. Moreover, the mechanisms by which individual members divide their labors and their labor time are first seen most appropriately in the context of the *total* productive output of households.

Of course, one could well study relative household investments in market and domestic work as a substantive issue in their own right. As socially meaningful units of productive activity, households might fruitfully be examined for how they allocate their efforts to home and market, and for what forces affect those allocations. Indeed, an understanding of the exogenous forces that "push" households toward, or "repel" them from, greater efforts in the household and the market can convey a good deal about the organization of daily life in American families.

In one sense, then, this chapter addresses the household effort devoted to domestic labor and market work as an end in itself, but more important, the analysis will serve as a route to understanding the terrain on which household members negotiate and establish their particular contributions to household and market work. In prior discussion, I suggested that the determinants of "what gets done" may be markedly different from the determinants of "who does what." Yet, in failing to distinguish these two quite different dimensions, past research has treated the two as substantively identical. In fact, it may be that what tasks a household accomplishes, who accomplishes them, and how much time members allocate to them are all determined by slightly different forces or show their effects to slightly different degrees. Without a clear sense of the former, the latter questions necessarily remain obscure. This initial examination of the total work of the household provides a foundation for the later analyses of the contributions of individual household members to the productive collectivities that are their families. In short, we must first attend to the "what" of "who does what."

To that end, this chapter begins the analysis of household and market labor by posing two related questions. First, what are the primary exogenous determinants of the size of the household "pie"? The metaphor of the pie is an apt choice because it conveys the notion that before there is any apportionment of labor to individual members, households must establish a "whole": an array of finite tasks that the members understand as routine household labor, and to which they devote a relatively fixed amount of time. Of course, households face not only decisions surrounding how many household labor tasks to undertake on a routine basis, and how much time to devote to them, but must also establish the total time that their members will spend on productive activities *outside* the home. Hence, the determinants of the two parts of the household "pie"—market and domestic labor—are of critical concern here. Simply put, I will focus on exogenous sources of variation in (1) the number of tasks done each month by households; (2) the total time devoted to them; and (3) the time allocated to employment. Whereas market effort will be measured in terms of time, household effort will be measured initially by the number of tasks accomplished monthly, and then by the number of minutes per day spent on household labor. Given the strong possibility that these two dimensions of household labor can yield somewhat different effects, two nonrecursive, structural models are presented and analyzed. One explores the determinants of total household labor *tasks* and total household market time. The other, in large part a replication of the first, specifies the determinants of total household labor *time* and total household market time.

As important, the market and home labors of members constitute sets of activities that may well determine each other. Thus, the second question addressed by this analysis centers on the *reciprocal* relation between household domestic and market work efforts.[1]

It should be obvious by now that this chapter is not concerned explicitly with the contributions of *individual* members to household or market activity, nor does it examine the mechanisms by which work tasks or time is apportioned among them. To reiterate, households *per se* are the unit of analysis; the division of labor within, with respect to either household or market activities, is ignored. In this chapter, one must pretend that the social relations within the household productive unit, which critically shape both the nature of work and its allocation, are hidden from view. To return to the earlier metaphor, households establish a total household "pie," made up of all the market and domestic chores that they will undertake and the time required for them. Only after that "pie" is created can it be sliced and the pieces doled out to individual members.[2]

The household and market pie defined and described here can be roughly conceptualized as the total productive capacity of the household, or as the result of a pooling of individual talents and resources. Indeed, were a measure of the time available for *leisure* incorporated into the measure of the pie, the household's full income (budget) constraint (i.e., the total productive potential of the household) could be described. Because this analysis has no measure of leisure time, does not employ time as the primary metric, and cannot handle multiple products from a single production process, it concerns itself with a kind of productive potential different from (but related to) the full income constraint. Namely, total household market time describes the household's ability to command market goods and services. The measures of total household tasks and time tap the production of household goods and services.

Thus, this chapter can be usefully thought of as explaining variation

---

[1]Without attention to the joint determination of the effort spent on domestic and market work, one risks serious problems of misspecification. (For discussion and empirical support, see Heckman, 1980; Presser and Baldwin, 1980; Waite, 1980; Berk and Berk, 1983.) Ideally, one might want to explore the reciprocal relations among the total tasks defined as household labor (or the total time devoted to them), market time, *and* leisure. In this analysis, there are no adequate measures of leisure activities or, more accurately, "non"-household work activities. An understanding of the reciprocal effects of leisure activities on household and market work must remain here a neglected empirical question.

[2]This is analogous to the classic problem of cost minimization found in textbook discussions of the theory of the firm (e.g., Henderson and Quandt, 1971, pp. 76–78). A given level of output is determined, and then the role of input factors is addressed.

in the household's *capacity* for household and market production, or what determines the productive potential across the household.[3] The task and time contributions of the *individual* members are addressed in later chapters and draw much of their meaning from the pie analysis. Those subsequent analyses consider how households allocate their productive resources *within* the overall productive capability revealed here.

Yet, when the household is conceived of as being a single unit of production, a good deal of information is lost. For example, one will see at the outset that, although it is perfectly adequate for some purposes to view the household as a single decision-making unit, such a view masks real variation in the allocation of efforts to home and market spheres by individual members. Because all the endogenous variables used in the models for this chapter represent the *summed* measures of the wives' and the husbands' efforts, it will be difficult to ignore hints of the lopsided allocation of market and domestic work so obviously revealed by the descriptive statistics of the last chapter. From the first glimpse of the model to be specified, through the discussion of the findings, there will be a strong temptation to ignore this initial view of the household. But for now, the individual work lives within households, and the social relations surrounding them must go unexamined while these more elementary questions are addressed.

DESCRIBING THE HOUSEHOLD "PIE"

• Table 4.1 displays the means and standard deviations for each variable contained in the models specified for total household market time and total household commodity production. Some of the descriptive characteristics of the sample that appear in Table 4.1 were discussed in the last chapter. However, particular attention is directed to the variables reflecting total household market investments and total household labor tasks and time. Each of these four variables was constructed from

---

[3]In this analysis, I assume that households use their full productive capacity; capacity is empirically indistinguishable from total output. This follows both from the maximization hypothesis and from common sense. Because household commodities include activities normally thought of as leisure (e.g., watching television), what is asserted here is that *all* household resources are allocated to some kind of action that adds to well-being. One could imagine in the extreme a household that allocated all of its productive resources to recreation, and such a household would be producing household commodities at full capacity. Thus, I am *not* asserting that, for households to produce at full capacity, all resources must be allocated to household chores.

TABLE 4.1

Means and Standard Deviations for Endogenous and Exogenous Variables

Endogenous variables		
Variable	Mean	SD
Total household market time (hours/month)	166.94	91.92
Total household market time (minutes/day)	614.02	343.21
Total number household work tasks (×frequency/month)	1,220.93	456.02
Total household work time (minutes/day)	693.96	324.23
Exogenous variables		
Variable	Mean	SD
Number of rooms	7.54	2.51
Number of household work appliances (0–7)	3.87	1.74
Yard (dummy, 1 = yes)	0.95	0.22
Own dwelling (dummy, 1 = yes)	0.67	0.47
Laundry done at home (dummy, 1 = yes)	0.87	0.33
Older wives (dummy, 1 if > 54 yrs)	0.16	0.37
Older husbands (dummy, 1 if > 54 yrs)	0.22	0.41
Number of infants (< 2 yrs)	0.15	0.39
Number of young children (2–5 yrs)	0.38	0.67
Number of older daughters (6–20 yrs)	0.52	0.83
Number of older sons (6–20 yrs)	0.48	0.85
Wives' schooling (0–9 levels)	3.76	1.78
Husbands' schooling (0–9 levels)	4.07	2.21
Wives' occupation: Professional/technical/managerial (actual and expected; dummy, 1 = yes)	0.24	0.43
Husbands' occupation: Professional/technical (actual and expected; dummy, 1 = yes)	0.22	0.41
Husbands' occupation: Managerial (actual and expected; dummy, 1 = yes)	0.16	0.37
Wives' wage (actual and expected; dollars/month)	632.67	556.91
Husbands' wage (actual and expected; dollars/month)	1,345.72	506.24
Wives' wage (actual and expected; dollars/hour)	3.95	3.48
Husbands' wage (actual and expected; dollars/hour)	8.41	3.16
"Other" household income (dollars/year)	189.75	331.49
Wives' serious illness or injury in past year affecting ability to do household work (dummy, 1 = yes)	0.19	0.39
Household work rationale: Importance of being a good homemaker (0–2 ordinal)	1.47	0.66
Household work rationale: Importance of family's overall well-being (0–2 ordinal)	1.73	0.54
Household work rationale: Importance of the way it was done when wife was growing up (0–2 ordinal)	0.72	0.78
Household work rationale: Importance of getting it over with (0–2 ordinal)	1.25	0.73
Household work rationale: Importance of satisfying self (0–2 ordinal)	1.40	0.70
Household work rationale: Importance of having little choice (0–2 ordinal)	0.89	0.76

[a]N = 335.

the measures of individual wives' and husbands' activities in home and market labors, discussed at length in the previous chapter.

For the "market" side of the household, two endogenous variables are intended to capture the total amount of market time spent by households (wives and husbands). And each was constructed through the simple addition of the total time that husbands and wives reported for their employment. Thus, the variable "Total household market time (hours/month)" is the sum of the two variables for wives' and husbands' monthly employment hours. Similarly, the variable "Total household market time (minutes/day)" represents the sum of the two measures of the length of the employment day for wives and husbands, drawn from the estimation of elapsed time between leaving for and returning from work.

The means for the total hours per month and the total minutes per day spent by sample households on market activities show roughly comparable results (given that 46 households had no one employed, and 16% of wives were employed part time). If we assume that there are approximately 20 working days in a month, the mean figure of 166.94 hours per month (8.35 hours per day) is comparable to the total of 614 minutes of market time (10 hours per day). The difference in the way in which employment time was operationalized in the two measures can easily explain the slightly larger mean for the minutes-per-day variable.

Table 4.1 also contains the means for the variables that describe the tasks and the time of household labor. The table first shows a mean of over 200 for the total number of household work tasks accomplished, weighted by the frequency with which each task was undertaken per month. Recall that this variable was constructed from the wives' task card-sorts and reported task frequency. Given that the card sorts included only a representative, and not an exhaustive, list of all the household labor tasks that the families might undertake, this figure suggests a vast and no doubt complicated work process. For example, given a 30-day month, a monthly "output" of almost 1,200 tasks means that at least 40 tasks per day would constitute an "average" level for these households.

The final endogenous variable describes the total amount of time spent on household tasks. Recall that this variable was constructed as the summed total of diary-reported task durations by wives and husbands, and that it stands as an alternative to the endogenous variable of the total number of household tasks. For the full sample of households, the total number of minutes that wives and husbands spent on household labor was 694, or over 11 hours per day. Of course, this figure ignores the very different levels at which individual members contributed household labor time. For the present, what concerns us is simply the level at which total household production took place.

A comparison of the means for the variables describing tasks and time returns us to the discussion in the last chapter where some potential differences between the measurement of household tasks and household time were first mentioned. As one indicator of those differences, the simple zero-order correlation between the total number of tasks undertaken in households and the total time spent on household labor is likely to be positive, but far from perfect. Not surprisingly, then, the correlation between the two variables is .39. Such a relatively low correlation does indeed suggest that there may be significant *substantive* differences between household tasks and household time revealed in the findings to come.

The remaining variables listed in Table 4.1 constitute those exogenous variables to be included in this chapter's two nonrecursive models. In the discussion that follows, the two models are outlined, and some underlying empirical expectations are explored.

MODEL SPECIFICATION

Two models of the determinants of the household pie were developed for analysis, and each contains two equations. In each, one equation regresses a measure of market time against independent factors that may affect it, and the other equation regresses a measure of household commodity production against independent factors. In both models, dependent measures also serve as endogenous causes for each other, allowing for reciprocal relations between household market time and household labor efforts. In the first model, the endogenous variables are household market time, as measured in the hours per month spent on market activity, and household labor efforts, as measured by the total number of household tasks undertaken, weighted by the frequency per month of their accomplishment. In the second model, the endogenous variables are household market time, as measured by the minutes per day spent on market activity, and household labor time, as measured by the total minutes per day that the households devoted to it. The two models differ only with respect to the measurement of the endogenous variables;

they are identical in their specification of explanatory variables. In the following discussion, then, the rationale for model specification is presented, with particular attention paid to the empirical expectations of the effects of the determinants of total household market time and total household commodity production.[4]

Explaining Variation in Total Household Market Time

Total household market time is represented in the two models by two different dependent measures. In the first model, it appears in an "hours-per-month" metric, and in the second model, it is represented through a "minutes-per-day" metric. The exogenous variables employed to explain variation in the market time portion of the household pie center primarily on those members' characteristics that enhance or inhibit a household's market efforts. Guided by the New Home Economics, the equations for household market time capture the impact of (1) attributes valued in the market; (2) the opportunity costs of labor force participation; and (3) tastes for household and market work.

At least for the moment, the assumption that households operate as a unit to maximize their overall well-being, or household utility (Becker, 1974, 1976b), is critical to the specification of these initial models. We have yet to open the "black box" of the household to examine the particular effects of individual members on household labor and market activities. Thus, the task of anticipating the sign and/or the magnitude of the effects on total household efforts is often quite difficult. And notwithstanding the problem of anticipating how combined individual characteristics determine total household production, some exogenous variables included in the models often present the possibility of *competing* effects on market time allocations.

The first two explanatory variables for household market time (whether in the hours or the minutes metric) are related in part to the impact of age on market productivity. Age may also be a proxy for changes in tastes and for the opportunity costs associated with life-cycle

---

[4]Those who wish to skip to this chapter's "punchline" may simply consult Table 4.2 and the subsequent discussion of the findings.

variation. First, a dummy variable was constructed for each respondent, with 55 years of age as the cutoff point; the goal was to reflect the common distinction between those of "prime" working age and those approaching retirement. Table 4.1 indicates that for the full sample of households, 16% of wives and 22% of husbands were 55 years or older. Moreover, the dummy variable implies that a discrete, downward shift in the intercept should be expected for both wives and husbands. That is, households with older wives or older husbands, or both, should show reduced household market time.[5]

Second, the levels of wives' and husbands' schooling are included, and again, variation in market productivity, opportunity costs, and tastes may be involved. As a consequence, clear-cut theoretical expectations of the overall effects exerted by schooling are difficult to develop. Past empirical research offers no clear leads, as prior research is characterized by conflicting conclusions about how schooling affects market time investments for men and women (e.g., Bridges and Berk, 1974). For example, it has been observed that women receive smaller market-sector returns on their education than do men. As a consequence, women's schooling may be less strongly tied to occupational aspirations, with smaller effects a result. I assume that wives' and husbands' schooling exerted a positive effect on overall household market time, yet perhaps the effects were larger for husbands. Schooling was measured in 10 levels and thus (formally) took an ordinal form. Table 4.1 shows that the mean levels of schooling for wives and husbands were similar; wives' mean schooling level was 3.76 (slightly more than a high-school education), and the mean schooling level for husbands was 4.07 (slightly more than vocational training).

Three dummy variables that describe a high occupational classification for wives and husbands appear in both models. For those respondents who were employed at the time of the survey, the best measure of their occupation was the job that they currently held. For those who were then unemployed, the job that they *thought* they could get was taken

[5]A variety of specifications for the "older" age variable for wives and husbands was attempted, with a number of cutoff points chosen. The cutoff point of age 55 for the dummy variable proved the best choice, as it seemed to capture the effects of both traditional retirement and voluntary reductions in time commitments to employment.

as a measure of occupation.[6] That is, regardless of current employment status, the occupational dummy variable of professional/technical/managerial work for wives and the two dummy variables of professional/technical and managerial work for husbands are included as surrogates for individual and occupational characteristics that may well have pulled the households toward greater market time. The logic behind the inclusion of these dummy variables is quite straightforward: occupation (actual or expected) stands as a proxy for marketable skills, training, the quality of work life, long-run earning potential, and a certain level of commitment to market activities. There is thus reason to expect positive effects for each of the three occupational variables.[7] Table 4.1 indicates that 24% of wives were found in the higher level occupational category (i.e., professional/technical/ managerial), 22% of husbands were professionals, and 16% were managers.

Through a related logic, wives' and husbands' actual or expected wage is included in the equations explaining household market time. The respondents were asked their current wage or were asked to estimate the wage that they would *expect* to receive if they were currently employed. In the same fashion as in the construction of the occupational dummy variables, the wage variables combine actual and potential wage levels.[8]

[6]If the occupational variables reflected only the occupations of wives and husbands who were currently employed, it would have been necessary to include a dummy variable for employment within the model. Obviously, this inclusion would have resulted in a large amount of variance in market time explained simply by employment. Instead, this specification allows for the particular effects of high-level occupational identification unencumbered by the potentially overpowering impact of employment alone. Alternatively, one could in principle throw out all the women who were unemployed and, as a consequence, ignore their households. In trade, one would introduce a sample selection bias (for discussion, see Heckman, 1980). Correcting for the bias is particularly difficult (and often intractable) within a multiple-equation system. The logic behind the handling of the occupational variables also applies to the construction of the wage variables discussed shortly.

[7]It should be noted that the gender inequality always operating to determine the occupational levels of women and men does not undermine the logic of including employment variables in this form. Such social processes no doubt play a part in determining the size of the household "pie." For now, however, the impact of gender on the individual household members' contributions to home and market are not addressed in the models.

[8]The present formulation within the household production function implies that people make rational decisions about how best to allocate their time and resources. Hence, ex-

Table 4.1 shows that the mean monthly wage (actual and expected) for wives was $632.67; for husbands, the mean wage was considerably higher, at $1345.72.[9]

Anticipating the effects of wages on market time is notoriously difficult. (For discussion, see Nicholson, 1978, pp. 443–462.) Moreover, such problems are exacerbated when one is trying to anticipate the overall effects of wives' and husbands' wages on *household* market time. It might seem as if the effect of wages would be obvious; the higher the wages a household can command in the labor market, the more time will be devoted to employment. Households able to earn high wages will substitute market time for household time. Such *substitution* effects would mean that, with increasing household wages, the price of the time devoted to household work, leisure, or employment is higher. But the wage is obtained for employment, and not for household activities. Thus, households might well be inclined to substitute market time for household time. With higher wages, the "cost" of engaging in household labor (or leisure) is greater (i.e., through wages forgone).

Yet, just as reasonable is the expectation that *income* effects will surface. When a household experiences an increase in wages for one or more of its members, the household unit has more income at its disposal. If one compared two households—one with higher wages and one with lower wages—the former would have more income to spend. But in either case (in principle), greater income would be used to "purchase" any sources of utility, including household commodities. This implies that, with greater income, there is a greater potential investment in household production (and leisure) and a reduced investment in market activities. Thus, wages can induce a substitution effect, toward greater market time,

---

pectations about the returns from household and market labor are crucial to actual decisions. In particular, expectations about wages are far more important than actual wages. For employed individuals, I assume that the expected wage was the actual wage. For unemployed individuals, I assume that statements about the wages that they thought they could earn are excellent measures of the expected wage.

[9]In the first market-time equation, the wage variables are reported in a monthly metric, because the corresponding equation for household labor regresses the total number of tasks accomplished per month. In the second model, the wage variables reflect an hourly metric, because the corresponding household-work equation centers on the number of household work minutes per day.

or an income effect, away from market time. In short, depending on the levels at which households "mix" their home and market time commitments, higher wages may foster greater market time to get more of a good thing (i.e., wages) or less market time to gain other good things (i.e., non-market utility).

The final exogenous variable in both models measures "other" yearly income. The respondents were asked how much money their households received each year from such sources as social security, pension benefits, investments, and the like. Table 4.1 indicates that the sample households receive a mean of $189.75 per year from such sources. Anticipating the effect of this variable is less complicated than anticipating that of wages because, unlike wages, this income is *unrelated* to active employment, or to time spent in the market. Substitution effects should no longer be relevant, as the price of household market time is unchanged. As a consequence, only an income effect can be expected, where the larger the amount of "other" household income, the less time households will devote to market activities.

Finally, as an *endogenous* explanatory variable, household commodity production (as measured through task or time) is expected to exert a significant negative effect on household market time. Households are to be thought of as single productive units. They can't always "earn" their "pie" and eat it too; households must clearly choose between their ongoing commitments to home and market. The broad patterns of such choices should appear as a negative relation between household commodity production and overall household market time.

In each model, the two different operational definitions of market time are similar enough to suggest a good correspondence when the effects of exogenous variables on hours employed per month or the length of the employment day are examined. However, this may not be the case for the two equations specified for household commodity production. The specification and rationale for these equations are presented below.

Explaining Variation in Total Household Commodity Production

The second equation in each of the two models turns on an endogenous variable reflecting either the total number of household tasks undertaken each month or the total amount of time devoted each day to household labor tasks.[10]

The first equation defines household labor through the number of tasks undertaken each month. The second equation defines household labor through the time spent on the tasks. The exogenous variables of household labor tasks and time remain the same across the two models, but the results may well differ along critical substantive dimensions. For example, those same forces that may have generated an increase in the number of *tasks* undertaken by households may not necessarily have increased the *time* devoted to household labor. Indeed, some resources available to the household and adapted to the household work environment may have posed new tasks for the members, yet may have lessened the total time commitment necessary for completion of those tasks. Thus, in the discussion of anticipated effects exerted by the exogenous variables, some attention must be given to the potential differences between the task and time equations.

To begin, in both household labor equations, four exogenous variables are included that center on the number of children in the households. The four variables are (1) the number of infants (children under 2); (2) the number of young children (2–5 years old); (3) the number of older daughters (6–20 years old); and (4) the number of older sons (6–20 years old). It is assumed that each of these variables exerted positive and significant effects on both the total number of tasks undertaken by the households and the total time spent by the households on domestic labor tasks. Common sense alone would argue that infants and young children can be viewed as important generators of work, or *objects* of labor. The additional tasks they bring to the household profoundly alter both the content of household labor and the total time necessary to complete tasks. (For discussion, see Berk and Berk, 1979.) Older children pose a more complex set of expectations. Like their younger siblings, older sons

---

[10]The reader will note that the endogenous variables for neither household market time nor household labor time incorporate the contributions of the children. This is unavoidable; yet, it does render the notion of "household" market and domestic labor time misleading. However, it should prove some consolation to learn that the household-labor contributions of the children are explicitly addressed when the apportionment of tasks is analyzed in the next chapter. It is only for the present analysis of the household "pie" that this limited conceptualization of household contributors is employed.

and daughters are also objects of labor; they too generate more work for the household. Yet, they may also contribute labor, particularly as they approach adolescence. Nevertheless, this should not change the expectation that children (regardless of age) will increase both the number of household tasks and the time devoted to them. Moreover, it is through the impact of children on household labor tasks and time that a concomitant (albeit indirect) effect on the market time of adult members may be discerned.[11]

Next, five exogenous variables are included describing characteristics of the household work site that had the potential to affect the number of tasks undertaken and the time devoted to them. The number of rooms in the household was the first of these. Table 4.1 indicates that the mean number of rooms within the sample households was about $7\frac{1}{2}$. Other things being equal, one might expect that the larger the household work environment (roughly measured by the number of rooms), the greater the number of household work tasks, and the more time spent on household labor.

The second variable addressing potentially critical features of the household labor environment is the number of "household work" appliances. Constructed from a checklist of 7 household work appliances presented to the respondents, the variable shows a mean of 3.87 appliances per household. It is not immediately apparent what magnitude or even direction of effect to expect for this variable. Depending on the cir-

---

[11]In an initial specification of the market time equations, variables covering the full range of the children's ages were included. A preliminary expectation was that, particularly for the younger children (ages 0–5), the household faced demands for vast time investments in the children, over and above the actual number of household tasks undertaken. However, an examination of the correlations among the regression coefficients suggests a serious problem of correlated regressors among household labor tasks and the number of children. For example, the coefficients for both young-children variables (children less than 2 years old and children 2–5 years old) are correlated with the coefficient for household labor tasks at levels approaching $-.90$. This implies that the number of infants and young children in households and what wives reported as the total number of tasks involved in their household labor are variables measuring virtually the same thing. If one were to include these variables in the same equation, one would find that infants and young children exerted no effects on market time, once the number of household work tasks was held constant. This is not to say that no such effects exist, only that the impact of children and the number of household work tasks accomplished cannot be statistically unraveled. From a substantive standpoint as well, it may be that the impact of children on the market time investments of households is best seen *through* their impact on household labor activities. It is this assumption that is reflected in the present model specification.

cumstances, appliances may effectively combine or eliminate tasks (e.g., a self-cleaning oven or a dishwasher); add new tasks to the household; or substitute new or more frequent tasks for old ones (e.g., a clothes dryer). Because such effects may well cancel each other out with respect to the total number of tasks undertaken, perhaps a positive (but nonsignificant) finding will result. In contrast, with a greater number of appliances, the amount of *time* devoted to household labor should increase. There is certainly strong historical evidence to suggest that appliances alter the content of household work tasks but ultimately increase the time spent on them. (For discussion, see Vanek, 1974; Robinson, 1980; Strasser, 1982.) For example, a clothes washer and dryer allows household workers the "luxury" of doing laundry once a day. Without such appliances, household members may well have their clothes washed less frequently. Thus, this variable's impact may vary, depending on whether the task or the time is the metric.

A third measure concerning household work resources is a dummy variable indicating whether the household laundry is done within the home. Table 4.1 shows that 87% of the respondent households did their laundry tasks at home, rather than, for example, in a shared laundry facility or in a laundromat. It was difficult to anticipate the effects of this variable on the two dimensions of household labor. Because the household task variable deliberately incorporates a measure of frequency, a positive effect may result if laundry done at home is done more often. Yet, time may be saved through the close proximity of a washer and dryer, and thus a negative effect might be found for the time devoted to domestic chores. As a result of this ambiguity, there was a firm expectation that the total number of household tasks would increase were laundry done at home, but no particular effects were anticipated for the impact on household labor time.

Two final dummy variables were included to capture some additional effects of the household work environment: whether the respondents own their own dwelling and whether there was a yard attached to the household. Both variables were expected to increase the total number of tasks accomplished, as well as the time spent to accomplish them. Table 4.1 indicates that 67% of the sample households owned their own dwelling, and fully 95% of the households had a yard. Ownership of a home brings with it extra household responsibilities that many renters do not face; one is responsible for all maintenance of the dwelling. Similarly, the presence of a yard extends the household work sphere and the number of necessary tasks. Thus, both variables were expected to exert positive effects on household labor tasks and time.

A third group of exogenous variables centers on the characteristics of the individual household members. Anticipating their effects on *total* household labor investments is certainly tricky, and the difficulty itself illustrates the need for conceptualizing households as more than the sum of their parts. Those ambiguities notwithstanding, the first two regressors are the dummy variables for wives and husbands 55 years or older (seen earlier in the market time equation) and are intended to represent the effects of the life cycle on household labor productivity. Of course, these are hardly perfect measures of the social "age" of households, as they reflect the age only of the adult members and are only rough indicators of the timing of major life-course events (e.g., pregnancy, children leaving home, and retirement). Nevertheless, one might well ask whether households with older couples take on fewer household labor tasks or devote less time to them. However, it is not immediately obvious whether these variables exert their own strong effects over and above (i.e., *ceteris paribus*) the other variables included in the equation (e.g., the number of children, the age groups of children, and market time), nor is it clear what effects the two variables will have as they tap the different meaning of life-cycle changes for men and women. But on the basis of simply marginal productivity, or "seniority" considerations, older couples should initiate fewer tasks and invest less time in them. Yet, it is impossible to anticipate precisely the magnitude, strength, or differences between the effects of these two variables.

Wives' and husbands' levels of schooling were also variables included to reflect household characteristics that might impinge on the tasks and the time of household labor. Earlier, these two variables were expected to increase household market time. In the present equations, where market time is held constant, schooling may reflect less the pragmatic trade-offs between household and market activities, and more a general "attitude" (i.e., taste) toward the degree of effort needed to maintain a household. Thus, the tentative expectation was that the higher the level of schooling for wives, the fewer the number of household tasks undertaken by the household as a whole, and the less time that households devoted to them. (For a related analysis, see Leibowitz, 1975.) The expectation for the husbands' schooling was roughly the same. However, because, in general, husbands' characteristics should exert weaker effects on household labor than those of wives, it should be the case here that the husbands' level of schooling had less impact on household tasks and time.

The centrality of wives to the overall level at which households accomplished their tasks is explicitly acknowledged in a dummy variable for whether wives had experienced a serious illness or injury in the past year (affecting their ability to do household work). One might well wonder about the effect on the total level of commodity production when the "first team" is disabled in some fashion. Of the sample wives, 19% reported a recent serious illness or injury that affected their ability to undertake household work. When anticipating the effect of this variable, it is important to remember again that the dependent variables in these equations describe total *household* labor tasks and time. Obviously, were one interested only in the productive output of wives, one would expect a decrease in both the wives' tasks and the time they devoted to them. However, as it is the household's labor that is at issue, something will certainly be lost in the translation from individual characteristics to total household output. Despite some real uncertainty, one can anticipate that if wives' productivity is reduced in absolute or relative terms, investments in overall household labor efforts (whether measured by task or by time) would also drop.

A final set of variables relates to very different household considerations. Like the others, however, these variables constitute less than perfect measures of *household* decision-making and are concerned with the qualities of individual members. Recall that, in the introductory chapter, it was argued that an understanding of household investments in market and home involves more than simple economic concerns. Particularly with respect to the work site of the household, the members' normative understandings of how household labor should be allocated can be as important as any more pragmatic consideration. (For a discussion of the complicated normative issues surrounding household labor, see Rowbotham, 1973; Oakley, 1974; Berk and Berheide, 1977.) With this in mind, six variables were included that tapped the wives' normative orientations to or general rationales for the ways in which they accomplished household labor.

Just as the variable for the wives' serious illness was included because it was presumed that a change in the level of work done by the primary worker would alter total household output, so, too, was the inclusion of the last six variables based on assumptions about the wives' unique household-work contributions. Here, I assumed that not only was it likely that wives undertook the vast majority of household tasks and devoted more time to them, but additionally, in taking *responsibility* for household labor, they set the work *style* for their particular families. We have all known families where household labor seems to get done, but in a haphazard and unsystematic way. In other households, work styles are markedly different, illustrating real variation in how workers orient themselves to, as well as organize, the work. It is just these considerations that the wives' household-work rationales were intended to address.

Each of the six rationales listed in Table 4.1 were based on specific questions asking the wives "how important" particular reasons were in "explaining how you actually go about your household work." The ordinal scale for the importance of each rationale ranged from 0 ("not at all important"), to 1 ("somewhat important"), to 2 ("very important"). The standard deviations listed in Table 4.1 clearly indicate that wives varied considerably in their normative orientations to household work styles, with rationales centering on the household unit (e.g., "being a good homemaker" and the "family's well-being") and rationales centering on the needs of the worker herself (e.g., "getting it over with" and "satisfying self") garnering the most frequent responses of "very important."[12]

The inclusion of these variables in the household labor equations represents a radical departure from even an ecumenical economic model of the household production function. The heresy derives from the fact that such rationales are akin to the explicit inclusion of tastes; in traditional models preferences are presumed to be fixed, and thus, tastes are virtually ignored. It is here, therefore, that the first "collision" (and, one hopes, "collusion") occurs between microeconomic and sociological approaches. Unfortunately, it is difficult to anticipate the effect that tastes will have on total household labor tasks and time. The only genuine expectations would argue for a positive effect for those rationales reflecting a more "other"-directed orientation with respect to domestic labor (e.g. "being a good homemaker" and the "family's well-being"), and per-

---

[12]I did not attempt to scale these variables because there was no reason to assume that they were unidimensional, or that they would affect the endogenous variables in a similar fashion. Moreover, although each item is coded in easily understood units, it is not at all clear what meaning the units of some aggregate scale would have. There is no point fixing something unless it is broken.

haps for a negative effect for those rationales that are more "self"-directed (e.g., "getting it over with" and "satisfying self").[13]

In sum, the exogenous variables for household labor tasks and time focus on (1) the characteristics of the household work environment that are likely to generate work (e.g., the number of infants and young children); (2) the characteristics of households and their resources that may alter either the number of tasks undertaken or the time needed to accomplish them (e.g., the number of rooms and the presence of yard); (3) the characteristics of individual members that may reflect particular relations to household labor (e.g., schooling and age); and (4) the respondents' assessments of orientation toward, or accounts for, particular household work styles (i.e., household labor rationales). In addition, the endogenous variable of household market time was included to capture the other side of the reciprocal relation between market and household labor production. It was expected that the greater the overall household investment in domestic labors, the less would be the market time invested overall; thus, household market time and household labor would be placed in a negative reciprocal relationship.

To provide a more complete summary of the models explaining market time and household work tasks and time, Table 4.2 is presented. For the market and household labor equations, I have noted the anticipated directions of effect associated with each variable. Note that even though the two market-time equations have endogenous variables that are operationalized differently, the *a priori* expectations for these equations are identical. This is obviously not the case for the two household labor equa-

---

[13]Of the eight rationales employed in this question, six suggested sufficient exogeneity to be included as variables. They are (1) "trying to be a good homemaker"; (2) "trying to do the most possible for the overall well-being of your family"; (3) "trying to do household work the way it was done in your home when you were growing up"; (4) "simply getting it over with so you can go on to other things"; (5) "satisfying yourself almost apart from what your family may think or feel"; and (6) "the fact that you may really have little choice about how you go about your household work, one way or another." One could properly be concerned about the exogeneity of these items. One helpful reviewer suggested that these measures might actually have been tapping a *post hoc* justification for existing household-work arrangements. There is no compelling answer to these questions. If such rationalization processes were operating, however, they must have been quite elaborate. In addition, even if the respondents' work orientations were shaped by existing household arrangements, it is reasonable to assert that those orientations would then have served to reinforce the status quo. At worst, therefore, the causal relations were reciprocal. Thus, the equations are *not* misspecified as written, but the results may be subject to simultaneous equation bias. How large that bias is likely to be, however, is unclear.

Table 4.2

Anticipated Direction of Effects on Market Time,
Household Labor Tasks, and Household Labor Time

	Anticipated effects on		
Predetermined variable	Market time	Household tasks	Household time
Total household market time (hours/month or minutes/day)	X[c]	− [b]	−
Total number household work tasks (times frequency/month)	−	X	X
Total household work time (minutes/day)	−	X	X
Older wives (dummy, 1 if > 54 yrs)	−	−	−
Older husbands (dummy, 1 if > 54 yrs)	−	−	−
Wives' schooling (0–9 levels)	+ [a]	−	−
Husbands' schooling (0–9 levels)	+	−	−
Husbands' occupation: Professional/technical (actual and expected; dummy, 1 = yes)	+	X	X
Husbands' occupation: Managerial (actual and expected; dummy, 1 = yes)	+	X	X
Wives' occupation: Professional/technical/ managerial (actual and expected; dummy, 1 = yes)	+	X	X
Husbands' wage (per month or hour; actual and expected	?[d]	X	X
Wives' wage (per month or hour; actual and expected)	?	X	X
"Other" yearly income	−	X	X
Number of infants (< 2 yrs)	X	+	+
Number of young children (2–5 yrs)	X	+	+
Number of older daughters (6–20 yrs)	X	+	+
Number of older sons (6–20 yrs)	X	+	+
Number of rooms	X	+	+
Number of "household work" appliances (0–7)	X	+	+
Household laundry done at home (dummy, 1 = yes)	X	+	?
Own dwelling (dummy, 1 = yes)	X	+	+
Yard (dummy, 1 = yes)	X	+	+
Wives' serious injury or illness (dummy, 1 = yes)	X	−	−
Household work rationales			
Being a good homemaker	X	+	+
Family's well-being	X	+	+
Way when growing up	X	+	?
Getting it over with	X	−	−
Satisfying self	X	−	−
Having little choice	X	−	?

[a] + = Positive effect expected.
[b] − = Negative effect expected.
[c] X = Variable not in equation.
[d] ? = No expectation.

tions, and as a result, Table 4.2 lists two columns of expectations for household labor tasks and time. If the expectation for any given predetermined variable is a significant positive effect, a plus sign appears in the table. If a significant negative effect is anticipated, a minus sign appears. If there is no *a priori* expectation attached to a variable, the table shows, appropriately enough, a question mark. The table reiterates the previous discussion of the models.

MODEL 1: MARKET TIME AND HOUSEHOLD TASKS

The first model establishes the determinants of the size of the household pie, as measured by monthly hours of employment and the number of household tasks undertaken each month (weighted by the frequency with which they were accomplished). Tables 4.3 and 4.4 present estimates of the metric regression coefficients and t values from the three-stage least-squares procedures.[14] Reduced-form equations are not presented, but their R squares show 34% of the variance in market hours and 53% of the variance in household tasks per month explained by the model's exogenous variables. Before the picture is complicated by a consideration of reciprocal effects, the two equations will be discussed as if market and home were independent.

Employment Hours

Recall that the equations for market time were designed to reflect, for the household as a whole, human capital, opportunity costs, and tastes. From Table 4.3 and the exogenous variables for total household market hours per month, it is clear that a few characteristics of households and household members exert a significant influence on market time. To begin, the dummy variables describing the transition of wives and husbands into older age did result in the anticipated negative effects on household market hours per month. However, it was only for older

---

[14]Three-stage least-squares was used to obtain parameter estimates for the models. Alternatively, two-stage least-squares analysis also produces consistent estimates, although they are less efficient. In essence, three-stage least-squares techniques allow one to take advantage of information contained in the correlated residuals across equations. Although both forms of analysis were applied to these data, only the three-stage results are reported because (1) the results proved highly stable across techniques, and (2) the statistical efficiency gained from estimation through three-stage least-squares techniques was helpful (Kmenta, 1971, pp. 573–579).

TABLE 4.3
Metric Parameter Estimates and t Values for Household Market Time (Hours/Month)[a]

Variable	Parameter estimate	t Value
Total number household work tasks (×frequency/month)	−0.030	−2.08*
Older wives (dummy, 1 if >54 yrs)	−63.194	−3.17*
Older husbands (dummy, 1 if >54 yrs)	−28.222	−1.57
Wives' schooling (0–9 levels)	4.703	1.32
Husbands' schooling (0–9 levels)	9.770	3.26*
Wives' occupation: Professional/technical/managerial (actual and expected; dummy, 1 = yes)	−1.866	−0.16
Husbands' occupation: Professional/technical (actual and expected; dummy, 1 = yes)	−27.650	−2.15**
Husbands' occupation: Managerial (actual and expected; dummy, 1 = yes)	−11.777	−0.97
Wives' wage (actual and expected; dollars/month)	0.011	1.40
Husbands' wage (actual and expected; dollars/month)	−0.016	−1.88
"Other" household income (dollars/year)	−0.062	−4.36*
Constant	198.735	8.05

[a]$N = 335$; R^2 (reduced form) = .34.
*$p < .05$ (one-tailed test).
**$p < .05$ (two-tailed test).

wives that the negative result was significant. If wives were 55 years or older, the total household market time per month dropped by about 63 hours, a drop that suggests a decline in employment hours with advancing years and perhaps a preference for fewer hours at work. The effect for husbands was nonsignificant and considerably smaller. Raising the cutoff to age 60 made little difference; thus, these gender differences may constitute a general phenomenon. On the other hand, the two age dummy variables are highly correlated, and it may be that separate age effects for husbands and wives cannot be disentangled. Such issues are more appropriately discussed in the chapter to follow, where the effects for family members are disaggregated.

Second, it was expected that with higher levels of wives' and husbands' schooling would come an increase in market hours. At the same time, one might also expect that, although both effects would be positive, the magnitudes of the coefficients would differ. Table 4.3 shows that, for husbands only, higher levels of schooling generated positive effects on household market time. (Although the impact of the wives' schooling shows a small positive effect, it is not significant.) In contrast, for every additional level of the husbands' schooling, total household market time increased by approximately 10 hours per month.

Apart from the effects of occupational level, greater amounts of schooling for husbands can result in greater lifetime market earnings (i.e., a higher earnings "stream"). Moreover, if one conceives of education as an investment in human capital, higher levels of schooling may be sought by those with an initial "taste" for employment, or by those who can combine education with other human capital assets (e.g., intelligence). Thus, schooling may indicate a long-term commitment to market activity and may manifest itself in greater household investments in employment time. Yet, Table 4.3 may also reflect the process by which gender inequality intervenes to retard the effect of wives' schooling on household market time. Thus, the positive, but nonsignificant, finding for the sample wives is consistent with the notion that despite their human capital investments, women experience smaller returns than do men. (For a much more extensive and general discussion of these issues, see Schultz, 1972; Becker, 1975; Lloyd and Niemi, 1979; Lloyd, Andrews, and

TABLE 4.4

Metric Parameter Estimates and
t Values for Total Number of Household Work Tasks (Times Frequency/Month)[a]

Variable	Parameter estimate	t Value
Total household market time (hours/month)	0.850	0.98
Number of infants (<2 yrs)	412.328	8.07*
Number of young children (2–5 yrs)	295.301	9,43*
Number of older daughters (6–20 yrs)	109.325	4.22*
Number of older sons (6–20 yrs)	61.978	2.48*
Number of rooms	14.940	1.41
Number of household work appliances (0–7)	11.644	0.79
Yard (dummy, 1 = yes)	−46.655	−0.50
Own dwelling (dummy, 1 = yes)	−37.028	−0.70
Laundry done at home (dummy, 1 = yes)	114.278	1.70*
Older wives (dummy, 1 if >54 yrs)	−9.314	−0.08
Older husbands (dummy, 1 if >54 yrs)	−53.935	−0.60
Wives' schooling (0–9 levels)	−28.43	−1.79*
Husbands' schooling (0–9 levels)	2.511	0.20
Wives' serious illness or injury (dummy, 1 = yes)	67.92	1.40
Household work rationales		
Being a good homemaker	49.152	1.51
Family's well-being	105.220	2.71*
Way when wife was growing up	1.209	0.04
Getting it over with	45.517	1.63
Satisfying self	−48.855	−1.67*
Having little choice	−30.554	−1.14
Constant	510.571	2.72

[a]$N = 335$; R^2 (reduced form) = .53.
*$p < .05$ (one-tailed test).

Gilroy, 1979; J.P. Smith, 1980.) Again, however, as the contributions of families are aggregated, such explanations risk the ecological fallacy.

Third, a parallel pattern can be seen for the impact of occupations. Although the effects of wives' and husbands' high occupational status had the same sign, the effect for husbands in the professional/technical category was the only one of significance. And in every case, the anticipated direction of effect for wives' and husbands' high occupational status was contradicted by the data. For husbands, membership in the high occupational position of professional/technical generated a *decrease* of about 28 hours per month in household labor activity, *when the effects of education and wage are held constant.* It is important to remind ourselves here that characteristics of *individuals* (e.g., what jobs they held) were being examined for their impact on *household* market totals. Given that significant negative effects were not found for the wives' high occupational status, nor for the husbands' managerial status, there must be something especially distinctive about the influence of husbands' highest occupational levels on *household* market time commitments. The next chapter's analysis may shed some light on the differences in the influence of individual members' characteristics.

Fourth, the impact of wives' and husbands' wages illustrates quite different overall effects for total household market hours per month. Recall, it was difficult to anticipate what wage effects would surface, given the likelihood of income or substitution effects, and given the necessity of using the individual members' wages to predict the household market time totals. Table 4.3 suggests that the uncertainty was well founded. The effect on total household market time exerted by the wives' wages was positive, but not significant. The effect for the husbands' wages was not significant either, but it suggests that increases in wages bring a decrease in market time. Although the formal conceptualization demands that we view household income as pooled income that generates utility for the family unit, there is a hint in these data that real life is different. It may be that, in the context of structured occupational and wage inequality, wives' higher wages can have greater (marginal) symbolic *and* monetary value for wives, and this would produce substitution effects. In contrast, higher wages for husbands may yield smaller marginal returns and thus may induce income, rather than substitution effects. (That is, as husbands already have a lot of income compared to wives, the next income unit may be worth less to them.) Of course, this would necessarily imply individual utility functions and would fundamentally violate the assumptions underlying the household production function.

An explanation of those sorts of violations must await a more detailed examination of the market and home activities of *individuals*.

The firm expectation of an income effect for the final exogenous variable of "other" income (households' "buying" household production and leisure) was supported by the findings in Table 4.3. For every additional dollar accruing to the households from these sources of income, market time dropped by .06 hours, or about 4 minutes per month. If the mean level of income from these sources is used as a reference point, a yearly "other" income of $189.75 resulted in a decrease of almost 12 hours per month of total household market time.

The results of the market time equation are broadly consistent with previous research. They indicate that a good deal of the household's market-time commitment is explained by the characteristics of husbands, reflecting their human capital, opportunity costs, and tastes. Further, the results argue strongly that in the relation between household labor and market time, the *individual* (and sometimes contradictory) effects of wives' and husbands' activities are of critical importance. In chapters to come, these issues constitute the primary focus.

With the presentation of the exogenous variables behind us, we can now consider the impact of household tasks on market time. Table 4.3 shows a significant negative effect for total household labor tasks on total household market hours per month. For every additional household work task undertaken each month, the total household market time dropped by about .03 hours per month, or about 2 minutes. Despite its statistical significance, this finding may seem trivial from a practical standpoint. However, the descriptive statistics of Table 4.1 serve as a reminder that a great many tasks can easily be added or subtracted from the household, with corresponding substantial effects on household market time. For example, an increase of even one tenth of the mean of 1,200 tasks would decrease household market time by almost 4 hours per month, if the effects of the other regressors are held constant. Later on, it will become clear how likely *combinations* of endogenous and exogenous effects can profoundly alter work levels in the home and the labor force.

Household Tasks

The equation for the total number of household labor tasks accomplished stands in some contrast to its companion equation for employment hours. Earlier discussion made clear that this equation is concerned less with the individual characteristics of the members and focuses more on the features of the work environment that would alter the demand for household work, or that would facilitate its accomplishment. In addition, characteristics of wives and husbands, as well as the wives' rationales for their household work styles, were assumed to be important in explaining variation in this portion of the household pie. And again, the reciprocal relation between household market time and household labor tasks will be discussed only after the findings from the exogenous variables are examined.

First, Table 4.4 indicates that all four of the exogenous variables describing the number and ages of children significantly influenced the total number of household tasks undertaken monthly. These findings are fully consistent with earlier expectations concerning the work generated by children, with infants and young children exerting the largest effects. Every additional infant (a child less than 2 years old) increased the size of this portion of the household pie by 412 tasks per month. Similarly, every additional child between the ages of 2 and 5 added approximately 295 tasks per month to households. It is important to remember that the variable for the number of household tasks incorporates a frequency weighting. This means that the increases generated by children may have represented a *combination* of more diverse household-work content (where new tasks were added) and a greater frequency of the accomplishment of certain other tasks. Yet, to put these two findings in perspective, one should recall that the overall mean of 1,200 household tasks equals about 40 tasks per day. Thus, one can see that an infant adds approximately 10 days' "worth" of tasks per month to the household, and that a small child adds about 5 days' "worth." As any mother with young children can attest, this constitutes no small change in the work life of household members. The number of older daughters and sons also signficantly affected the total tasks of households. For every additional daughter between the ages of 6 and 20, 109 tasks were added to the household's monthly total; every additional older son brought approximately 62 additional tasks.

It is probably a mistake to conclude that the findings for younger and older children represent identical phenomena. It is, of course, likely that the positive effects found for infants and small children represented a vast increase in both the kind and the frequency of tasks. However, older children not only generated a demand for new tasks and a greater frequency of task accomplishment but also may have increased the total number of tasks through their own *contribution* to household labor. (For a preliminary discussion, see Berk, 1976; Berk and Berk, 1978.) Again, these issues are better explored in the chapters to come, but the contribution of older children may well explain the difference in the coefficients for older daughters and sons. That is, daughters may have *provided* more labor than their brothers, and thus their presence may have resulted in a greater number of tasks overall. This gender difference between sons and daughters is fully consistent with the earlier descriptive picture revealed in the last chapter.

Next, five features of the household work environment are represented in this equation; they describe (1) the number of rooms; (2) the number of household work appliances; (3) whether the household had a yard; (4) whether the family owned its own home, and (5) whether the laundry was done at home. Recall that earlier expectations of the effects of these variables differed, depending on whether household labor was measured by task or time. With the "task-per-month" specification, a significant and positive effect was anticipated for all the variables that describe features of the household labor environment. Nevertheless, only one of the five variables resulted in confirmation of *a priori* expectations. Clearly, physical changes in the household labor "terrain" have little significant effect on the total number of household tasks undertaken.[15] (For a related discussion, see Berk, 1980.)

Yet, some physical features mattered. *A priori,* it seemed reasonable to expect that, as home laundry facilities would make doing laundry less onerous, or at least more convenient, its frequency of accomplishment would increase, thereby increasing the total number of tasks undertaken. As anticipated, Table 4.4 shows that if the laundry was done at home, an additional 114 household labor tasks per month resulted.

Turning now to some specific characteristics of wives and husbands, we begin with the findings for older couples. For both older wives and the older husbands, a reduction was expected in the number of household tasks undertaken per month. Table 4.4 shows that, although the direction of effect was negative for both wives and husbands 55 years or older, neither effect is statistically significant. Perhaps age *per se* is relatively insensitive to the life-cycle changes of household work, distinct from changes in, for example, household composition.

---

[15]Of course, this holds only for the kind of "terrain" found in these data. For example, no one-room efficiency apartments or fifty-room mansions were found.

A priori expectations are supported by the results for the wives' schooling. An increase in the wives' schooling generated a significant negative effect on the number of monthly household tasks. Over and above the effect of household market time, each additional level of the wives' schooling decreased total household task accomplishment by about 28 tasks per month (for a maximum effect of 252 tasks). This finding reflects the poorly articulated, but consistently supported, notion that education fosters attitudes toward household labor which lower investments in it (e.g., Leibowitz, 1975). Table 4.4 also supports the earlier hunch that it would be the wives' schooling only that would critically affect the number of tasks households undertook. The table also substantiates an assumption made throughout this discussion, namely, that the wives' activities are more important to the work life of the household, and thus, their attitudes should operate to influence the household's work more strongly than those of other members.

The last variable describing the characteristics of an individual household member is one that taps the effects of the wives' illness or injury on overall household labor efforts. Although the expectation for this variable was tentative, it was anticipated that, in general, household productivity would drop were wives' ability to undertake household labor diminished to any significant degree. Table 4.4 shows that, in fact, the coefficient was positive, but not significant.

The final six exogenous variables in the equation are those concerning the wives' orientation to household work. The findings for these variables reproduce the mixed bag of results so characteristic of variables whose actual meaning, let alone exogeneity, is less than clear. Four of the six variables did not generate significant effects on household labor tasks. The two rationales that did show significant effects were among those to which *a priori* expectations had been attached. From the wives' perspective, a unit change in the importance of a family's well-being, as a justification for the way in which household labor was done, resulted in an increase of 105 household tasks per month. In contrast, a unit increase in the importance of satisfying oneself, as an explanation for a wife's household work style, brought a *decrease* of almost 50 tasks per month. Interestingly, these two "taste" variables that resulted in unambiguous and statistically significant effects are the two rationales that are the least equivocal in their emphasis on others or oneself. This may foreshadow some later (and less ambiguous) findings about *individual* contributions to household labor.

In summary, the exogenous variables that do the most to determine the size of the household labor portion of the pie center primarily on the presence and number of household members who, first, generate work for the household and, second, provide household labor. Indeed, this equation suggests that a great deal of information about the domestic work life of households is captured simply by the number and the ages of the children. Second, and of much less importance, the one "resource" of home laundry facilities, the particular stance toward household labor implied by higher levels in the wives' schooling, and the wives' "self"- or "other"-directed rationales for their household labor all exerted significant effects.

Finally, Table 4.4 displays the somewhat surprising, and certainly unanticipated, finding that virtually no impact was exerted by household market hours per month on the total number of household labor tasks per month. (I will return to this finding shortly.) Now that the first model has been examined, it is impossible to resist some preliminary speculation on the different attachments that wives and husbands have to the labor force and to the household. Some brief remarks are in order, if only to anticipate the findings of the next chapter and to better clarify the unexpected relationship found here between household market time and household labor tasks.

Anticipating Effects for Husbands and Wives

Throughout this discussion, it has been prudent to examine household and market activities unencumbered by considerations of individual members' contributions or of the mechanisms by which work is allocated to them. The conceptualization of the household as a single decision-making unit has proved a useful frame for an initial analysis of the household's relation to market and domestic labors. Moreover, it has been relatively easy to describe those forces that determine the size of the household pie, as they require only measures of household "output" (i.e., task and time) in the market and home spheres. Nevertheless, any reasonable interpretation of the *reciprocal* relation between market and home work, as well as any analysis that rests on the notion that the two spheres are inextricably *related,* demands at least a quick glance inside the "black box" of the social relations that determine the output described in this chapter. Specifically, some acknowledgment of the profound differences between wives and husbands as household and market workers is necessary.

When summarizing the findings from Tables 4.3 and 4.4, it is impossible to ignore the general impression that husbands' employment activities and the individual characteristics that establish husbands in the occupational sphere are the most critical determinants of total household market time. Likewise, it is wives' characteristics and their attachment to the domestic sphere that in large part determine the size of the "domestic" portion of the household pie. This was at least implicit in a number of findings from the nonrecursive model just presented. For example, only the husbands' schooling and the husbands' occupational level proved critical to the establishment of total household market time. Moreover, apart from the central role played by the number and the ages of the children, it was only the wives' schooling and the wives' orientation to household labor that had significant effects on the establishment of total household labor tasks.

Finally, the reciprocal relation between the two outcome variables of market and household work illustrated that the total number of household work tasks decreases household commitment to employment hours, yet market time commitments have no discernible effect on total household commodity production. To interpret these findings, and to anticipate those that may emerge in the next chapter, we come face-to-face with the very different social "locations" of wives and husbands.

A number of well-documented—even well-worn—observations provide the backdrop necessary to addressing these findings. First, a great many women are employed, but in numbers and hours well below those of men. Second, few married men engage in significant amounts of household labor and child care. Third, when women are employed, few substantial changes in their contributions to household work and child care result. Indeed, the "normalization of the double day" is fast becoming an old saw in sociological circles. Given these observations, it is little wonder that it is the individual characteristics of husbands, their wages, and their occupational levels that explain most of the variance in household market time. In general, husbands are more firmly attached to the labor force, and command higher wages, more resources, and higher occupational status than their wives. An enhancement of any of these would therefore have significantly greater marginal impact on the household than those same changes in wives' employment characteristics.

Additionally, it is understandable that there exists an inverse relation between total household commodity production and total household market time. Imagine an "ordinary" household where both wife and husband are employed. If for any reason (e.g., the demands of young children) it becomes necessary to increase household work, it is likely to be the wife who reduces her employment time, thus generating a drop in the total time spent by the household in labor market hours per month. In fact, it is possible to work through such an example from the data at hand. From Table 4.3, we know that every additional domestic task decreases total household market time by about .03 hours per month (i.e., 1.8 minutes). In addition, we can say that every additional infant in the household generates a drop of approximately 12$\frac{1}{2}$ hours of market time per month (412 × .03). In the context of an extremely high correlation between the number of infants in the household and the number of monthly household labor tasks, we might well conclude that it is *wives'* activities that explain the negative relation between household work and market time. Of course, it can also be argued that events which lead to a decrease in household labor tasks (e.g., children's leaving home) may well be responded to by increases in wives' commitment to employment.

Finally, the null relation between changes in market time and household task accomplishment can also be accounted for. To return to our "ordinary" household, if there is reason for the husband to increase the hours that he spends in market work (e.g., lower wages, necessitating two jobs), his fewer hours spent in the household will have little effect on total household labor. From the descriptive statistics (Table 4.1), we might assume that our "ordinary" husband is not doing enough household work in the first place (relative to the size of the pie), so that doing less would not make much difference. So, for husbands, a *floor* effect operates. In contrast, an increase in the market time of the "ordinary" employed wife (perhaps necessitated by an ability to command higher wages) will make almost no dent in total household labor tasks; someone still has to do them, and the job (as we will show in more detail later) will "naturally" fall to her.

Consider the reverse. When one or more factors motivates the husband to *withdraw* from the labor force (i.e., to work fewer hours), household work is still not the alternative activity to which he is likely to turn his attention. It is, after all, "woman's work" and, for him, not the best source of psychic rewards outside employment. Similarly, when the wife withdraws from the market and works fewer hours, an increase in household labor is not probable either. With respect to task accomplishment, our "ordinary" wife cannot do very much more than she has been doing already. Here, a *ceiling* effect is found, so that little may change in wives' household labor when their market time drops. In short, effects on "total" household effort mask real differences between individual members' efforts.

This brief discussion anticipates the very concerns that motivate the chapters to follow. Yet, it is important to appreciate that even when it is solely the determinants of the size of the household pie that are at issue, the social relations behind the production of family and market resources intrude as powerful (if mysterious) mechanisms by which households operate. In the following discussion, the alternative model of market- and household-labor minutes per day is presented, and some similarities to and departures from the earlier model are explored.

MODEL 2: THE MINUTES PER DAY OF MARKET AND HOUSEHOLD LABOR

As discussed earlier, the alternative model for exploring the determinants of the household pie differs from the original only with respect to the definition of the endogenous outcome variables. Rather than the original "hours per month" of market time, as measured by reports of formal employment hours, this model defines household market time as the summed durations of wives' and husbands' time spent on employment-related activities (i.e., the difference between the time one leaves for and returns from work). In addition, as an alternative definition of household labor as the number of monthly tasks undertaken, here wives' and husbands' diaries provided the summed total minutes per day spent on household labor.

Table 4.2 indicates that the anticipated effects of the predetermined variables on market time are the same for both definitions of the endogenous variable. But the table also reflects the uncertainty surrounding expectations for this alternative measure of household work time. Specifically, the effects exerted by home laundry facilities and some wives' rationales for how household labor is done are impossible to foresee.

Yet, apart from the particular similarities and differences that one might anticipate, it is also the case that, for reasons not immediately apparent, these alternative measures may yield some new insights. To begin, the two measures of market time for wives and husbands differed along at least one critical dimension. The measurement of market time through the elapsed time between leaving for and returning from work confounds employment with other activities (e.g., commuting). Thus, the effects of regressors related to distance from the workplace, for example, would be confounded with effects linked to employment time. The definition of household labor as minutes per day may also produce some new substantive findings. To a large extent, the exogenous variables concern routine, "normal" events and characteristics that hold over time. Yet, the measure of household labor time was drawn from the wives' and the husbands' diaries, and thus, at the very least, the amount of explained variance should decline. More important, unlike measures of task accomplishment, the elapsed time for the entries in the wives' diaries was *calculated* from the disparity between task starting and ending times. Consequently, the time measure is far less likely to tap norms and expectations about the "proper" mix of household activities. One result is that the regressors for the subjective orientations to household work, in particular, may be far less important than previously.

In sum, both alternative measures—elapsed market time and elapsed household time—at a minimum appear to have much more "noise." Overall then, less variance should be explained, and statistical power should decline. In fact, the reduced-form equations reveal that 39% of the variance in market minutes per day and 21% of the variance in household labor minutes per day are explained by the exogenous variables in this alternative specification, as opposed to the 34% and 53% of the variance explained earlier.

Household-Market Minutes Per day

Table 4.5 lists the metric parameter estimates and *t* values for the equation that explains the wives' and the husbands' total market minutes per day. Table 4.5 indicates that, as in the original model, the dummy variable for the wives' older age exerts a significant negative impact on household market minutes. Households with wives 55 years or older may expect a decrease of approximately 307 minutes per day (or about 5 hours) devoted to market activities. In the earlier model, it was only the husbands' schooling that significantly affected the household's market time. The same pattern appears for this specification as well. For every unit increase in the level of the husbands' schooling, the household market minutes increased by almost one half hour per day. This means, for example, that, over and above the impact of occupation, husbands with

TABLE 4.5
*Metric Parameter Estimates and t Values for Total Household Market Time
(Minutes/Day)[a]*

Variable	Parameter estimate	t Value
Total household work time (minutes/day)	−0.174	−0.40
Older wives (dummy, 1 if >54 yrs)	−307.400	−4.22*
Older husbands (dummy, 1 if >54 yrs)	−46.159	−0.69
Wives' schooling (0–9 levels)	11.403	0.88
Husbands' schooling (0–9 levels)	27.478	2.50**
Wives' occupation: Professional/technical/managerial (actual and expected; dummy, 1 = yes)	−9.477	−0.22
Husbands' occupation: Professional/technical (actual and expected; dummy, 1 = yes)	−42.635	−0.90
Husbands' occupation: Managerial (actual and expected; dummy, 1 = yes)	1.181	0.03
Wives' wage (actual and expected; dollars/month)	12.174	2.64**
Husbands' wage (actual and expected; dollars/month)	−19.659	−3.52**
"Other" household income (dollars/year)	−0.228	−4.42*
Constant	812.382	9.20

[a]$N = 335$; R^2 (reduced form) = .39.
*$p < .05$ (one-tailed test).
**$p < .05$ (two-tailed test).

a college degree (rather than, say, a high-school diploma) enhanced their household's investment in the market by approximately one hour per day. This finding supports the notion that such human capital investments (particularly for men) may be associated with a long-term commitment to employment, as well as a prediliction for devoting greater time to it. However, it may also be the case that more highly educated husbands were likely to spend more time commuting (or socializing before or after work). Therefore, the positive effects of education were perhaps inflated by the underlying effects of time spent on employment-related, but "nonwork," activities.

The absence of significant effects for the husbands' occupational variables suggests some unanticipated substantive differences tapped by the shift in outcome measure. In the previous market-time equation, all the husbands' occupational variables appeared to exert negative effects on household market time, with only the "Professional/technical" category proving significant. Here, two of the three occupational variables exert negative effects, but none appears to be significant. In addition, in the prior model, only husbands' wage exerted significant and negative effects on total household market hours per month, whereas the impact of the wives' wage was positive ($t = 1.40$). In this equation, wives' and husbands' wage rates again exert opposite effects, but both are statistically significant. An increase of one dollar per hour in wives' wages generated an increase of about 12 minutes in the length of the household's employment day. An equivalent increase in husbands' wages resulted in a significant decrease in household market time. For example, a five-dollar increase in husbands' hourly wages lowered household-market minutes per day by one hour. That same wage increase for wives increased market time for the household by an additional hour per day. In short, if the wives' and husbands' wage rates were equal, their substitution and income effects, respectively, would virtually cancel each other out.

In general, one would expect that this more broadly defined measure of household market time would make it more difficult for the traditional employment-centered exogenous variables to generate clear effects. For example, if one assumes that the endogenous variable confounds actual work time with time spent on commuting, then the high occupational variables (as surrogates for high socioeconomic status) would also, perhaps, capture the effects of the longer commutes. As a result, there would be a positive bias in market time for those with higher SES occupations. This may help to explain why most of the occupational variables once again show strong negative effects, but none of significance. Likewise, one might assert that jobs commanding higher wages are located further from the household. Therefore, when women take such jobs, the small positive (substitution) effects found in the earlier model are here enhanced. It may be that the negative (income) effects for husbands' wage are enhanced as well. If higher wage jobs for men are located further from their households and thus require greater commuting times, then a greater "decline" in market time activity would result when higher wages are used to "buy back" leisure and home-centered activities.

Related arguments could be made for "other" household income, but overall, a (negative) income effect is to be expected. Table 4.5 shows that an additional dollar per year of "other" income results in a decrease of .23 minutes of household market time per day. Were a household at the mean level of income for this sample ($189.75), compared to those households with no "other" income, its market time would drop by about 44 minutes per day. If we assume that a month has approximately 20 working days, this effect is greater (14.5 hours per month) than in the earlier model (11.4 hours per month). In any case, income effects are clearly present: households "buy" leisure (including greater household time) and thus decrease their investments in market time, whether that time is measured through hours per month of employment, or through the minutes of the employment day.

For these equations, I anticipated that household-market minutes per day would be influenced by household-labor minutes per day. Even though the measures of market minutes were drawn from estimates of employment day durations and from household labor minutes drawn directly from wives' and husbands' construction of ongoing accounts of their days, one could reasonably expect a significant negative relationship to result. In fact, the minutes per day spent by wives and husbands on household labor exerted no significant impact on the total time devoted to employment-related activities. The negative sign suggests some time trade-offs, but a more important insight emerges from this null finding. Namely, household-market time investments are most affected by the demands of *task* accomplishment, and only secondarily by time commitments to them. In other words, the household pie has two great slices to be allocated to members: the time spent in employment and the *tasks* that constitute household labor. A discussion of the implications of this finding follows shortly.

Household-Labor Minutes Per Day

Table 4.6 presents the metric parameter estimates and *t* values for the final equation explaining the number of household-labor minutes per day. In the earlier discussion of model specification, I argued that, although the overall results for the two equations for household labor tasks and time may well be comparable, the particular effects of some exogenous variables might differ. Table 4.6 indicates that this is indeed the case.

To begin, three of the four variables describing the number of children within households exerted positive and significant effects on total household-labor minutes per day. In the earlier model, we found that every additional infant increased the number of total monthly household *tasks* by well over 400. Table 4.6 indicates that each additional infant also generated an increase of over 105 minutes in the household workday. Likewise, whereas an additional 295 tasks per month were added to the household by the demands of each child between the ages of 2 and 5, here one finds a corresponding increase of 115 minutes of household la-

TABLE 4.6
Metric Parameter Estimates and t Values for Total Household Work Time (Minutes/Day)[a]

Variable	Parameter estimate	t Value
Total household market time (minutes/day)	−0.186	−1.13
Number of infants (<2 yrs)	105.279	2.38*
Number of young children (2–5 yrs)	115.425	4.29*
Number of older daughters (6–20 yrs)	69.785	3.00*
Number of older sons (6–20 yrs)	23.550	1.08
Number of rooms	11.726	1.28
Number of "household work" appliances (0–7)	20.158	1.57
Yard (dummy, 1 = yes)	−21.041	−0.84
Own dwelling (dummy, 1 = yes)	−58.071	−0.71
Household laundry done at home (dummy, 1 = yes)	23.966	0.41
Older wives (dummy, 1 if >54 yrs)	35.479	0.35
Older husbands (dummy, 1 if >54 yrs)	−92.921	−1.26
Wives' schooling (0–9 levels)	−10.009	−0.76
Husbands' schooling (0–9 levels)	11.601	1.11
Wives' serious injury or illness (dummy, 1 = yes)	−46.959	−1.09
Household work rationales		
Being a good homemaker	−6.750	−0.24
Family's well-being	−4.325	−0.13
Way when wife was growing up	13.060	0.52
Getting it over with	36.724	1.57
Satisfying self	−12.082	−0.48
Having little choice	−23.902	−1.02
Constant	585.583	3.39

[a]$N = 335$; R^2 (reduced form) = .21.
*$p < .05$ (one-tailed test).

bor per day for each small child. Finally, where older daughters and (secondarily) older sons were found to increase household labor output both through their demands and through their own contributions, the total time that households devoted to domestic labor significantly increased only as the number of older *daughters* increased. Each older daughter increased total household-labor minutes per day by well over an hour; their brothers' presence exerted no such significant effects. Thus, small children made more work for the household, and older daughters provided more work to the household. In both cases, the size of the pie increased.

Table 4.6 indicates that no other characteristic of the household work environment, wives, or husbands does much to explain the total time devoted to household labor. Of particular interest, and consistent with earlier hunches about how time was measured, none of the normative, or "taste," regressors surfaced. That is, orientations to household labor did not prove salient when household work time was calculated from diary data.

At the same time, if we exercise some speculative license, an additional substantive story is suggested. Earlier, I argued that household work appliances would show few clear effects on the number of tasks undertaken, as they serve to recombine some tasks, to eliminate others, and perhaps even to increase the frequency of still others. Recall that, indeed, the t value for "appliances" was less than 1.0. However, with respect to the effect of appliances on the *time* spent, it was expected that appliances would increase the necessary time devoted to household labor. Moreover, such a result would corroborate prior studies of both historical (e.g., Vanek, 1974; Strasser, 1982) and current patterns of household labor (e.g., Berk, 1980). Table 4.6 hints that each additional household work appliance lengthens the household work day by about 20 minutes. (This conclusion, however, turns on one's taking seriously a regression coefficient with a t value of 1.57; $p = .06$ for a one-tailed test.) With an increase in the number of household labor appliances comes the potential for an escalation in standards and a greater investment of time in household labor. This finding may also reflect an *a priori* commitment to the domestic work undertaken, in turn, with lots of "gadgets." Of course, such a commitment would have to reflect tastes not already captured through the attitude variables included in the model. Regardless, the data appear to extend the past findings: the idea that appliances are "labor-saving" should not necessarily imply that they are also "time-saving." To equate the two is to ignore the very real differences between the frequency with which tasks are accomplished and the time demanded for them.

To recapitulate, the findings from the two household labor equations in the two models speak to the important differences between the task and the time metrics of household labor itself. For example, a comparison of the two equations demonstrates that children can importantly determine how much *and* how long households will engage in household labor. In contrast, the number of household work appliances may make little overall difference to how much households do but may well affect how much time is spent on tasks. Last, although the underlying rationales for household labor styles may affect how many and how often household work tasks are elected in the first place, they may not have much effect on how much time is spent on them. Of course, here both substantive and methodological issues may be implied.

Finally, in the prior model, the reciprocal relation between the two endogenous variables was such that the total number of tasks accomplished by the sample households was relatively impervious to changes in market time commitments. Yet, tasks from the domestic sphere significantly altered household investments in market time. In the present model, it was expected that a negative reciprocal relation would appear; instead, an inconclusive but intriguing finding emerged. At the risk of interpreting a result that might well have occurred by chance, I will turn briefly to a coefficient found significant in only the two-stage least-squares result.

Table 4.6 shows no statistically significant effect for the reciprocal relation between total household-labor time and market time. But let us presume that total household-market time is negatively related to total household-labor time, where increases in household market time decrease household work time. Were this the case, the difference between the reciprocal relations of the two models highlights a *substantive* difference between household tasks and household time. These two dimensions of household labor may reflect the nature of the discretion attached to household labor.

The discretion necessary for a potential alteration in the domestic work of households may not revolve primarily around the choice of tasks, how many tasks to undertake, or even how often tasks are accomplished. Such decisions are determined quite forcefully by the demands of household members themselves, especially children. Moreover, there are certain routine tasks that virtually all households must undertake with some regularity (e.g., meal preparation). Hence, real discretion in the level at which households engage in domestic labor is found in the amount of time invested. As a consequence, market demands placed on households affect domestic labor largely through the dimension of "how long" and not "how much"—through time and not task. Similarly, the demands of the household take their toll on market commitments through the somewhat rigid mix of domestic tasks. The relative inflexibility of household tasks and the little discretion available to members to alter them can exert a strong effect on household market time. Thus, demands that increase how much household labor is done result in a drop in the commitment of the household to employment.

In sum, Tables 4.3–4.6 suggest that any new demands that of necessity increase the number of household labor tasks can significantly alter the market time commitments of some household members. In contrast, demands that foster an increase in household market time may alter not the tasks of the household, but instead the *time* that the members devote to them.

OVERVIEW AND CONCLUSIONS: THE HOUSEHOLD "PIE"

This analysis began with two seemingly simple questions. It first asked what determines households' investments in the labor market (as measured by two estimates of market time) and households' investments in domestic work (as measured by task and time). The second question addressed the relation between the spheres of employment and domestic labor. Figures 1 and 2 provide a pictorial representation of the important explanatory variables for the household "pie." Figure 1 shows the key coefficients for the initial model; Figure 2 shows the findings for the alternative model. In the figures, the mean for each variable is listed in parentheses. The regression coefficients are listed along each arrow leading to the household pie. With the exception of the causal link between total household-market minutes per day and total household work time, each regression coefficient listed represents a statistically significant effect.

Much of what is striking about the figures has been discussed in greater detail in the preceding sections. However, some general observations bear reiteration here. To begin, the figures affirm that a greater number of exogenous factors affect the number of household tasks than affect household work time. Likewise, there are more significant determinants of the time committed to employment when "official" employment hours are used as the operational definition of market time. One explanation is the greater "noise" generated in the endogenous variables when they are defined by (1) the duration of the employment day or (2) household minutes per day from diaries. In addition, the definition of household work as tasks may produce a more interesting set of effects because of the normative and expectational components incorporated in them.

Neverthelesss, for both measures of total household labor output, for example, the number of children in particular age categories was critical to the determination of how much domestic work would be elected

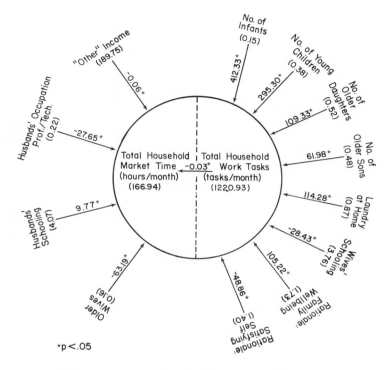

FIGURE 1. Total household-market time and tasks $(N = 335)$.

by the sample households. Figures 1 and 2 suggest that regardless of how household commodity production is defined, children make the crucial difference in total household labor effort, with selected features of the work site and perhaps wives' preferences exerting secondary effects. Similarly, general conclusions can be drawn from the two market-time equations. Those forces that attract household members to and repel them from the market sector center on the trinity of human capital, opportunity costs, and tastes.

A consideration of the relation *between* the two spheres that constitute the household pie poses a greater challenge to a meaningful comparison of the models. Figure 1 shows clearly that the household exerts its influence over the market commitments of its members through the establishment of the tasks of the household. The tasks then serve to modify a household's formal investment in employment, rather than day-to-day variation in the time of market-related activities. As a result, an increase

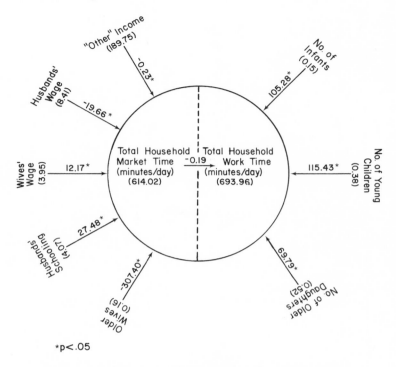

*p<.05

FIGURE 2. Total household market and work time (N = 335).

in the total number of household tasks undertaken per month generated a decrease in the total number of household employment hours per month. But, the reverse relation did not emerge. Figure 1 illustrates this asymmetric link between domestic and market labors. At the same time, as is illustrated by Figure 2, there is the suggestion of a "missing" reciprocal relation between household market time and domestic labor time. That is, the specific day-to-day time that households spend at their already established market commitments may influence the work of the household through the time devoted to *already-established* domestic tasks.

This seeming contradiction between the findings of the two models first suggests that both the total number of household labor tasks established per month and the total household market time per month are "lumpy"; they are relatively more fixed, more stable, and less flexible than the daily *minutes* devoted to either activity. That is, household members may be committed to a particular level of employment, and the number of tasks undertaken by the households may not be subject to large amounts of discretion. For example, one cannot choose to "cut back" on the tasks required to care for young children. Likewise, few jobs are organized to allow for flexible hours for workers to respond to the demands of the household. Thus, the imperatives of domestic work may well take some members out of the market altogether or may substantially decrease their formal attachment to it. In contrast, the employment commitments of household members can have little impact on the relatively fixed requirements of household labor.

I have argued, albeit more tentatively, that the opposite story may emerge when the household labor day and the market day are expressed in *minutes.* Although, in general, the tasks of the household may be more fixed, the number of minutes that households can spend on those tasks is no doubt more variable and is more subject to individual household discretion. I have speculated that, as a consequence, the relatively inflexible demands of employment can critically influence how many minutes per day household members devote to household labor. In households where the members make some fixed commitment to the market (given the "lumpy" domestic labor tasks), any particular day can find a decrease in the time spent on household labor as a function of the demands of employment. To return to a previous example, we see that the demands of infant care must be met through a great number of tasks for the household. However, that does not preclude some discretion in how much time is devoted to those tasks.

The dual specification of the household pie has thus revealed two somewhat different, yet complementary, dimensions of the same phenomenon. The result is two views of how employment can influence the accomplishment of household labor, and how the establishment of household tasks places very real demands on the members' formal commitments to market work. In summary, the demands of household labor, presented to the members as the array of tasks that must be accomplished, can exclude a household member (or members) from the world of employment and may thus significantly lower the total household commitment to employment. Yet, once that market commitment is made, the constraints imposed may also reduce the time devoted to household tasks. Thus, market work perhaps has little power over how *much* is done in the household, and the time spent on household labor perhaps has little power over the relatively fixed *length* of the household's employment day.

Finally, Figures 1 and 2 summarize a story that carries significant implications for the more detailed analysis to follow. Thus far, the exogenous variables reflecting the sample husbands' characteristics have typically played a larger role in the determination of household market time, and the wives' characteristics have proved more important for total household labor efforts. Just as compelling are the barely masked individual gender differences operating in the reciprocal relations between the two work sites.

For example, the asymmetric relation between household tasks and market time operates in interesting ways when households face change. When the demand of household tasks goes up, it is likely to be wives who will decrease their labor market participation. That is, husbands will not be responsive to household demands and will thus not alter their employment commitments. After all, the market time of husbands is very likely to be the more valuable to the household as a whole, and thus a "maximizing" household (ceteris paribus) is one in which the wives respond first to household demands. Yet, when the total household market commitment goes up, one sees little change in husbands' or wives' households efforts because (1) the husbands' efforts are small to begin with, and (2) the wives' efforts must remain the same, regardless of employment. When household labor time and household market time were examined, the same sorts of principles could be applied. Namely, market demands may lower the total time spent on household labor (as wives adjust to the "double day"), but when household labor requires more time, this need is translated into new demands placed on wives and has little impact on the total time spent by the household on employment. Clearly, there is something operating here beyond the rational considerations of households seeking to maximize utility.

As I will turn shortly to the mechanisms that explain variation in the allocation of household and market work to individual household members, the broader determinants of the household pie will remain a critical backdrop. It is possible to examine how variance in the division of household labor is determined, conditional on the effects found here for total household capability at work and at home. In forthcoming chapters, the overall task and time commitments to household labor and market activities are treated as the initial condition under which the apportionment of work is negotiated and established.

More specifically, an analysis of the particular contributions of wives, husbands, sons, and daughters to the work of the household will assume the size and the determinants of that portion of the household pie as the context in which the members' efforts are realized. Likewise, the particular impact of the members' characteristics on their labor-market attachments will be viewed as conditional on the total household investment in market work. Finally, the reciprocal relations among individual members' contributions to home and market will be analyzed only in light of the overall commitments that households make to employment and domestic labor.

For the examination of the division of household labor (as measured by task or time) and the division of market labors (as measured by market time) the household pie will be "sliced." The next two chapters delineate the mechanisms by which the household pie is apportioned, and the explanation of variation in that apportionment constitutes the primary focus. Chapter 5 examines how household tasks and market time are allocated; Chapter 6 supplements that analysis with a look at wives' household and market time.

CHAPTER 5

Dividing It Up
The Mechanisms of Asymmetry

INTRODUCTION

Up to now, considerable time has been spent on the argument that an understanding of the division of household labor turns on at least two critical components: (1) a clear distinction between household productive capacity and its allocation among household members and (2) formal acknowledgement of the reciprocal relation between household and market labor investments. These two dimensions of household production have done the most to inform the organization and analysis of the data. For example, the conceptual distinction between the household "pie" (made up of domestic and market labors) and the efforts of individual members has led to both methodological and substantive departures from earlier efforts. It has also meant some theoretical dependence on the New Home Economics, as well as taking some empirical liberties with it. In particular, households are conceptualized as *both* productive units and collections of separate individuals. It is in this chapter, where the household-task and market-time contributions of individual members will be examined, that the merits of this conceptualization can be demonstrated.

In the last chapter, theoretical notions from the household production function led to a specification of a two-equation model. Each coefficient estimated represented the change in total household market time or commodity production, given a unit change in some aspect of household productivity or opportunity cost. Thus, for example, we saw that (other things being equal) the respondent husbands' "professional or technical" occupations served to decrease total household market time by

27.65 hours per month, compared to those not in that occupational category. Likewise, households with an infant initiated an additional 400 tasks compared to those without an infant. In short, a model was posed to explain variation in the household's productive capacity to command market goods and services, and to produce household goods and services.

When the focus shifts to individual efforts, the model is interpreted differently, as the household pie (whether it be the portion that is market time or the portion that is tasks) provides the *context* in which to view task apportionment. More specifically, we can now consider how households allocate the productive capacity (i.e., the pie) examined in the last chapter. The labor provided by each member operates within that overall productive capacity. Thus, the relevant question for this analysis is, *conditional on* total household productivity, what determines the apportionment of productive resources? For example, we will see the effect that daughters have on the number of tasks their mothers undertake per month, in the context of their effect on the establishment of the household's total number of tasks. Or whereas earlier we saw that a variable exerted little or no effect on a household's command of market goods and services (total household market time), that same variable may prove significant to an individual's market time, conditional on household productive capacity. More difficult to accept, perhaps, will be those instances in which variables (e.g., education) that are traditionally assumed to *directly* affect the household activities of individuals in fact influence individuals through *total* household effort. Nevertheless, in this more rigorous specification, each variable exercises its effect in *interaction* with the overall capacity already established by household. Conceptualizing the apportionment of individual labors this way means that the specific effects of particular regressors on members' market time or tasks can be related to changes in the *proportion* contributed by that household member.[1] In other words, to return to the pie metaphor more directly, the explanatory variables operate on each individual's "slice" of the

---

[1]Consider a simplified version of one of the equations:

$$Y = B0 + B1(D2) + B2(D3) + B3(X)^*P + e,$$

where: Y = the contribution of the person in question; X = any regressor of substantive interest; P = the size of a portion of the pie (e.g., number of tasks); $D1$ = dummy variable if portion of pie is small (excluded); $D2$ = dummy variable if portion of pie is "average"; and $D3$ = dummy variable if portion of pie is "large."

Now, divide both sides by P:

$$Y/P = B0^*1/P + B1^*(D2)/P + B2^*(D3)/P + B3(X)^*P/P + e/P$$

household pie, the slice sizes vary among the members, and are themselves affected by factors both exogenous and endogenous to the pie itself.[2]

Yet, despite this marked departure from the last chapter's conceptualization of the model, the variables included are often the same. By and large, the equations still involve issues of marginal productivity (e.g., age); the opportunity costs of household or market contribution (e.g. wage); and household work "tastes" (e.g., "rationale" variables). There are some new twists in the specification of these models, and they are discussed in more detail below. For the moment, it is only important to remember that *every* effect on the contribution of individual members to time in the labor market or the tasks of the household takes as *given* the already-established level for household market hours or the already-established level for monthly household tasks. In short, as we now know what makes a difference in realizing total household productive capacity, we can ask what makes a difference in realizing individual resources for the market and the household.

THE MODEL

The equations specified for the allocation of monthly employment hours and the number of monthly household work tasks constitute the model for the allocation of household market time and household labor. Table 5.1 is included as a general reminder of the variables in the five equations of the model. The table simply lists the relevant endogenous and exogenous variables (along with their means and their standard devi-

---

Therefore: (1) Because $P/P = 1$ and Y/P is a proportion, $B3$ is now the change in the proportion done by the member for a one unit change in X. (2) $B0$ captures the impact of "1/pie," a new variable but is of no substantive interest and is likely to be close to zero in practice. (3) $B1$ *or* $B2$ will be the new intercept, depending on whether the size of the "pie" falls at $D2$ or $D3$, then, $D2/P = 1/1$, or $D3/P = 1/1$. When the size of the "pie" falls at $D1$, the intercept is zero.

[2]The technique through which the "proportion" effect is captured requires the construction of interaction terms where total commodity production, or total household market time, is the context in which the members divide their tasks and/or time. A more formal "proportion" analysis was attempted at a preliminary stage, where the endogenous variables to be estimated were actual proportions (proportion done by wives, husbands, sons, and so on). This method was eventually abandoned, in part because it was plagued by heteroskedasticity; the disturbance variance was necessarily larger for the households that divided the work more evenly. In addition, a richer story can be told from the present formulation.

TABLE 5.1

Means and Standard Deviations for Endogenous and Exogenous Variables[a]

Endogenous variables		
Variable	Mean	SD
Total household market time (hours/month)	178.82	83.60
Wives' market time (hours/month)	37.85	64.82
Husbands' market time (hours/month)	140.97	51.88
Total number household work tasks (times frequency/month)	1,234.36	450.30
Wives' household task contribution (wives' report)	1,149.39	458.94
Husbands' household task contribution (husbands' report)	374.61	325.64
Daughters' household task contribution (wives' report)	136.86	266.88
Sons' household task contribution (wives' report)	66.20	142.32

Exogenous variables		
Variable	Mean	SD
Middle-aged wives (dummy, 1 if 30–50 yrs)	0.44	0.50
Older wives (dummy, 1 if >50 yrs)	0.19	0.39
Middle-aged husbands (dummy, 1 if 30–50 yrs)	0.49	0.50
Older husbands (dummy, 1 if >50 yrs)	0.24	0.42
Wives' schooling (0–9 levels)	3.85	1.78
Husband's schooling (0–9 levels)	4.19	2.19
Wives' occupation: Professional/technical/managerial (actual and expected; dummy, 1 = yes)	0.24	0.43
Wives' wage (actual and expected; dollars/month)	633.89	561.32
Husbands' wage (actual and expected; dollars/month)	1,348.89	524.69
"Other" household income (dollars/year)	175.26	334.15
Wives' serious illness or injury in past year affecting ability to do household work (dummy, 1 = yes)	0.19	0.39
Household work rationale: Importance of being a good homemaker (0–2 ordinal)	1.46	0.67
Household work rationale: Importance of family's overall well-being (0–2 ordinal)	1.73	0.54
Household work rationale: Importance of the way it was done when wife was growing up (0–2 ordinal)	0.72	0.78
Household work rationale: Importance of getting it over with (0–2 ordinal)	1.26	0.73
Household work rationale: Importance of satisfying self (0–2 ordinal)	1.42	0.70
Household work rationale: Importance of having little choice (0–2 ordinal)	0.89	0.77
Mean household task importance (0–9 levels; wives' report)	6.85	1.32
Mean household task importance (0–9 levels; husbands' report)	6.76	1.12
Mean household task pleasantness (0–9 levels; wives' report)	5.15	1.03

Continued

TABLE 5.1 *(continued)*

Mean household task pleasantness (0–9 levels; husbands' report)	4.89	0.94
Daughter in household, 6–20 yrs (dummy, 1 = yes)	0.32	0.48
Number of daughters, 6–10 yrs	0.24	0.51
Number of daughters, 11–15 yrs	0.18	0.47
Number of daughters, 16–20 yrs	0.12	0.35
Son in Household, 6–20 yrs (dummy, 1 = yes)	0.32	0.47
Number of sons, 6–10 yrs	0.20	0.48
Number of sons, 11–15 yrs	0.20	0.48
Number of sons, 16–20 yrs	0.10	0.35

[a]$N = 311$.

ations). One will notice two modifications of the earlier models. First, compared to that in the last chapter, the sample size has decreased from 335 to 311. Preliminary analysis ran afoul of a few "outlier" couples where the husbands were unemployed, *and* did virtually no household labor (i.e., fewer than 75 tasks per month). As a consequence, it was necessary to drop 24 couples from the analysis. A glance at the means for this "new" sample will show that there is virtually no difference generated by the exclusion of these couples. Second, one will note that the table includes the two market- and household-labor pie measures. These will be used to construct product variables tapping interaction effects.

Rather than belaboring the preliminary discussion with details from each individual equation, some general comments will suffice as a guide to the specification of the model. More specific discussion of each equation follows, of course, with the presentation of the findings themselves.

The Allocation of Wives' Market Hours

The present model cannot include equations for both wives' and husbands' employment time. Recall from the last chapter that the variable for total household market hours was defined arithmetically by summing the employment hours for wives and husbands. Unlike the variable for total household tasks, it did not represent a "stand-alone" measure of total output. Being essentially mirror images of each other, the individual market time contributions of wives and husbands cannot be estimated in the same model.[3] Because there was more variance in the factors that attracted wives to or repelled them from the market, their market time is estimated in the model. (One might just as easily argue for an estimation of the husband's market time equation.) It should be emphasized that from a substantive point of view, a good deal of information about the "missing" partner's market time is conveyed indirectly, although the precise coefficients remain unestimated.

The equation explaining wives' employment hours per month should look familiar, as it is largely the "wives' " portion of the equation estimated for total household market hours. Guided by the New Home Economics, that equation contained variables reflecting the household members' marginal productivity (e.g., schooling and age) or the opportunity costs of household market time (e.g., wages and occupation). Here, such variables account for the individual wives' contribution in interaction with, and thus conditional on, the market portion of the household pie. Moreover, although they may take a somewhat different form, these regressors should be reminiscent of a great deal of earlier work mentioned in the first chapter (e.g., Becker, 1976b, 1981; Berk and Berk, 1978).

The first of the variables in the equation reflect the market portion of the pie through three dummy variables for total household market

[3]Consider the following simplified example:

$$H = A0 + A1(P) + A2(P)^*W + A3(P)^*X + e1 \tag{1}$$
$$W = B0 + B1(P) + B3(P)^*X + B4(P)^*Z + e2 \tag{2}$$
$$P = H + W \text{ or } H = P - W \tag{3}$$

where: H = husbands' contribution; W = wives' contribution; P = household task portion of pie; W, X, and Z = typical regressors.

Now:

$$H = P - W = A0 + A1(P) + A2(P)^*W + A3(P)^*X + e1 \tag{4}$$
$$- W = A0 - P + A1(P) + A2(P)^*W + A3(P)^*X + e1$$
$$W = -A0 + P - A1(P) - A2(P)^*W - A3(P)^*X - e1$$
$$W = -A0 + (1 - A1)(P) - A2(P)^*W - A3(P)^*X - e1$$

Because Equation 2 must equal Equation 4, we can equate the corresponding terms:

$$B0 = -A0,$$
$$B1 = (1 - A1),$$
$$0 = -A2,$$
$$B3 = -A3,$$
$$B4 = 0.$$

Therefore: (1) The two equations must include identical regressors; (2) The coefficients in the two equations are related in a linear fashion and, generally, are mirror images of each other.

time.[4] The dummy variables describe various levels of employment time achieved by the households, approximating units in the convenient (and more grounded) metric of "full-time job" (e.g., less than one full-time "job," less than two full-time "jobs," more than two full-time "jobs"). At any level, however, it was anticipated that the market portion of the pie would exert a positive effect on wives' market time; as the total increased, so, too, would wives' contribution to it. Yet, defining the variable in this form also provides for the possibility that the effect on wives' market time would be curvilinear. Perhaps at high *and* low levels of total market time, wives' participation increases.[5]

Second, the variable for wives' household tasks, in interaction with total household market time, was expected to generate a negative effect on wives' market time. Third, exogenous variables are included for the wives' age level (30–50 years; older than 50 years), schooling, and wages; the husbands' wages; the wives' occupation in professional, technical or managerial fields; and "other" household income. Of these, the variables for the wives' middle age (30–50 years), the husbands' wages, and "other" household income were expected to exert negative effects on the wives' market time. It was anticipated that wives of an age to be "working" at childbearing and child rearing (roughly 30–50 years) might exhibit a smaller investment in labor force participation. Likewise, both the husbands' wages and "other" household income were expected to exert negative effects on the wives' time in the market. In either case, income provided by higher husband wages or household income unrelated to employment could "buy" the market time of wives. In contrast, the wives' "older" age (older than 50 years), the wives' schooling, a high-level occupation, or a higher wage would generate positive effects, as they each

[4]The careful reader has probably noticed that by placing the market portion of the household pie (and later the total household pie) on the right-hand side of the equation, one introduces part of the endogenous variable on both sides of the equals sign. The statistical consequences are clear: all of the regressors are, in principle, correlated with the disturbance term, which, in turn, leads to biased and inconsistent estimates of the regression coefficients. In response, I constructed instruments for the pie variables whether used alone or in product form, and I reran the equations. The story was virtually the same, although the *t* values were, on the average, reduced, just as one would expect (because the regressors had less variance and were more highly correlated). When the results are reported without the instruments, the reader is not misled, however. Indeed, the reported estimates may be "better" in the sense of having a smaller mean squared error. That is, a bit of bias is introduced in exchange for a substantial reduction in estimator variance.

[5]The four dummy variables describing total market time were defined as (1) greater than zero, but less than or equal to 80 hours per month; (2) greater than 80, but less than or equal to 161 hours per month; (3) greater than 161, but less than or equal to 241 hours per month; and (4) greater than 241 hours per month. They are interpreted in a metric of "full-time job." The first dummy variable is the excluded comparison variable.

represent a pull toward wives' market time rather than wives' household time.[6] Together, these variables will serve to explain variation in the wives' market hours per month and, by implication, also speak to the relationship between the wives' and the husbands' market time.

Table 5.2 displays the variables included in all the model's equations and shows the *a priori* expectations for them. It will also guide a brief discussion of four features of the equations estimating the members' household task allocations: (1) the role of the household task portion of the pie; (2) the role of the members' market time; (3) the reciprocal relations among members efforts; and finally (4) the exogenous interaction terms. These last include some variables consistent with the concerns of the New Home Economics and Becker's household production function, as well as variables more "sociological" in character. Of course, it bears reiterating that, with the exception of the variables representing the market or task portions of the pie, *every* variable listed in Table 5.2 is an interaction term, incorporating its conditional relationship with the pie. However, for ease of exposition, I will not burden the text with constant references to the interaction terms.

The Role of Household Commodity Production

Through the symbols for expected directions of effect, Table 5.2 indicates the variables contained in the equation for the members' household-task contributions. Moving down the columns under the "Household tasks" heading ("W," "H," "D," "S"), one can first see the presence of variables constructed to reflect the effect of the total household commodity production on the individual members' efforts. Like its market counterpart, the household task portion of the pie is represented by three dummy variables and may generate positive but curvilinear effects on the members' contributions.[7]

---

[6]The more specific dummy variables for age (younger than 30 years; 30–50 years; older than 50 years) also appear in the household labor equations for wives and husbands. The simpler age variable included in Chapter 4 was intended to tap only the difference between the pre- and postretirement activities of couples. The dummy variables included here are expected to reflect other, more subtle life-cycle effects (e.g., childbearing and child rearing).

[7]The four dummy variables describing total household tasks were defined as (1) greater than or equal to 234, but less than 734 tasks per month; (2) greater than or equal to 735, but less than 1,234 tasks per month; (3) greater than or equal to 1,234, but less than or equal to 1,735 tasks per month; and (4) greater than 1,735 tasks per month. These divisions seemed to best capture the range of total tasks undertaken by the sample households. The first dummy variable is the excluded comparison variable.

TABLE 5.2
*Anticipated Directions of Effects on Wives' Market
Time and Members' Household Labor Tasks*

Predetermined variable	Wives' market time	Household tasks W	H	D	S
			Household tasks		
Total household market time (3 dummy variables	$+^a$	X^c	X	X	X
Total household work tasks (3 dummy variables)	X	+	+	+	+
Wives' market time	X	$-^b$	X	X	X
Husbands' market time	X	X	−	X	X
Wives' household task contribution	−	X	X	X	X
Husbands' household task contribution	X	X	X	−	−
Daughters' household task contribution	X	−	−	X	−
Sons' household task contribution	X	−	−	−	X
Middle-aged wives (30–50 yrs)	−	+	X	X	X
Older wives (>50 yrs)	+	−	X	X	X
Middle-aged husbands (30–50 yrs)	X	X	−	X	X
Older husbands (>50 yrs)	X	X	−	X	X
Wives' schooling	+	−	X	X	X
Husbands' schooling	X	X	+	X	X
Wives' wage	+	X	X	X	X
Husbands' wage	−	X	X	X	X
Wives' occupation: Professional/technical/managerial	+	X	X	X	X
"Other" household income	−	X	X	X	X
Wives' serious illness or injury	X	−	X	X	X
Daughter in household (6–20 yrs)	X	X	X	+	X
Number of daughters, 6–10 yrs	X	X	X	+	X
Number of daughters, 11–15 yrs	X	X	X	+	X
Number of daughters, 16–20 yrs	X	X	X	+	X
Son in household (6–20 yrs)	X	X	X	X	+
Number of sons, 6–10 yrs	X	X	X	X	+
Number of sons, 11–15 yrs	X	X	X	X	+
Number of sons, 16–20 yrs	X	X	X	X	+
Household work rationales					
Being a good homemaker	X	+	−	−	−
Family's well-being	X	+	−	−	−
Way done when wife was growing up	X	+	−	+	−
Getting it over with	X	−	+	$?^d$	?
Satisfying self	X	?	?	?	?
Having little choice	X	+	?	?	?
Mean household task importance	X	+	+	?	?
Mean household task pleasantness	X	+	+	?	?

^{a} + = Positive effect expected
^{b} − = Negative effect expected
^{c} X = Variable not in equation
^{d} ? = No expectation.

The Role of Members' Market Time

Just as the equation for wives' market hours incorporated an inter-action term for wives' household labor tasks (conditional on total employment time), the wives' and the husbands' household-task equations contain measures of their market hours (conditional on some level of total household task accomplishment). As indicated in Table 5.2, for both wives and husbands it was assumed that the time each invested in employment exerted a negative effect on the number of household tasks each undertook. However, it was also expected that the magnitude of these effects might well differ from one another.

One might wonder why the wives' or the husbands' market time is not included in equations other than those for their "own" contributions. For example, wives' employment hours are present in the equation for the wives' household-task contribution, but they are not allowed to have direct effects on husbands' or children's household-task contributions. Such relationships were not suggested by either the theoretical standpoint taken nor some preliminary empirical models. Instead, it is more logical to assume that any effect one member's market time may have on another's household task contribution will be felt indirectly or will operate *through* the relations between the task contributions of each member. For example, any effect that mothers' employment may have on children's contributions should be experienced through (and thus reflected by) a change in the mothers' *household labor.* This would likewise be true of all other reciprocal effects between members' household labor efforts.

Reciprocal Relations among Members' Contributions

The effect that one member's efforts have on another's is clearly critical to any model concerned primarily with the division of household labor. Moreover, the assumption that the work of each household member is at least minimally substitutable lies at the heart of the household production function. In theory, then, the variables representing the members' task contributions both are essential to the model and are presumed to stand in negative relation to one another. That is, as one member does more in the household, another does less. Unfortunately, constructing such a model in theory and constructing it in reality can be quite different propositions. In fact, Table 5.2 indicates that a variable for the wives' household tasks is not placed in reciprocal relation to any other members' efforts, and that the variable for the husbands' tasks is missing as a determinant of the wives' household tasks.

The absence of a measure for the wives' tasks in all equations is necessitated by a very high (.95) zero-order correlation between the total of the household tasks accomplished and the wives' individual contributions. This should come as no surprise, as the earlier descriptive statistics certainly support the observation that the total done and what wives do are often virtually the same thing. A more puzzling set of observations lies behind the decision to remove the variable for the husbands' tasks from the wives' equation. The exclusion of the husbands' task variable was necessitated by a nagging, quite robust cross-correlation of −.70 between the residuals for the wives' and the husbands' household task contributions, as an artifact of the husbands' contributions.[8] These compromises notwithstanding, one would anticipate effects just as economists would: because the members' household efforts are, in principle, substitutable, they stand in negative reciprocal relation to one another.

The final introductory note on the model concerns the exogenous terms in the household task equations. After brief mention of some variables missing from the equations, three sorts of exogenous variables are discussed in turn.

The Exogenous Components

As a reminder that the establishment and the allocation of market time and household tasks are quite different processes, Table 5.2 indicates that some variables from the prior specifications for the household pie are conspicuous in their absence from the present equations. First, where some physical characteristics of the household (e.g., laundry done at home and number of rooms) were seen as important to the establishment of the household's productive capacity, it is difficult to argue that they would significantly affect the apportionment of those tasks. Ordinar-

[8]The problem surfaced initially when a *positive* effect was found for the impact of the husband's task contributions on the wife's task contributions: the more he did, the more she did. This effect was perplexing and troubling as well, because of the large correlation between the residuals of the two equations. With all of the interaction terms, one is constantly teetering on the brink of serious multicollinearity anyway, and the positive effect, as well as the high cross-correlation, seemed to be a statistical artifact. By fixing the regression coefficient for the impact of the husbands' task contributions to various levels and reestimating the model, it became apparent that the two were associated, and that by constraining the regression coefficient to a small number, the cross-correlation could be made to disappear. Thus, it seemed sensible to simply drop the variable for the husbands' tasks from the equation estimated for the wives' tasks.

ily, their impact would be felt indirectly, *through* the size of the pie itself. Thus, all such variables were excluded from the equations specified for the members' household-task contributions.

A second exclusion is that of small children. Although the presence of both infants and small children had a profound effect on the size of the household labor portion of the pie, it may be that they have no effect on the allocation of household tasks. Thus, variables describing the presence of small children should not be included in the equations for household members' task contributions. On the other hand, it may be that, particularly for wives, the presence of infants and small children makes a difference in the mothers' contributions that sheer numbers of tasks could never fully capture. Unfortunately, and at the risk of some misspecification, it was impossible to include total tasks accomplished and the young children variables in the same equation. What may have begun as a relatively innocuous zero-order correlation between total tasks and infants (.38), or between total tasks and the number of small children (.50), developed into a full-blown collinearity problem through the construction of the necessary instruments for the total tasks and the wives' contributions. Thus, for the equations explaining variance in the members' contributions, the effect of infants and small children will continue to work through the household labor portion of the pie.

What remains is a relatively straightforward and simple set of four equations, containing three different sorts of predetermined variables (constructed as interaction terms): (1) those that tap member differences in marginal productivity; (2) those that describe an available "labor pool" of children; and (3) those that may address some of the effects of the norms and the psychic rewards surrounding household work.

To begin, the exogenous variables describing wives' and husbands' age levels and schooling serve as the direct "representatives" of properties of the household production function. Their presence in the equations for wives' and husbands' household-task contribution maintains that, as the marginal productivity of any household member increases, so, too, should that member's relative contribution. Likewise, and quite obviously, as marginal productivity decreases, the contribution should decrease. For example, in the case of middle-aged wives, accumulated household skills over time would lead one to expect an increased relative task contribution, as wives become more and more "practiced" as household workers. For husbands, the characteristic of age *without* practice is more likely and might result in a negative effect on the husbands' task contributions. This expectation is fully consistent with an assertion recently articulated by Becker (1981), namely, that over time the "optimizing" household comes to "specialize" the efforts of its members. Yet, any age variable may confound the two processes and may consequently show quite different effects. One could be tapping enhanced household productivity through experience, or reduced productivity through aging, or both. Thus, the age variable was constructed as three dummy variables (i.e., younger than 30 years, 30–50 years, older than 50 years), with the first age variable excluded for comparison.

The exogenous variables for husbands' and wives' schooling were also expected to show opposite effects, but perhaps for more complicated reasons. Recall that in the last chapter higher levels of schooling for wives and husbands decreased the number of tasks undertaken by the household (and this finding was partially borne out by the data). Here, however, relative contribution must be anticipated, given some already-established level of household productivity. An economist might argue that schooling would lead to more knowledge, and thus to heightened "productivity" in household work. One might then expect positive effects for highly educated wives and husbands. (Were we talking about time spent, however, the story might take a different turn.) Yet, if a "taste" for household labor is operating here, more highly educated wives might do fewer household tasks, and more highly educated husbands would undertake a greater number. Whether such effects reflect a stronger preference for leisure, changes in long- or short-term opportunity costs, or both, is never clear. A third and final variable intended to measure the marginal productivity of wives is the dummy variable for whether wives had experienced a serious illness or injury in the past year. Here, one would expect a significant negative effect on the wives' task contribution; marginal productivity would surely have suffered under such conditions.

If we turn next to a very simple set of variables that constitute the equations explaining daughters' and sons' contributions, two dummy variables are introduced to control for the presence of an "older" son or daughter (6–20 years). Thereafter, the interaction terms describe the number of sons or daughters in three age ranges. In each, one would anticipate that the greater the number of children in any age range, *ceteris paribus*, the greater the relative contribution of children. (For a recent empirical examination, see Cogle and and Tasker, 1982.) Moreover, one can here begin to appreciate the strategy of disembedding the members' contributions from the effects on the total of tasks undertaken. Because the household task portion of the pie is incorporated into the term, the resulting coefficients reflect not the tasks *generated* by the presence of children, but only the children's contribution as part of a household labor "pool."

Just as in the last chapter, six household-work "rationales" ("How important to the way you do household work") elicited from wives are included as exogenous variables in members' household-task equations. For the purposes of including some measure of the norms surrounding household labor, these variables tap the preferences surrounding household commodity production by the "primary" worker but may directly affect the contributions of each member. And just as in the last chapter, the *a priori* expectations for these variables are more tentative than for some others. Although I earlier guessed at what the wives' household work "styles" might do to the total household tasks undertaken, it is even more difficult to know the effect that such attitudes would have on individual household members *other* than wives. For example, in the last chapter, doing household work in particular ways to "satisfy self, almost apart from what others may think or feel," proved significant to a decrease in the number of household tasks elected by households. Yet, what might this variable mean in relation to individual household members' contributions? Even as it *decreases* total household tasks, it might also increase wives', husbands', or children's relative contributions. Regardless, one would expect that, if these variables did anything, they affected the wives' household-task contributions most strongly, and in general, had a smaller impact on the other members' labors.

Finally, Table 5.2 shows two "taste" variables added to each household member's equation. Like those for the household work "rationales," these two variables capture the effects of the preferences on the allocation of household work. The rationale variables expand on the notion that the division of household labor is affected by other than the straightforward concerns of marginal productivity and opportunity costs. These two variables represent the mean rankings by wives and husbands for (1) the importance, and (2) the pleasantness associated with household tasks. Recall that as an additional requirement of the card-sorting procedure, wives and husbands were asked to rank those tasks they said were accomplished in their households (regardless of who did them) along a 9-point "importance" scale and a 9-point "pleasantness" scale. That is, each task, sorted as accomplished in households, was then sorted for "how important it is to maintaining the household" and "how pleasant" it was to accomplish. The variables resulting from the card sorts represent the overall mean importance and mean pleasantness rankings received for household tasks.[9] Particularly with respect to mean task pleasantness, the presence of the variables fundamentally departs from Becker's model of the household production function. Recall that no psychic rewards or consequences operate in the labor process of Becker's model household. Rewards can be reaped only through consumption, not through production. Yet these additional measures of taste constitute a vital extension of the model.

Table 5.2 indicates the *a priori* expectation that for both wives and husbands, a high mean ranking for task importance or task pleasantness (conditional on productive capacity) will bring greater contributions by them. This is not to suggest that these variables measure the same phenomenon, only that, when tasks are perceived as important to household maintenance *or* when their accomplishment produces psychic value, members will be more likely to elect the tasks themselves. No particular expectation for children was anticipated *a priori,* as one can build good arguments for why high importance or pleasantness might either retard or enhance the contributions of children.

Taken together, the exogenous variables listed in Table 5.2 support an assertion that who does what in the market and the household is a function of (1) the marginal productivity of the members; (2) the available household labor "pools"; and (3) both normative and psychic considerations. An examination of the results of these equations follows.

SLICING THE "PIE"

As the findings are presented, it will become clear that in short order the picture can become quite complicated. In the interests of exploring that complication with some clarity, a series of tables and figures are used to reconstruct productive household relations, and to facilitate a discussion of their implications.

As each of the equations is discussed in turn, the findings will be in-

[9]Recall also that, for these variables, the wives' mean rankings are used as "exogenous" variables only in equations addressing the wives' task contributions. Likewise, it is the *husbands'* mean task-importance and -pleasantness rankings that are found in equations explaining the husbands' tasks. Moreover, these variables are newly introduced for this analysis because they are interpreted as characteristics of the household as a whole. Earlier, when the establishment of the household pie was at issue, they could not be treated as exogenous.

terpreted as conditional on the relevant portion of the household pie (employment hours or number of tasks) at some specific level. It is only through this technique, or a similar one, that the results can assume a grounded interpretation. Thus, in all the tables and figures that follow, the coefficients resulting from interaction terms are interpreted at the *mean* level for market time or tasks.

Wives' Market Hours

For the wives' market time, Table 5.3 presents the estimates of the metric regression coefficients and t values from the three-stage least-squares procedures. The reduced-form equation for this endogenous variable resulted in an R^2 of .82. A glance at Table 5.3 is all that is necessary for one to conclude that it was the household's total market hours that were the critical determinant of the wives' market time. When the total household market time fell somewhere in the range of the rough equivalent of one to two "full-time jobs," the wives' market hours increased by over 47 hours per month. Even more dramatic effects occur when the total household market time exceeded the two "full-time job" level; the wives' market hours per month increased by 140.

With one exception, the other exogenous variables had no discernible effect on the wives' market time. The exception is the variable for whether wives are older than 50. Assuming households at the mean level for total household market hours (178.82), wives falling in this age category were employed an additional 11 hours per month. (Middle-aged wives were expected to be employed significantly fewer hours than the younger women; this did not prove significant to the market time equation.) Just as interesting, of course, is the *absence* of effects for those variables that earlier made a difference to total household market time. For example, it was at least reasonable to expect the wives' wages and occupation to affect their market hours, "net" of the impact those variables might have on the household's capacity to command market resources.

To make the necessary links between the establishment of total household market hours and the allocation of them, Figure 3 is presented. It combines the significant findings from the last chapter with those of the present one, to show both the market portion of the pie and what determined the portion allocated to the wives.

In the last chapter, we saw that the particular stage of the household

TABLE 5.3
Metric Parameter Estimates and t Values for Wives' Market Time
(Hours/Month)[a]

Variable	Parameter estimate	Effect at mean	t Value
(Wives' household tasks/month) × (Total household market time)	− 0.00001	− 0.003	− 0.67
Total household market time < one full-time "job" (dummy, 1 if 80 < market time ≤ 161)	− 7.224	dna[b]	− 0.93
Total household market time < two full-time "jobs" (dummy, 1 if 161 < market time ≤ 241)	46.045	dna	4.44*
Total household market time > two full-time "jobs" (dummy, 1 if market time > 241)	137.338	dna	11.71*
[Middle-aged wives (1 if 30–50 yrs)] × (Total household market time)	0.022	3.93	1.22
[Older wives (1 if > 50 yrs)] × (Total household market time)	0.061	10.91	2.13*
[Wives' schooling (0–9 levels)] × (Total household market time)	0.005	0.89	0.97
[Wives' wage (actual and expected; dollars/month)] × (Total household market time)	− 0.00002	− 0.004	− 1.17
[Husbands' wage (actual and expected; dollars/month)] × (Total household market time)	0.000015	0.003	0.96
[Wives' occupation: Profession/technical/ managerial (actual and expected)] × (Total household market time)	0.023	4.11	1.07
["Other" household income (dollars/year)] × (Total household market time)	0.000011	0.002	0.35
Constant	5.35		1.05

[a]$N = 311$; R^2 (reduced form) = .82.
[b]dna = does not apply.
*$p < .05$ (one-tailed test).
**$p < .05$ (two-tailed test).

members' life cycle (i.e., the "older wives" variable), husbands' schooling, high occupation, and available income unrelated to employment all influenced total market productivity. Its size, in turn, determined the wives' (and the husbands') market time. Not surprisingly, the data show that there was no effect on the wives' market time when the market portion of the "pie" was at a relatively low level (less than one "full-time job"). Because the wives' and the husbands' market hours were mirror images of each other, the wives' "secondary" position as contributors of market time is reflected. That is, the exogenous and endogenous factors that establish household market hours result in an initial allocation of market hours to husbands. Thereafter, increases in the market portion of the pie result in wives' increased market hours.

Moreover, when one compares the two "older wives" findings shown in Figure 3, they appear to be in contradiction. In fact, here we may be seeing another reflection of changes in the husbands' market time. Earlier, the households with "older" wives showed a significant decrease in total market time. This finding was taken to be a reflection of a household's gradual decline in labor force participation as the members approached retirement age, as well as of a declining "taste" for employment during this stage of the life cycle. Moreover, an economist might argue that, with a shortening of the time horizon, households may choose to invest less in job-specific human capital. Yet, conditional on this smaller time investment, husbands may "pull out" of the labor market earlier, or to a greater degree than wives, hence the positive finding for the respondent wives over age 50 or, had the alternative equation been estimated, a negative finding for the husbands.

The implications of the allocation of market hours seen here will be investigated after the findings for the apportionment of household tasks are considered.

Wives' Household Tasks

Table 5.4 shows the metric parameter estimates and t values for the number of household tasks done by wives. The table shows only the third-stage results, but the reduced-form estimation for the wives' household tasks resulted in an R^2 of .87.

If we turn first to the findings for the exogenous variables, the most striking result is the dramatic linear effect of the household labor portion of the pie. As anticipated, Table 5.4 shows unequivocally that, when there was more household labor to accomplish, the wives' took on more. That is, as the total productive capacity moved from "low" to "moderate" (or "average"), the wives' monthly tasks increased from 250 to 537, and with an increase to "high," 773 additional tasks were undertaken by wives. Thus, any increase, at any level, of total household-task accom-

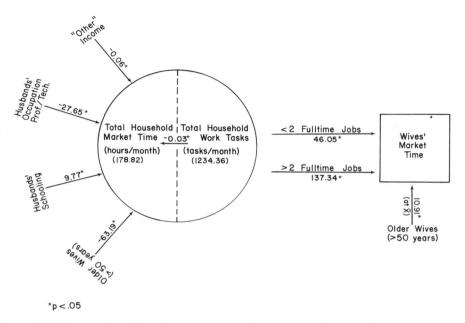

*p < .05

FIGURE 3. Total household market time and the wives' market time (N = 311; 335).

plishment had a profound effect on the wives' work at home. Of course, this finding will take on more meaning when the influence of the pie is estimated for other household members. For now, it is enough to note, from one more vantage point, the intimate relation between the tasks to be done and what wives do.

Additional (and unexpected) effects were generated by wives' schooling. Based on the women's differential "tastes" for household tasks, the *a priori* expectation was that the higher the level of the wives' schooling, the fewer would be the tasks contributed by wives. Instead, what resulted was a positive and significant finding; assuming a household at the mean level of household commodity production (1,234.36 tasks), every increase in the wives' schooling brought them an additional 21 tasks per month. I will return to this finding when the husbands' contributions are discussed, but it is apparent that, in relative terms, the effect of the wives' schooling was modest. Indeed, the maximum effect (assuming a household at the mean for monthly tasks, and a wife with an advanced degree) was only 189 tasks per month.[10]

---

[10] It should be mentioned also that this finding could constitute an artifact of the more highly educated respondents' being more thorough in their reporting of task accomplishment.

TABLE 5.4
Metric Parameter Estimates and t Values for Wives' Household Task Contribution (Tasks/Month)[a]

Variable	Parameter estimate	Effect at mean	t Value
(Daughters' household tasks/month) × (Total household work tasks)	−0.0002	−0.247	−3.12*
(Sons' household tasks/month) × (Total household work tasks)	−0.0001	−0.123	−1.10
[Wives' market time (hours/month)] × (Total household work tasks)	−0.0001	−0.123	−0.80
Total household work tasks at "low" level ($\geq 735 < \bar{X}$)	250.176	dna	6.84*
Total household work tasks at "average" level ($\geq \bar{X} \leq 1,735$)	537.159	dna	10.37*
Total household work tasks at "high" level ($> 1,735$)	773.234	dna	10.53*
[Middle-aged wives (1 if 30–50 yrs)] × (Total household work tasks)	0.043	53.078	2.06*
[Older wives (1 if >50 yrs) × (Total household work tasks)	−0.014	−17.281	−0.44
[Wives' schooling (0–9 levels)] × (Total household work tasks)	0.017	20.984	3.67**
[Wives' serious illness or injury (1 = yes)] × (Total household work tasks)	0.004	4.937	0.23
Household work rationales			
(Being a good homemaker) × (Total household work tasks)	0.036	44.437	2.65*
(Family's well-being) × (Total household work tasks)	0.021	25.922	1.28
(Way when growing up) × (Total household work tasks)	0.020	24.687	1.81*
(Getting it over with) × (Total household work tasks)	0.024	29.625	2.15**
(Satisfying self) × (Total household work tasks)	0.001	1.234	0.12
(Having little choice) × (Total household work tasks)	−0.011	−13.578	−1.02
(Mean household task importance) × (Total household work tasks)	0.024	29.625	3.78*

Continued

TABLE 5.4 *(continued)*

Variable	Parameter estimate	Effect at mean	*t* Value
(Mean household task pleasantness) × (Total household work tasks)	0.015	18.515	1.96*
Constant	251.550		7.05

[a]$N = 311$; R^2 (reduced form) = .87.
[b]dna = does not apply.
*$p < .05$ (one-tailed test).
**$p < .05$ (two-tailed test).

In preliminary work, a single dichotomous variable for the wives' age (55 or more years) proved to be of no significance to the wives' tasks. But once reconstructed as two dummy variables for middle-aged (30–50 years) and older (older than 50 years) wives, one significant finding emerged as anticipated. Compared to the younger wives, and conditional on a mean level for household tasks, the middle-aged wives elected about 53 additional tasks per month. Indeed, with respect to typical life-cycle-related events, such women had probably reached the height of family and household demands.

The remaining significant exogenous predictors of the wives' tasks all derive from the group of variables intended to measure the preferences surrounding the work. And it was thought that, of the items tapping normative orientations to household labor, most would exert positive effects on the number of tasks wives accomplished. Of the variables that measure the importance of various household work "rationales," three proved significant. Assuming households at the mean level of task accomplishment, an increase of one level in the perceived importance of "being a good homemaker" or "the way it was done when growing up" generated an increase of 44 and 24 tasks per month, respectively, in the wives' contribution. This also implies maximum (and modest) effects of 132 and 72 tasks per month, respectively. An additional but unanticipated effect was generated by the rationale of "getting it over with." A one-level increase in its importance to wives brought them an additional 30 tasks per month (or a maximum of 90 tasks per month). Perhaps all these effects imply as much a taste for certain *allocations* of household labor as for household labor itself. That is, all may have tapped a normative notion on the part of wives that it was they who should be routinely accomplishing the tasks. Whether household work was identified with "being a good homemaker," was justified as having been done that way when the wife was "growing up," or was done because it was easier to do it oneself than to argue about it (i.e., "getting it over with"), the result was the same: a bigger slice of the household labor pie for wives. Because of such normative notions, the wives' contributions took on a unique status and could be defined as labor for which no substitutes could be easily found.

Finally, the wives' perceptions of household tasks as more important, or more pleasant, increased their contribution. For household task importance, the effect of a single-level increase in the wives' ranking (conditional on a mean level for total household tasks) was almost 30 more tasks per month. The maximum effect (10 levels of importance × 30) was approximately 300 more tasks per month. The effects for the pleasantness scale were of smaller magnitude but were nonetheless significant. Conditional on a mean level for household tasks, a one-unit increase in the wives' mean task-pleasantness rankings resulted in an increase of about 19 additional tasks per month, with a possible maximum effect of 190 tasks per month. In short, and despite neglect by the household production function, both norms and psychic rewards were the source of preferences that proved significant in household task apportionment.

We can now return to the impact of more endogenous forces. It was anticipated that, *ceteris paribus,* a greater slice of one portion of the pie (i.e., market time) might decrease the size of the slice taken from the other portion (i.e., household tasks). Obviously, this expectation was ill founded, as there seems to have been no significant relationship between the apportionment of market time and household tasks to wives. We return to the implications of this a little later.

Finally, the unequivocal expectation of a negative relation between all the members' household-task contributions led quite obviously to the *a priori* expectation that the children's contributions would substitute for their mothers'. (I cannot speak to the direct effect of the husbands' tasks on the wives', although it was not significant in the preliminary and problematic equation.) Table 5.4 indicates that it was only the daughters' tasks that seemed to substitute for the wives' tasks. Assuming that the households were at a mean level of task contribution, a daughter's household task took away about one fourth (.25) of a task from each one done by her mother. This finding is interesting because, in theory, such relationships are expected to at least approximate a one-to-one substitution. In practice, they clearly do not. Nevertheless, it once again suggests that critical relations are not determined solely by considerations of marginal productivity and opportunities forgone.

Figure 4 gives a sense of the relationships among the significant de-terminants of the household labor portion of the pie and the resulting al-location of tasks to wives. The figure ignores other members' household work and attends exclusively to wives. Figure 4 underscores the story told by Table 5.4, namely, that once the determinants of total tasks are al-lowed to operate, a great deal is immediately known about the level at which wives contributed. For example, the addition of a small child to the household (or, for that matter, the presence of any child, of any age) could easily increase the total level of household commodity production anywhere from 60 to 400 tasks. This increase could surely catapult a household from the "low" end of the household-commodity-production continuum to the "moderate" or even the "high" end. Thus, Figure 4 shows the repercussions for the wives' work. From a practical standpoint, then, the impact of the other exogenous variables (e.g., household work rationales and the wives' schooling) made some difference, but they ul-timately paled in comparison to the impact of the household task portion of the pie on the wives' labors.

The findings for the next equation—the husbands' task contributions—are critical to our understanding of wives' work. From them one can get a sense of how wives and husbands orchestrated their household labor.

Husbands' Household Tasks

Table 5.5 presents the findings for the husbands' monthly task con-tributions. This equation is distinguished for how much it *fails* to explain. The reduced-form R^2 for this endogenous variable (.13) stands in stark contrast to the explained variance of the last equation. Moreover, we see that none of the endogenous variables proved significant in explaining what husbands contributed. Most striking perhaps is the absence of the household labor portion of the pie as a predictor for the husbands' task contribution. Even as we saw an inextricable link between household work routinely done and how much the wives undertook, for husbands the relationship is at least orthogonal. Indeed, there is a slight suggestion of a *negative* relationship, where, with an increase in the household task total, the wives' may have reacted by increasing their work load, and hus-

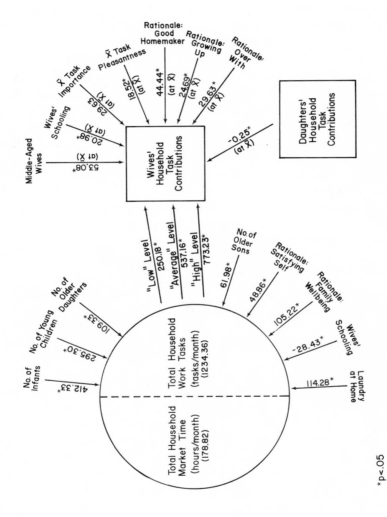

FIGURE 4. Total household work tasks and the wives' household task contributions ($N = 311; 335$).

*p < .05

TABLE 5.5
Metric Parameter Estimates and t Values for Husbands' Household Task Contribution (Tasks/Month)[a]

Variable	Parameter estimate	Effect at mean	t Value
(Daughters' household tasks/month) × (Total household work tasks	− 0.00007	− 0.093	− 0.67
(Sons' household tasks/month) × (Total household work tasks)	− 0.00004	− 0.049	− 0.22
[Husbands' market time (hours/month)] × (Total household work tasks)	− 0.0003	− 0.370	− 0.70
Total household work tasks at "low" level ($\geq 735 < X$)	− 41.612	dna	− 0.60
Total household work tasks at "average" level ($\geq \bar{X} \leq 1,735$)	− 14.184	dna	− 0.13
Total household work tasks at "high" level ($> 1,735$)	− 140.391	dna	− 0.91
[Middle-aged husbands (1 if 30–50 yrs)] × (Total household work tasks)	0.047	58.015	1.14
[Older husbands (1 if > 50 yrs) × (Total household work tasks)	− 0.022	− 27.156	− 0.29
[Husbands' schooling (0–9 levels)] × (Total household work tasks)	0.012	14.812	1.69*
Household work rationales			
(Being a good homemaker) × (Total household work tasks)	0.023	28.390	0.94
(Family's well-being) × (Total household work tasks)	0.022	27.156	0.72
(Way when growing up) × (Total household work tasks)	− 0.029	− 35.796	− 1.44
(Getting it over with) × (Total household work tasks)	0.019	23.453	0.90
(Satisfying self) × (Total household work tasks)	− 0.040	− 49.374	− 1.89**
(Having little choice) × (Total household work tasks)	0.035	43.203	1.69
(Mean household task importance) × (Total household work tasks)	0.024	29.625	1.81*

Continued

TABLE 5.5 (continued)

Variable	Parameter estimate	Effect at mean	t Value
(Mean household task pleasantness) × (Total household work tasks)	0.004	4.937	0.26
Constant	100.329		1.44

[a]$N = 311$; R^2 (reduced form) = .13.
[b]dna = does not apply.
*$p < .05$ (one-tailed test).
**$p < .05$ (two-tailed test).

bands may have responded by undertaking fewer tasks. I return to this relationship shortly.

The variables that do prove significant to the husbands' task accomplishment seem to center on the husbands' household-labor "tastes." Again, assuming a mean level for household productivity, a one-unit increase in the husbands' schooling increased their monthly tasks by about 15. At its maximum, this effect could mean an increase of 135 tasks per month for "postgraduate" husbands. This is certainly not an earth-shaking effect, even at its maximum. As expected, an additional positive effect was exerted by the husbands' ranking of task importance. A one-unit increase in mean task importance brought almost 30 additional tasks to the husbands' share of household labor (and a maximum possible effect of an additional 300 tasks). With so little variance explained (and so little to explain), these findings seem to raise more questions than they answer. Nevertheless, they imply a good deal about the relationship between wives' and husbands' work relations. The next figure facilitates some brief speculations.

Figure 5 combines the findings for wives' and husbands' household-task contributions with the now familiar determinants of the household pie. It represents a simple elaboration of the earlier figures and illustrates the absence of a relationship between the husbands' household-task contribution and the household work pie, as well as the effects of the two exogenous variables on the husbands' household labor. Obviously, the figure can show no direct relationship between husbands' and wives' household labor, but that does not mean that the two were unrelated.

Note that both of the exogenous variables that provided some explanation for the level at which husbands contributed reiterates a variable significant to the wives' household work. Earlier, the wives' schooling

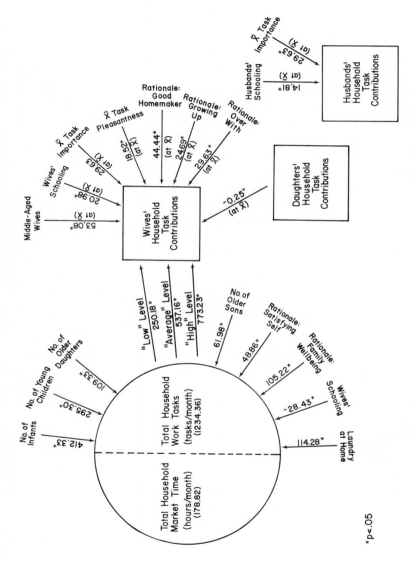

FIGURE 5. Total household work tasks; Wives' and husbands' household task contributions ($N = 311$; 335).

exerted a significant, if modest, effect on their household tasks. And just as an increase in the wives' contribution to household labor resulted when wives ranked tasks as being of higher importance, here there is an almost identical effect for the husbands' task contributions.

That these findings are comparable provides us the opportunity to distinguish between a quite obvious independence between wives' and husbands' task contributions, as well as a more subtle relationship of *shared* or complementary labor between them. First, the overwhelming salience of the wives' labor was conveyed quite clearly by the relative impact of the household labor pie on wives' and husbands' tasks. Every increase in total household-commodity production brought an increase in wives' labor, while leaving the husbands' contributions either unchanged or even decreased. Thus, as the pie got bigger, wives did more, almost as if they were the only source of household labor. For example, an infant could increase the size of the household labor portion of the pie by over 400 tasks. Judging from the earlier descriptive statistics, it is likely that the wives' labor absorbed virtually all of the tasks that the presence of an infant introduced into the household. At the same time, husbands were likely to take on virtually no, or very few, new tasks.[11] Thus, an increase in the size of the household labor pie certainly produced a direct effect on the wives' work load: as the productive output of the household increased, the wives' output increased. Of course, it is important to reiterate that, although the productive capacity of the household was affected primarily by the presence of children, it was also determined by the wives' characteristics (i.e., schooling) and preferences (i.e., household labor rationales).

Nevertheless, it would be a mistake to conclude that husbands have no relation to household labor, or to their wives as household workers. Indeed, two significant exogenous variables had similar effects on wives *and* husbands: both schooling and mean task importance increased the contributions of wives and husbands. This does not mean that more highly educated couples or couples who viewed household tasks as more important took on more *total* tasks. That would be reflected in the findings of the pie itself. Instead, it means that the couples with these characteristics, net of the total, engaged in more household tasks *together*. Thus, the relationship between wives and husbands is accurately represented as being both one of independence, with the particular level depending on the total demanded of the household, and one of complementarity,

---

[11]As one respondent said, "I'd like my husband to share more with me. We're working on it now. I'll be honest with you. I do 90%–100% with the baby. I've done a lot."

where one partner stepped in to share labor with the other. Of course, it is important to the story to emphasize that this relationship was not one of substitution, and that it was the *wives'* labor that was complemented by the husbands' occasional contributions. Such patterns certainly argue against the likelihood of a "genderless" system, where any patterns of specialization are motivated primarily by the principles of maximization (see Becker, 1981, for an elaboration). However, further discussion of this point must await the incorporation of the children's labor into the model.

The Contributions of Daughters and Sons

Tables 5.6 and 5.7 show the metric parameter estimates for the daughters' and the sons' task contributions. The reduced-form equations for these variables explained .41 and .39 of the variance, respectively. It is possible to present and discuss the contributions of sons and daughters together, as one may assume that their status as household workers was similar. That is, the children's labor (regardless of gender) was subject to unique age and status constraints that the adults' household work was not. At the same time, gender may have produced real differences in how the children's labor was used. These differences are surely illustrated by the *kind* of household tasks undertaken by children (see the discussion in Chapter 3). But apart from these obvious and well-documented differences, it may well be that gender intervened more subtly to affect the level of the children's participation in household work.

A brief look at the two tables together suggests many more similarities than differences in the factors that explain the sons' and the daughters' "share" of the household labor portion of the pie. Figure 6 shows this even more clearly, and for the purposes of clarity, it can be introduced here.

First, and perhaps most interesting, are the positive and significant effects for the relationship between daughters' and sons' efforts. It was anticipated that all the members' task contributions would stand in negative relation to one another; as one did more, the others would do less. Yet, with the children, the exact opposite phenomenon obtained: their labors seem only to have complemented each other. Perhaps the households could be characterized by whether or not they called on the labors of the children; if the children's labor was available, all the children of an appropriate age were pressed into service, or all escaped household chores.

Second, the variables that do the most to explain the children's task

TABLE 5.6

Metric Parameter Estimates and t Values for Daughters' Household Work Contribution (Tasks/Month)[a]

Variable	Parameter estimate	Effect at mean	t Value
(Husbands' household tasks/month) × (Total household work tasks)	−0.000007	−0.009	−0.09
(Sons' household tasks/month) × (Total household work tasks)	0.0006	0.704	6.40**
Total household work tasks at "low" level (≥735<X)	12.216	dna	0.29
Total household work tasks at "average" level (≥X≤1,735)	−42.316	dna	−0.66
Total household work tasks at "high" level (>1,735)	−60.641	dna	−0.70
[Daughter in household (6–20 yrs)] × (Total household work tasks)	0.098	120.97	3.03*
(No. of daughters, 6–10 yrs) × (Total household work tasks)	0.005	6.172	0.23
(No. of daughters, 11–15 yrs) × (Total household work tasks)	0.065	80.233	3.11*
(No. of daughters, 16–20 yrs) × (Total household work tasks)	0.022	27.156	0.68
Household work rationales			
(Being a good homemaker) × (Total household work tasks)	0.035	43.203	2.21**
(Family's well-being) × (Total household work tasks)	0.012	14.812	0.58
(Way when growing up) × (Total household work tasks)	−0.019	−23.453	−1.40
(Getting it over with) × (Total household work tasks)	−0.020	−24.687	−1.48
(Satisfying self) × (Total household work tasks)	−0.036	−44.437	−2.81**
(Having little choice) × (Total household work tasks)	0.023	28.390	1.72*
(Mean household task importance) × (Total household work tasks)	0.002	2.469	0.27

Continued

TABLE 5.6 (continued)

Variable	Parameter estimate	Effect at mean	t Value
(Mean household task pleasantness) × (Total household work tasks)	0.005	6.172	0.53
Constant	− 16.318		− 0.42

[a]N = 311; R^2 (reduced form) = .42.
[b]dna = does not apply.
*p < .05 (one-tailed test).
**p < .05 (two-tailed test).

contributions are those that establish the availability of their labor in the household. Presuming a total household task level at the mean for all households, simply *having* a daughter between the ages of 6 and 20 was "worth" over 121 tasks per month. Moreover, every additional daughter or son between the ages of 11 and 15 significantly increased the number of tasks done by them (80 and 60 tasks, respectively). Each additional son between the ages of 16 and 20 in the household brought an increase of almost 94 tasks per month to sons. Particularly for sons and daughters between the ages of 11 and 15, it can be argued that this age represents the optimal time to "collect" on children's ability to labor. Children have yet to expend their energies on work outside the home and do not roam far for very long, and most important, it is at this age that household chores are easily defined as "character builders"—when the sheer *accomplishment* of household work is defined as beneficial to children. (For a discussion of this point in another context, see Wittner, 1980.) In short, it is at this time that children's ability *to* labor, "meets" an ideology *about* children's labors.[12] The result is household chores. Of course, this again violates a model that does not allow joint production (e.g., a "clean" room *and* a "responsible" child), but this seems essential to any real understanding of children's contributions to the household.

Just as important in this study was the absence of any influence exerted by total task accomplishment. For both daughters and sons, changes

[12]One mother illustrated this point quite clearly when she said, "You'll probably think this is unfair. I don't give my son any allowance. He has to learn that to get money you have to work for it. He empties the garbage and scoops the dog poop. We pay him 50 cents a week for that. He baby-sits for 25 cents an hour. Last week, he made 4 dollars. He's responsible for keeping his room neat and his bed made."

TABLE 5.7
Metric Parameter Estimates and t Values for Sons' Household Work Contribution (Tasks/Month)[a]

Variable	Parameter estimate	Effect at mean	t Value
(Husbands' household tasks/month) × (Total household work tasks)	0.00003	0.031	0.59
(Daughters' household tasks/month) × (Total household work tasks)	0.0001	0.123	4.44**
Total household work tasks at "low" level ($\geq 735 < \bar{X}$)	26.337	dna	1.16
Total household work tasks at "average" level ($\geq \bar{X} \leq 1,735$)	27.270	dna	0.80
Total household work tasks at "high" level ($> 1,735$)	55.671	dna	1.18
[Son in household (6–20 yrs)] × (Total household work tasks)	0.022	27.156	1.22
(No. of sons, 6–10 yrs) × (Total household work tasks)	0.011	13.578	0.84
(No. of sons, 11–15 yrs) × (Total household work tasks)	0.049	60.484	3.66*
(No. of sons, 16-20 yrs) × (Total household work tasks)	0.076	93.811	4.91*
Household work rationales			
(Being a good homemaker) × (Total household work tasks)	−0.010	−12.344	−1.15
(Family's well-being) × (Total household work tasks)	−0.001	−1.234	−0.09
(Way when growing up) × (Total household work tasks)	−0.0004	−0.494	−0.05
(Getting it over with) × (Total household work tasks)	0.003	3.703	0.43
(Satisfying self) × (Total household work tasks)	0.011	13.578	1.58
(Having little choice) × (Total household work tasks)	−0.010	−12.344	−1.36
(Mean household task importance) × (Total household work tasks)	−0.009	−11.109	−2.07**
(Mean household task pleasantness) × (Total household work tasks)	0.002	2.469	0.39
Constant	33.321		1.56

[a]$N = 311$; R^2 (reduced form) = .39.
[b]dna = does not apply.
*$p < .05$ (one-tailed test).
**$p < .05$ (two-tailed test).

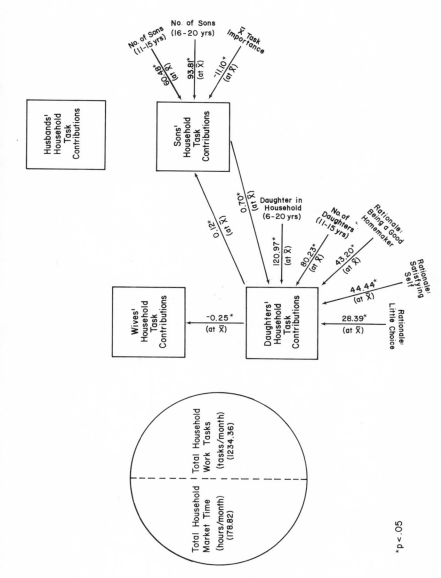

FIGURE 6. Total household work tasks; children's household task contributions ($N = 311$).

*$p < .05$

in the total tasks faced by households seem to have had no real effect on how much children did. Together with the prior finding, this suggests another dimension to the unique status of children in the household work system, namely, that the normative notions that propel children into household labor also serve as a check on their labors and probably limit the effect of the pie. Too few chores can certainly "spoil" the child, but too many introduce the folk wisdom of "all work and no play." Thus, a household's productive capability must take a back seat to the more exalted purpose of socializing the young.

Gender differences in the children's task accomplishment seemed to surface through the earlier finding of the differential impact of the dummy variables for the presence of a son or a daughter. Moreover, the effects of the wives' household-work rationales and mean task importance were not the same for daughters or sons. The daughters seem to have been subject to their mothers' orientations to household labor in a way that their brothers were not; three household work rationales proved significant in the daughters' task contributions, whereas none had any effect on the sons'. An increase in the wives' ranking of the importance of "being a good homemaker" or "having little choice" in the way that they accomplished household labor increased the number of tasks done by daughters. An opposite effect was generated by the rationale of "satisfying self." The point is not to attempt to divine the psychological processes of mothers and daughers to explain the *direction* of this effect, but to observe that only daughters were affected by a mother's household labor preferences; husbands and sons stood apart from such influences.

Finally, wives' assessments of mean task importance served to *decrease* the number of tasks done by sons. This finding may constitute another reflection of gender. The mothers who deemed household tasks to be of high importance may have been reluctant to grant their sons the responsibility of household tasks. Assuming our household at the task mean, a unit increase in mean household task importance "robbed" the sons of over 11 tasks per month. Moreover, this also implied a maximum effect of 110 fewer tasks per month accomplished by sons. Not so with daughters, who apparently were expected to do household work, even in households where the tasks were deemed more important. Coupled with the earlier finding that it was only daughters whose household labor tasks actually substituted for a portion of their mothers' tasks, these findings make clear that gender may well operate to link the household

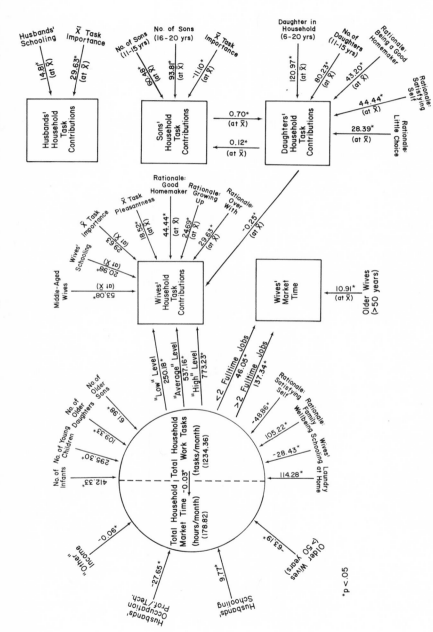

FIGURE 7. Establishment and allocation of market time and household tasks ($N = 311; 335$).

labor efforts of mothers and daughters more intimately than those of mothers and sons. In other words, and through the *ideological* overlays of household work, gender again emerges as a critical component in the mechanisms of task allocation.

A Brief Summary

Now that the findings have been presented, it is possible to step back and reflect on the larger story that they tell. To facilitate a useful summary, a final figure shows the full set of significant relations for market time and household tasks. Figure 7 puts all the pieces of the analysis of Chapters 4 and 5 together in one "grand" representation of the household pie and its apportionment to household members. It provides a point of reference for some general observations about how households first establish their overall productive capacity and then apportion their labors.

To begin, the salience of the market portion of the pie in its allocation was established. A variety of household members' characteristics that concern their marginal productivity in market work determined the total number of hours that our households devoted to employment and, in turn, affected the wives' (and, by implication, the husbands') market time. Specifically, the findings showed that the wives' employment time was critically affected by the total market time established in their households, and that it increased significantly when the market portion of the pie surpassed the rough equivalent of one full-time job. This implies a close relation between wives and husbands in the allocation of market work, with the wives' labor market contribution depending fundamentally on a moderate to high initial household commitment. This leads logically to a consideration of the relation between the wives' and the husbands' *household* work. It is obvious here again that, although the spheres of market and household labor are *analytically* separable, they are nonetheless fused in the real world and together establish the character of household members' work lives.

Turning to the wives' and the husbands' household labor, there was a clear bifurcation between their efforts and between the determinants of their relative contributions. Figure 7 illustrates that how much was done in the household was the overwhelming determinant only of how much *wives* undertook. Moreover, along with the variables of the wives' schooling (a relatively weak measure of accumulated human capital) and age, both norms and the psychic rewards surrounding household labor explained the wives' task contributions. Nevertheless, such variables make a difference only "around the edges"; it was the effect of the household task portion of the pie that told the story of the wives' household labor.

As powerful as was the effect of the household labor portion of the pie for the wives' work, it was insignificant to husbands' efforts. Indeed, very little could be found that affected how much husbands did. Only their level of schooling and their orientation to task importance explained some variance in their relative contribution. In short, what needed to be done and how wives responded seemed to have little effect on the husbands' work. Nevertheless, there is no denying the descriptive statistics showing the contributions that the husbands made to household labor. As has been demonstrated through other methods in past work (Berk, 1979), if husbands are at home, they may provide important, but nonetheless supplemental efforts coordinated with their wives' household chores.[13] Indeed, although the *levels* of participation were quite different, the *mechanisms* behind the allocation of market and household work to wives and husbands may have been similar. That is, wives certainly complemented and supplemented the market work of husbands, even as husbands complemented and supplemented the household labor and child care of wives. What is completely *unsupported,* especially in the household, is any real *substitution* between the efforts of wives and husbands. Shortly, a more grounded illustration of this is explored for its implications.

For the children's household efforts, the findings are quite straightforward. The relative contributions of sons and daughters first rested on the availability of their labor. If children were there and capable, their age and gender made a difference in the level of their contribution, as did their mothers' orientation to household labor. The effect of age (and, secondarily, gender) is here taken as a measure of the *normative* context that defines every child's life. Although the influence of the normative on the organization of work is not unique to children, it is especially obvious in how their labor is used. What children *should* be doing both defines and constrains the level at which they contribute to the work of the home.

---

[13]See Chapter 3 for a more lengthy discussion of "help" versus "responsibility." Of course, the measures of task contribution used here center on *routine* task accomplishment. They are thus a reflection more of "responsibility" than of "help." But to conclude from this that husbands (or sons) do "nothing" around the house is to seriously misapprehend the findings and their subtleties.

Accounting for Asymmetry

Figure 7 allows for some tentative conclusions concerning the mechanisms generating the effects found here. The New Home Economist and the sociologist might agree on what Figure 7 suggests: an optimal allocation of effort may result in household member "specialization." This notion simply maintains that household members (whoever they may be) must realize their best productive efforts through capitalizing on the skills that they bring to the household, that they hone over time, and through which they may demonstrate their greatest competence. This sort of "explanation" harks back to Parsons and Bales (1956), Blood and Wolfe (1960), and, more recently, Becker (1981). Indeed, what one might call the old Parsonian seduction, has been born again as the Becker ruse. Becker (1981) maintained in his most recent work that "at most one member of an efficient household would invest in both market and household capital and would allocate time to both sectors" (p. 4). Whatever the bottle, the wine is the same, and we are returned to a system of production where gender seems to play no theoretical role whatsoever. Or are we?

Let us assume a household that would seem familiar to Parsons, Blood and Wolfe, or Becker. We find an unemployed wife, attending almost completely to household production. Likewise, we find a husband who does almost no household work, as he specializes almost completely in market production. In Becker's latest work, this sort of arrangement is justified through a loose "bioeconomic" formulation. Becker (1981) observed that:

> women not only have a heavy biological commitment to the production and feeding of children, but they are also biologically committed to the care of children in other, more subtle ways. (p. 21)

Thus, although the labors of wives and husbands could in principle substitute for each other (e.g., in case of illness or death), such a substitution would clearly constitute a suboptimal arrangement. Husbands and wives have different comparative advantages, and to maximize overall household well-being, their labors serve as effective complements, not substitutes. Becker started, then, with the theorem that no more than one member should invest in both market and household. Next, invoking some unknown biological force, he argued that it usually turns out that the wife is the household "specialist." Consequently, for the household in which each member specializes in a *single area*, Becker's sex-linked predictions fit the data quite well.

But let us suppose that financial demands impinge on this arrangement (e.g., perhaps through an inflationary economy), so that more market time is needed from the household. Assuming declining marginal productivity, a point will be reached (if only through exhaustion) where one additional hour of a husband's market time is not as productive as an initial hour of a wife's market time. The result is an impact of the market portion of the pie on the wife's market time: when the household need is great enough, the wife will supplement the market time of the primary wage-earner.

Similarly, one should be able to apply such logic to household production. Presumably, at some point, an additional hour of a wife's household time (perhaps prompted by exhaustion) will be less productive than an *initial* hour of a husband's household time.[14] Yet, the data clearly show that, whereas wives make a significant contribution to market time in response to household need, there is virtually no level of household work demands that prompts a substantial contribution from husbands. Why should it necessarily be the case that wives will assume specialization in both areas? Biology again?

In accounting for these empirical patterns, the economist might first argue that wives are so productive in their household work that, when they near the point of very small marginal products, they still remain the more productive members. This position maintains that even dead on their feet, wives are more productive in the household than husbands. Second, the economist would have to argue that, nearly always, the net household gain when the wife trades the "next" household hour for a market hour exceeds the net gain to the household when the husband trades the "next" market hour for a household hour. There is no reason that this conclusion should necessarily follow; it would depend fundamentally on the precise production function, affected by such considerations as the rate at which marginal productivity declines. In any case, such arguments would rival even Becker's recent "bioeconomic" model

[14]Whether from art or life, we would recognize the conversations between husbands and wives that reflect this sort of decision making. The two conversations below are hypothetical, but should sound familiar:

WIFE: Look at you, you're exhausted! You're working two jobs, and now you're talking about a third! Please let me try to find something part-time. It would really help, and it would only be for a little while.
HUSBAND: I don't know, I just don't like the idea of your working. I guess it's OK for a while— we don't have much of a choice.

Another hypothetical conversation should also sound familiar:

HUSBAND: Look at you, you look terrible! Tell you what, while you finish the dishes I'll take the baby to the park or something. You should get off your feet.
WIFE: *Would* you? Just an hour or so would be wonderful!

for rampant adhoc-ery. Somewhat different speculations on the findings thus far conclude this chapter.

CONCLUSION: A "GENDERED" ALLOCATION SYSTEM

The analysis presented in Chapter 4 drew from the New Home Economics in its conceptualization of the household as a "tiny firm" that, according only to considerations of marginal productivity and opportunity costs, establishes its total productive output. Operating in concert, individual labors are combined and are presumed to approach an "optimal" mix of effort devoted to market and home. Some would argue (although others would disagree; see, for example, Brown, 1982) that the advantage of this model of household production is that it does not depend on determinants difficult (or impossible) to measure. The inputs into preferences—norms, psychic rewards and costs, and custom (the stuff of inequality)—so central to the *sociologist's* conceptualization of human collectivities are at best given short shrift by the New Home Economics.

Thus, in Chapter 4, with the help of the household production function, a "genderless" system of household and market labors was explored. And in many respects, it withstood the test of data pretty well; by and large, variables centering on household members' productivity or the opportunity costs of members' labors did prove significant in explaining variance in market and domestic work. It appears that, with respect to *what* gets done and how much time is spent, preferences usually take a back seat to the costs and the opportunities posed by occupation, education, children, age, and so on. Nevertheless, saying that households operate in this way did not necessarily imply that gender played no part in the process. Indeed, it was just as obvious from the data that one could make no real sense of the determinants of the household pie without a consideration of the perhaps complementary, but clearly distinct, "territories" of work occupied by husbands and wives. Thus, against a vague "gender backdrop," households seemed to be utility maximizers.

Therefore, one would anticipate that, if a household's productive capacity is affected by gender, so, too, would be the apportionment of work to individual members. Indeed, every sociologist who is worth her or his degree (and who studies household labor) has said as much. In 1978, my coauthor and I (Berk and Berk, 1978) argued "that the division of household labor is not solely, or even primarily, a function of productive capacity. *Who* you are matters as much as *what* you are able to contribute; age and gender count" (p. 462). We conceived of the household as a work site where there is certainly conflict, certainly gender inequality, and *certainly* a lopsided division of labor. At the same time, we presumed that family members engage in a process of "give and take" in their commitments to the work of household and market. Moreover, specifically with respect to domestic labor, some sort of "hydraulic" model might apply, namely, as one adult did more household labor, another would do less. Thus, each household "labored" along, negotiating the relative efforts of its members and its overall investments in market and home.

As an analysis of total productive efforts, Chapter 4 suggested that there is more to the pie than the maximization of utility. This chapter demonstrated that there is *less* to the division of labor than the system that we may fancy it to be: one marked primarily by rational specialization, substitution, and cooperation. Particularly with respect to the apportionment of household tasks, this chapter demonstrated that men and women may share a work environment but do not share much of its work, that they may share a living space, but that the maintenance of that space affects primarily the wives. Thus, this chapter ultimately suggests an intimate relation between work and gender that is revealed through the division of household and market labors. Specifically, it is not just that gender *influences* the division of household labor; gender both *affects* and is perhaps effected *through* the division of household labor. It is around household work that gender relations are produced and reproduced on a daily basis, and it is through these relations that work in the home assumes its uniquely constrained patterns of allocation, and thus its character.

These conclusions are explored more fully in the final chapter. First, however, a supplementary analysis of wives' market and household labor time is presented.

CHAPTER 6

Wives' Time

Another View

INTRODUCTION

In the earlier examination of the household "pie," it was possible to model household productive capacity through the metrics of household tasks and household time. This conceptualization was motivated by both opportunity and logic. No prior studies had employed comparable measures of both in analyses of household and market labor, and thus, the research design provided a unique data set. Moreover, a consideration of household labor as *work* demanded some formal acknowledgment of the fact that work time is "spent," and that it is spent on (and through) discrete and discernible tasks. In fact, in Chapter 2, I likened household tasks and time to a difference of input and output; time became the input of "labor power," and task the necessary form that labor must take to become realized as the output of household "commodities." For example, when one sets out to wash a kitchen floor, the ultimate "commodity" (if we ignore intermediate products) may be a "clean floor." But, the production of that discrete outcome requires the input of labor power, reflected through time.[1] This chapter focuses on the individual inputs of the wives' time: their daily minutes of employment and household work.

The findings of Chapter 4 implied that household tasks and employment hours are relatively constraining on household members. It prompted some speculation that there was little discretion attached to household and market work when they "appeared" in units of monthly

---

[1] Of course, this is a very loose analogy, because, strictly speaking, labor power is found only when labor can itself take commodity form (i.e., in a market).

hours and tasks. In some contrast, the *minutes* of household labor seemed to allow for greater discretion, and thus for sensitivity to other forces. At least in the case of household labor, the members may allocate tasks *first* and then "fine-tune" both the total work and their own contributions through the units of time. Although such disparities between the determinants of household task and of time are not earth-shattering, they are provocative enough to motivate the analysis presented here.

The analysis of time spent on home and market work in Chapter 4 suggested that, when the productive capacity of households is expressed through tasks, it may significantly alter household market capacity. Yet, it is not until that same productive capacity is expressed in the metric of time that the influence of the market can be discerned. When the demands of employment intervene to affect *household* labors, the number of tasks may remain fixed, and the amount of *time* spent on them may change. All this is worth reiterating only because this inherent difference in household discretion may well matter when *individual* allocations of work are discussed. Conditional on total household productive capability, how would a household member's time contributions be determined? Would the same allocation patterns that emerged for task contribution appear when time is the metric? This chapter provides some equivocal, but nevertheless useful, answers to these questions.

A PARTIAL MODEL

One mission of the analysis is to capitalize on the *comparability* of the dual measures used to capture the processes by which household and market labors are allocated. Thus, it is easy to imagine the ideal model for members' contributions to the time of home and market work, as it would be nearly identical to the model specified in the last chapter. Where earlier, household members' task contributions were the focus, here the time spent on those tasks is considered. Moreover, quite obviously, the exogenous variables employed in the prior analysis would remain the same.

Unfortunately, real-life models can differ substantially from ideal ones. In this case, not only do the old problems of comparability between the measures of time and task remain (see Chapter 2 for a discussion), but new compromises are introduced. In the last chapter, the market contributions of individual wives and husbands could not be included in the same model. Because the market portion of the "pie" was defined through the linear combination of wives' and husbands' market time, and because the total was included as a regressor, only one household member's contribution could be directly addressed. (See Chapter 5, Footnote 3, for a formal exposition.) The same sort of difficulty plagues the analysis here, but this time, it is germane to both the measures of market *and* household minutes per day. Recall that to achieve a measure of total *time* spent by the adult members on household labor, the total elapsed daily "diary" minutes spent by wives and husbands was summed. That sum (along with the one for the total minutes per day that the households spent on employment-related activity) made Chapter 4's analysis of the pie possible; yet, it will seriously limit the development of the present model. Coupled with a lack of data on the children's household time contributions, it means that only one household member's contributions to home and market can be modeled.

Just as in the last chapter, when faced with the necessary choice of examining only one adult member's market contributions, I will here elect to model the wives' employment and household time. And just as in the last chapter, this is an arbitrary choice. It may be argued, however, that the wives' market time is indeed the better choice because (1) it will facilitate comparisons with the analysis of the last chapter, and (2) there is greater variance in the time that wives spend on household labor, in comparison with the time spent by any other household members.

This solution hardly promises an exhaustive, or even a fully adequate, treatment of the allocation of household members' time to market and home. Still, given the definition of variables through linear combination, it is still the case that the "missing" member's efforts are (by definition) reflected in the direct effects that emerge. Moreover, significant comparisons can be drawn between the findings from the "task" analyses and those from the "time" analyses. For example, the determinants of the wives' employment hours per month (found in the last chapter) and those for the wives' market minutes per day estimated here are expected to be similar, just as one would expect a recapitulation of the earlier relationship between the market portion of the pie and the wives' market time. And again, in each relationship, the husbands' market contributions are at least implied.

Endogenous Variables

Table 6.1 lists the means and the standard deviations for the endogenous variables relevant to this abbreviated analysis of market and household time. Moreover, for purposes of clarity, the pie variables of market and household time are included along with the two endogenous

TABLE 6.1

Means and Standard Deviations for Endogenous Variables[a]

Variable	Mean	SD
Total household market time (minutes/day)	649.88	323.41
Wives' market time (minutes/day)	142.86	224.16
Husbands' market time (minutes/day)	507.02	232.31
Total household work time (minutes/day)	702.74	320.53
Wives' household work time (minutes/day)	509.28	263.06
Husbands' household work time (minutes/day)	193.46	185.67

[a] $N = 311$.

variables of the wives' market and household work time. All the exogenous variables remain identical to those in the prior analysis in Chapter 5, and they will be reviewed very briefly a little later on.

The descriptive statistics contained in Table 6.1 for the refined sample of 311 wives and husbands are virtually identical to those presented in Chapter 3 for the full sample of 335 couples. Comparable variables for husbands are included parenthetically and are there to round out the descriptive picture; they are not, of course, included in the formal model.

The levels indicated for wives' and husbands' time at market and household labors should seem quite familiar. In addition to the standard asymmetry in market and household time exhibited by wives and husbands, Table 6.1 also serves as a reminder that the means for husbands' household work time seem somewhat inflated. Recall that the effects of respondent-estimated task durations, as well as the relatively liberal operationalization of household labor, were mentioned earlier as an explanation. (See Chapter 3 for a discussion.)

Specifying a Model for Wives' Time

There are few surprises in the details of the model specification for the allocation of the wives' time to market and home. As mentioned earlier, the intention is to reproduce the prior model as closely as possible, and thus, the exogenous variables included are identical to those for the wives' equations in the last chapter. Of course, the logic underlying the specification of the model for task contribution applies to this model as well. The determinants of the household members' contributions (in this case, the wives' time) are allowed to operate only *conditional on* the total productive capacity of the household. In other words, the present model recapitulates the earlier one by placing the exogenous variables in each equation in interaction with the relevant portion of the household pie. Moreover, but unlike the earlier efforts of Chapter 4 and 5, *a priori* expectations are shaped directly by previous and clearly comparable results. Table 6.2 lists the predetermined variables for this analysis and the anticipated directions of effect for the wives' market- and household-time equations. It will be possible to briefly discuss the specification of the two equations together, as they are so similar to the wives' equations in the last chapter.

If we turn first to the variables that reflect the effects of the pie, Ta-

TABLE 6.2
Anticipated Direction of Effects on Wives' Market and Household Work Time

	Anticipated effects on[a]	
Predetermined variable	Wives' household market time	Wives' household work time
Total household market time (three dummy variables)	+[a]	X[c]
Total household work time (three dummy variables)	X	+
Wives' market time	X	−[b]
Wives' household work time	−	X
Middle-aged wives (dummy, 1 if 30–50 yrs)	−	+
Older wives (dummy, 1 if >50 yrs)	+	−
Wives' schooling	+	−(?[d])
Wives' occupation: Professional/techni-cal/managerial	+	X
Wives' wage	+	X
Husbands' wage	−	X
"Other" household income	−	X
Wives' serious illness or injury	X	−
Household work rationales		
Being a good homemaker	X	+
Family's well-being	X	+
Way when wife was growing up	X	+
Getting it over with	X	−
Satisfying self	X	?
Having little choice	X	−
Mean household task importance	X	+
Mean household task pleasantness	X	+

[a] + = Positive effect expected.
[b] − = Negative effect expected.
[c] X = Variable not in equation.
[d] ? = No expectations.

ble 6.2 indicates that both total household market time and total household labor time are expected to exert positive effects on the wives' market- and household-work time. Just as in the last chapter, the market and household portions of the pie are each reflected through four dummy variables. (For a brief discussion of some estimation issues, see Chapter 5, Footnote 4.) The dummy variables were constructed by dividing household employment time and household work time into quartiles. For both total household-market minutes per day and total household-work minutes per day, the dummy variables are labeled *low, average,* and *high.* In each case, the excluded comparison variable is "low" total market and "low" household time.[2]

The findings of the last chapter create additional expectations for the varying *levels* of total household-time commitments to market and home. For example, in Chapter 5, it was clear that the market portion of the pie significantly affected the wives' employment hours only when the total household commitment to the market was high. It should likewise be the case here, where "high" market time exerts a significant positive effect on the wives' market minutes per day.

It is important to remember that formal employment hours and the duration of the employment day are quite different variables. In Chapter 4, where some individual effects were intimated, the measure of market *minutes* per day perhaps tapped into some member discretion that was not captured through monthly employment hours. This may also be true for the impact of the household work portion of the pie. Judging from the findings of the last chapter, where tasks were the unit of analysis, one would expect that the greater the total household investment in household work time, the more time the wives would devote to it. Moreover, one would expect the effect to be strong—and linear. Yet, it is the case that the number of tasks undertaken and the elapsed time spent on

---

[2]The four dummy variables describing total market minutes per day were derived from quartile divisions of the frequency distribution and were defined as *small* (market time greater than zero and less than or equal to 525 minutes per day); *low* (greater than 525 and less than or equal to 590 minutes per day); *average* (greater than 590 and less than or equal to 810 minutes per day); and *high* (greater than 810 market minutes per day). The four dummy variables describing total household work minutes per day were also derived from quartile divisions and were defined as *small* (greater than or equal to 66 and less than or equal to 445 minutes per day); *low* (greater than 445 and less than or equal to 650 minutes per day); *average* (greater than 650 and less than or equal to 899 minutes per day); and *high* (greater than 899 household work minutes per day). In both instances, the dummy variable for *small* was excluded for comparison.

them may result in quite different magnitudes, if not directions, of effect. Therefore, although one would expect comparable findings, the precise impact of total household productive capacity on the wives' market and household time can only be guessed at.

Second, Table 6.2 indicates an obvious expectation for the reciprocal relation between wives' time in the household and employment. Even though a negative reciprocal relation between employment hours and the wives' household tasks (net of the impact of the pie) did not appear in Chapter 5, there is no reason to abandon the notion that time spent in one place may take away from time spent in another. Indeed, based on some hints in Chapter 4's pie analysis, one might expect that it is here, where market and household work are measured in minutes, that an inherent reciprocity can be better reflected. In any case, the wives' market minutes per day and their household minutes per day are expected to exert significant negative reciprocal effects.

Third, Table 6.2 lists all the explanatory variables found in the two equation model for the wives' time, and it indicates the *a priori* expectations for each variable's direction of effect. Given the elaborate justifications for model specification in Chapter 5, it is a relatively easy matter to anticipate the effects of at least some of the exogenous variables. Just as in the prior equation for the wives' monthly employment hours, the equation explaining variance in the length of the wives' employment day contains variables that capture the effects of the wives' age, wives' schooling, high occupation, family members' wages, and household income unrelated to current employment, all net of the effects of total household market time. The *a priori* expectations remain the same as they did in the earlier model; wives' older age (indicating fewer demands on household time), wives' higher schooling, the wives' high occupation, and higher wives' wages—presumably all reflect the wives' enhanced marginal productivity in employment. Negative effects are expected for the variables of wives' middle age, husbands' wages, and "other" household income. Each of those variables represents higher opportunity costs for investments in market activity—and thus a pull away from long hours (i.e., many minutes) on the job.

Table 6.2 shows the anticipated directions of effect for the exogenous variables explaining the wives' household work minutes per day. These, too, were included in the prior equations for the members' number of monthly household tasks, and each is placed in interaction with the household work portion of the pie. The question now becomes, conditional on the total productive time of the household, what determines the wives' "share" of household labor time? For virtually all the variables, the *a priori* expectations remain as they were in the last chapter.

The wives' ages, reflected in the dummy variables of "middle-aged" (30–50 years) and "older" wives (older than 50 years), are expected to show opposite effects from each other, with women 30–50 years spending significantly greater time (and older women less time) on household work each day. The expectation for the effect of the wives' schooling remains negative, on the assumption that more highly educated wives do not display a preference for household labor and thus spend less time on it. However, this *a priori* expectation is now much more tentative, because, earlier, wives' schooling exerted a significant *positive* effect on the number of wives' household labor tasks. Additionally, wives who had experienced a recent serious illness or injury were expected to limit their household work time, just as earlier they were expected to limit the number of tasks that they undertook.

All the variables tapping the "tastes" associated with household labor—the household labor "rationales," mean household-task importance, and mean household-task pleasantness—also carry the same *a priori* expectations that they did in the last chapter. An exception is the household work rationale of "having little choice." Where earlier I anticipated that this variable would cause the wives' to take on a greater number of tasks, here, when it is the minutes of the household day that are at issue, one can expect that such a rationale would hardly encourage the wives to linger over, or to luxuriate in, the pleasures of household work. Moreover, this rationale, in fact, did not cause the wives to elect greater numbers of tasks; the direction of effect was negative. For these reasons, one would expect wives with this orientation to "cut corners" in their household labor-time investments.

Finally, the rationale of "getting it over with" was expected to result in less household time for wives. Despite the finding in Chapter 5 that the rationale of "getting it over with" increased the number of the wives' tasks, this rationale may be just the one that motivates fewer minutes spent on tasks.

In sum, the model for the wives' market- and household-labor minutes per day recapitulates the earlier wives' equations for employment hours and household tasks. This time, however, the *a priori* expectations have both a theoretical and an empirical basis; one would expect quite similar results for both market hours and minutes, and for household tasks and minutes, but at the same time, one would anticipate differences posed by the metric of time.

FINDINGS AND DISCUSSION

The findings for the wives' market and household time are interpreted here in light of the earlier results for the wives' employment hours and household tasks.

Wives' Employment Day

Table 6.3 presents the findings for the metric parameter estimates and *t* values for the wives' market-minutes equation. Just as in the prior analysis, interaction terms are interpreted at the mean level of the relevant portion of the pie on which they are conditional. The reduced-form R^2 for the wives' market time is .61.

The most powerful effect is one that is reminiscent of an earlier finding. Just as was found for the wives' market hours, the level at which households committed time to employment profoundly affected the duration of the wives' employment days. Yet, in this case, only total household-market time at *high* levels proved significant to wives' market time. When household market time reached the "high" range, the wives' employment day increased by 278 minutes, or about 4.6 hours. This may be capturing the effect of the wives' part-time or full-time employment, but in any case, we see again that the wives' employment represented an additional household commitment that might (to take a longitudinal tone) have "followed" husbands' initial investment in employment time.

Among the other exogenous variables, two proved significant to the wives' market minutes per day, and both increased the wives' time. In the last chapter, it was found that women older than 50 years invested more time in employment, for a given *household* time commitment, and thus (assuming a mean level for household market time) increased the length of their employment days by almost three quarters of an hour. Additionally, as anticipated, wives with more schooling also extended the length of their employment day. Again assuming a mean level for household market time, a one-unit increase in the wives' schooling added about 14 minutes to the employment day. The maximum effect for this variable, when wives reached the highest level of schooling was an increase in market time of about 2 hours per day.

The schooling variable was included as a simple indicator of the effects of increased human capital on market time, and thus an incentive for longer employment hours. Yet, just as in Chapter 4, one must consider the unintended influences of class on this variable. Because the

TABLE 6.3

Metric Parameter Estimates and t Values for
Wives' Market Time (Minutes/Day), [a]

Variable	Parameter estimate	Effect at mean	t Value
(Wives' household work time) × (Total household market time)	−0.00018	−0.116	−3.06*
Total household market time: Low (dummy, 1 if > 525 < 590)	−40.869	dna[b]	−1.47
Total household market time: Average (dummy, 1 if > 590 < 810)	−7.085	dna	−0.25
Total household market time: High (dummy, 1 if > 810)	278.254	dna	7.77*
[Middle-aged wives (1 if 30–50 yrs)] × (Total household market time)	0.032	20.796	1.30
[Older wives (1 if > 50 yrs)] × (Total household market time)	0.064	41.592	1.68*
[Wives' schooling (0–9 levels)] × (Total household market time)	0.021	13.647	3.01*
[Wives' wage (actual and expected; dollars/month)] × (Total household market time)	0.0056	3.639	1.55
[Husbands' wage (actual and expected; dollars/month)] × (Total household market time)	0.0052	3.379	1.27
[Wives' occupation: Professional/technical/managerial (actual and expected)] × (Total household market time)	−0.016	−10.398	−0.56
["Other" household income (dollars/year)] × (Total household market time)	0.00007	0.045	1.54
Constant	22.759		1.16

[a] $N = 311$; R^2 (reduced form) = .61.
[b] dna = does not apply.
*$p < .05$ (one-tailed test).
**$p < .05$ (two-tailed test).

market-minutes-per-day measure is actually one of the elapsed time between going to and returning home from work, the effect of schooling may simply reflect the effects of the commuting time of the more well-to-do employed wives. At the same time, if the effect were contaminated by this "suburbia" influence, one would expect the other exogenous variables of wives' wages, husbands' wages, or wives' high-level occupation to reflect it as well. Because they do not, it is difficult to know what forces are operating here. Nevertheless, although the coefficient is significant, it is small.

The final significant result is one that was formally anticipated but was not found in Chapter 5's model for hours and tasks. Table 6.3 indicates that, with a mean level for total household market time, an additional minute of the wives' household work brought a reduction of about a tenth of a minute (.12) in the employment day. At the more meaningful level of, for example, a 2-hour increase in the wives' household labor time, market employment would have dropped by almost 15 minutes per day. This is certainly not a one-to-one trade-off, but that would be unlikely anyway; it is enough to show that some discretion can be exercised in shaping the duration of the employment day to respond to the demands of the household *net* of the total household commitment to the labor market. I will return shortly to this relationship and its connection to other endogenous forces.

Wives' Household Day

If we turn to the second and final equation in the two-equation model, Table 6.4 shows the estimates for the metric regression coefficients and *t* values for the number of minutes per day that wives spent on household labor. The reduced-form equation for this endogenous variable resulted in an R^2 of .72.

To begin, the strong linear effect for the household minutes portion of the pie should come as no surprise. An increase in the number of tasks undertaken by the household meant a greater burden to wives, and likewise, an increase in household labor *minutes* brought the wives longer household workdays. Once again, an increase in productive time from "small" to "average" or from "average" to "high" levels added an hour to the wives' household labor day. To anticipate the later discussion only a little, these findings for the effect of the household time pie demonstrate that the tasks of the household and the time demanded by them clearly operate in concert to influence the work lives of women.

The exogenous variables of the wives' age and schooling showed results in the direction opposite to the one expected. The finding for the wives' age category illustrates the difference between the number of household tasks the members undertook and the time they spent on them. Recall from Chapter 5 that wives 30–50 years old did significantly greater numbers of household tasks, for a given total, than did the youn-

TABLE 6.4

Metric Parameter Estimates and T *Values for Wives' Household Work Time (Minutes/Day)[a]*

Variable	Parameter estimate	Effect at mean	t Value
[Wives' market time (minutes/day)] × (Total household work time)	– 0.00039	– 0.027	4.33*
Total household work time: Low (dummy, 1 if > 445 < 650)	107.561	dna[b]	3.96*
Total household work time: Average (dummy, 1 if > 650 < 899)	179.202	dna	5.20*
Total household work time: High (dummy, 1 if > 899)	263.922	dna	5.11*
[Middle-aged wives (1 if 30–50 yrs)] × (Total household work time)	0.031	21.784	1.29
[Older wives (1 if > 50 yrs)] × (Total household work time)	0.075	52.706	2.22**
Wives' schooling (0–9 levels)] × (Total household work time)	0.029	20.379	4.32**
[Wives' serious illness or injury (1 = yes)] × (Total household work time)	– 0.041	– 28.812	– 1.35
Household work rationales			
(Being a good homemaker) × (Total household work time)	– 0.020	– 14.055	– 1.08
(Family's well-being) × (Total household work time)	0.005	3.514	0.24
(Way when growing up) × (Total household work time)	0.046	32.326	2.91*
(Getting it over with) × (Total household work time)	0.052	36.542	3.43**
(Satisfying self) × (Total household work time)	– 0.003	– 2.108	– 0.20
(Having little choice) × (Total household work time)	– 0.039	– 27.407	– 2.69**
(Mean household task importance) × (Total household work time)	0.024	16.866	2.75*
(Mean household task pleasantness) × (Total household work time)	0.010	7.027	0.86
Constant	132.300		5.35

[a]$N = 311$; R^2 (reduced form) $= .72$.
[b]dna = does not apply.
*p < .05 (one-tailed test).
**p < .05 (two-tailed test).

ger wives (under age 30). This finding was taken as a logical reflection of a life-cycle effect whereby the women of an age to be subject to high family demands (e.g., young children) took on more tasks. Moreover, this finding informed later expectations about household work *time,* that wives 30–50 years would also spend greater household-work minutes per day than did their younger sisters. Instead, Table 6.4 indicates that, although wives 30–50 years were subject to greater numbers of tasks, it was the *older* wives who spent the greatest time on them. Compared to the younger wives, and conditional on a mean level for household tasks, the older wives spent about 53 additional minutes a day on household labor tasks. (It is worth noting that wives who were 30–50 years old also spent more time, but not at a substantive or statistically significant level.) Perhaps this means that middle-aged wives do more tasks, more quickly, whereas older women do fewer tasks more slowly.

Table 6.4 also shows similarities to the prior model in the finding for wives' schooling: a one-unit increase in the wives' level of schooling (given a mean for total household labor time) increased their household work time by 20 minutes per day. Given the findings in Chapter 5, it is clear that the variable for the wives' schooling was simultaneously tapping multiple and perhaps counteracting forces. Perhaps this is just one more illustration that the preferences and incentives presumably associated with class are not one-dimensional, nor easily captured through single or even multiple measures such as schooling, occupation, and income. And, as has been obvious all along, the preferences associated with household labor are much more complicated than what is modeled here.

It was anticipated that among the household labor "rationales," the three that seemed to tap more traditional notions ("good homemaker," "family's well-being," "way when growing up") would exert positive effects, and that at least two of the remaining variables that seem to tap more individual concerns and tastes would generate negative effects. Of the rationale variables, three proved significant, two of the three in the expected direction. If we assume that households were at the mean level of household work time, an increase of one unit in the wives' perceived importance of doing household labor the "way it was done when they were growing up" added 32 minutes to their household day. Also as expected, the rationale of "having little choice" served to decrease the wives' household-work time. A one-unit increase in its importance (if we still assume a mean household level) decreased the wives' household work time by 27 minutes per day. These two findings also imply maximum effects of $+93$ and -81 minutes, respectively. In contradiction to the anticipated effect, but consistent with the findings of Chapter 5, the rationale of "getting it over with" exerted a positive and significant effect. A one-unit increase in the importance of this rationale increased the length of the household workday by almost 37 minutes, with a maximum effect possible of almost 2 hours per day. Of course, this also suggests the obvious possibility that the causal direction might go the other way: more time spent might lead to a belief in the greater importance of "getting it over with." (For a discussion of exogeniety, see Chapter 4, Footnote 13.)

Through these findings, we see that (1) wives are subject to normative considerations in the amount of the household's labor time that they assume, and (2) such normative forces affect not only the number of tasks allocated to household members, net of the total, but, as vitally, the time spent on those tasks. This is no better illustrated than through the finding for task importance. Both this variable and its companion—mean task pleasantness—tap the effects of preferences informed by normative and psychic consequences, respectively, on household labor time. Table 6.4 shows that a single-unit increase in the wives' mean ranking of task importance increased the time they spent on household labor by about 17 minutes per day. This result also implies a maximum effect (if we still assume a mean for total household work time) of over $2^{1}/_{2}$ hours per day (153 minutes). In contrast, mean task pleasantness showed virtually no effect on wives' household labor time, even though earlier it affected the relative number of tasks that fell to wives. Perhaps the initial *choice* of tasks (e.g., child care vs. cleaning the oven) reflects such preferences. Once the tasks are chosen, the decisions regarding time spent on them must attend to other than psychic or normative concerns.

CONCLUSIONS AND SPECULATIONS

The Allocation of Wives' Time

Figure 8 is included to facilitate a discussion of the findings for the wives' market and household minutes per day. Each of the significant variables affecting the establishment of the household pie and the wives' time is represented in it. The figure makes it easy to see that the primary determinant of the wives' market and household time was the level at which their households were "attached" to time in the market or at home. That is, when households reached a high level of employment time commitment, only then did the wives' market time become most seriously affected. Likewise, the greater the time demanded by household labor, the greater the time wives committed to it. Additional and not surprising effects on the wives' market time are found for the wives' age and schooling. Each of these findings reiterated a similar result from the

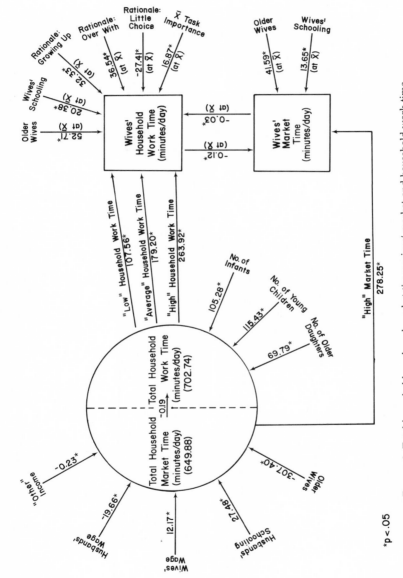

FIGURE 8. Total household work and market time; wives' market and household work time ($N = 311; 335$).

*p < .05

earlier, more elaborate model for market hours and household tasks. In that model, two variables proved important to the wives' monthly employment hours: the market portion of the household pie and the wives' age. The results are similar here, although schooling also exerted an effect on the wives' market minutes per day.

If we turn to household time, each significant result reminds one of a prior finding; what made the difference in the number of tasks elected by the wives was the household work portion of the pie, the wives' age and schooling, some of their rationales for household work accomplishment, and the normative (mean importance) or psychic (mean pleasantness) consequences associated with household tasks. Here, where household minutes are at issue, all but household task pleasantness appears to have been significant to the wives' time.

Of course, that also means that the null findings were nearly identical. A number of the wives' characteristics that might have operated to enhance their employment time (hours or minutes) did not prove significant in either model (e.g., the wives' occupation and the wives' wages). And in the household, where the model did slightly better in specifying the salient determinants of the wives' work, there was still a variable or two that a priori seemed good bets, but that proved otherwise (e.g., the wives' serious illness or injury and "satisfying self").

What differentiates the two models for the wives' market time and household work is what they convey about the relationship between the wives' work at home and on the job. In the model for the wives' employment time and household tasks, there was no apparent reciprocity between market and home; the relation between what wives did at "home" and what wives did at "work" was not reflected through the variables of hours and tasks. Another finding emerged when the dependent variables became household and market minutes. At that point, the negative reciprocal relation appeared: work at home took time away from employment, and time at work robbed the wives of household labor time. Moreover, the relation was not one-to-one; the impact of household demands on the wives' employment was four times greater than the impact of market time on wives' household labor time. Should one assume that the differences in the findings across the two models result *only* from measurement differences?

To address this question properly, it is necessary to return to Chapter 4's examination of the two portions of the pie. Recall that the market portion of the pie negatively influenced household time, but not household tasks. Yet, only household tasks exerted a negative effect on total household employment. I argued then that, rather than suggesting some measurement artifact, the seeming contradiction simply indicated two substantive dimensions of household work, and I offered the distinction between "lumpy" tasks and time. The former was more fixed, more stable, and less flexible, and the latter more fluid and manipulable. When we turn to this same phenomenon for the allocation of individual effort to home and market, it is necessary to ask what makes household tasks "lumpy." *Why* do wives' (and presumably others') household tasks have no effect on, and why are they not affected by, employment? I believe that the secret of task "lumpiness" lies in the familiar distinction between household "help" and "responsiblity." For wives, the routine accomplishment of household tasks (what was measured when the respondent wives and husbands did their card sorts) becomes a permanent feature of household relations. Come rain or shine, or even changes in employment, wives expect—and are expected—to assume a vastly greater share of household tasks than other household members. Of course, this means that a negative reciprocal relation between market hours and household tasks would not be forthcoming. To paraphrase the tired old saw, a woman's *first* place is in the home.

But quite a different relation can appear when one is no longer measuring formal hours of employment, or especially the rigid system of task allocation that was the story of Chapter 5. When market and household *minutes* are the focus, we can now imagine wives changing the "mix" of the time and the quality inputs into various tasks, other household members being pressed into service (if only for a moment) or even making a crucial contribution on any given day, in response to the demands of wives' market time. More important, once formal hours of employment are traded for the minutes of a workday, wives may more easily adjust their "at-work" time to respond to the demands of their "at-home" time.

In short, the specification of this chapter has introduced the flexibility of time and has allowed the influence of "help" from other members to be more clearly reflected. Thus, this additional dimension of the allocation of market and household work rounds out the picture first outlined in Chapter 4. Within a relatively inflexible and (I have argued) nearly intractable system of work relations lurk some discretion and flexibility made possible by the organization of employment and by the personal relations surrounding household labor.

This discussion quite logically brings us to a final set of speculations concerning the model for wives' market and household work time. Namely, what does the model say about other household members' work time?

The "Hidden" Household Workers

Recall that, when total household productivity (whether in employment or in the household) is defined as a linear combination of wives' and husbands' efforts, equations estimating one member's contribution tell a good deal about that of the other. Thus, this chapter has one more familiar ring to it, namely, that husbands' market-time contribution is most affected at levels other than (or, perhaps, "prior to") a "high" household-market-time commitment.

Much more interesting, perhaps, are the speculations one might offer about members' household labor time. To begin, Figure 8 indicates that however much Chapter 5 painted the contributions of members other than wives' as trivial, it was not an exaggeration. The figure speaks volumes when it shows that it was only the wives' household work minutes per day that were affected by the total household time given over to domestic labor.

Yet, it is logical to assume that if the model had been able to estimate equations for other members, we might well have found that the effects for daughters, and perhaps even for sons and husbands, were statistically significant and reciprocally related to one another. Some hints from Chapter 5 and a suggestion here of greater discretion in the members' management of household work time make this hunch an informed one. Such indirect evidence suggests that perhaps the daughters' and the sons' household work time was positively related, and that the daughters' help in the household could (as it did in the last chapter) lessen their mothers' household work time. It might also be safe to assume that when household time is the focus, even the husbands' aid may have made a significant difference to their wives. Although we cannot ultimately know from this model what *exogenous* variables would influence the household time of husbands (or children, for that matter), it is probably safe to assume that whatever the effects of these variables, their overall practical significance is limited. What sense household members make of the arrangements just analyzed is the initial concern of the final chapter.

CHAPTER 7

Conclusions
Work and Gender

INTRODUCTION AND REPRISE

I began with the well-worn story of "who does what" in the market and the household. Judging from the literature, and the descriptive statistics in Chapter 3, it looked as if there wasn't much variance, or even much of a story to tell: husbands are the primary breadwinners, so-called, and wives the household workers. When wives take outside jobs, they add those hours to their work in the home. Such generalizations are, of course, accurate, if imprecise. And that is where the analysis began.

Another story was unearthed by positing a set of work relations that operate within the household and are determined by the unexamined terrain of *household* productive capacity. That is, how much was done at home, at work, and who did it were conceived to be different, albeit related, phenomena. Moreover, how work was allocated was presumed to operate in the context of, and conditional on, the establishment of the total amount of household and market work.

The more accurate picture that emerged was still one of little variance, but the sources of that variation were revealed. First, a great deal of the variance in individual contributions to the home and to the labor market is captured by the context of the work itself. That is, the household "pie" places its own demands on household members and helps to determine household labor- and market-time allocations. Second, however, and just as crucial to an understanding of household work relations, is the vast (and largely uncharted) normative backdrop that influences the mechanisms by which work is apportioned to household members, and that renders household work relations, gender relations. Thus, as

185

only one example, the total amount of work established for the household had a large and significant bearing only on the wives' tasks and time. These findings cannot be dismissed simply by invoking some version of a "natural order"—of either an economic or a biological variety.

It is the premise of this final chapter that the division of household labor represents a process whereby both gender and work shape, and are shaped by, each other. Moreover, the results of this analysis demand a reconceptualization of household production that takes account of the imperatives of work and gender, and of the sense that the members make of them.

Given the data presented in the last few chapters, one cannot help wondering how much difference of opinion there is between wives and husbands about who should do what. Surely, a related question is how husbands and wives evaluate the equity of their present arrangements. Do household members necessarily define as inequitable the lopsided divisions of labor that they experience? To ground some final speculations on the nature of production and the potential for change in it, I turn initially to these questions. Although the data may not prove ideal for the questions posed, it is nevertheless important to end this examination where it began: at the direct experience of one manifestation of the "problem that has no name."

MANAGING THE DIVISION OF LABOR: CONSENSUS AND EQUITY

To address the members' assessments of their household work, four questionnaire items measured the differences of opinion held by our respondent wives and husbands about the perceived equity of their household-work arrangements. The supposition was that those households with the greatest number of tasks to accomplish (i.e., those with the bigger task pie) may also be those in which couples express the greatest differences of opinion about who should do what. Or, perhaps, employed wives have husbands whose answers to "how fair" their household work arrangements are differ markedly from those whose wives are not employed. Unfortunately, this brief analysis can be neither precise nor elaborate; the causal relationships between these items and any endogenous variables examined earlier are impossible to establish. As a consequence, both the *a priori* expectations about and the interpretation of the findings are tentative and speculative. Nevertheless, information about the degree to which the couples disagreed, how they resolved their disagreements, and what their perceptions of equity were can, as substantive correlates to the prior and more rigorous analysis, suggest some ways in which the allocation of work is understood by household members. In other words, these concluding questions speak more directly to how household members make sense of, and thus manage, the normative dimension of their household work lives.

After a brief consideration of the frequencies of the variables, their relationships to the endogenous variables that figured so importantly in the earlier analysis are explored. Two questions come to mind. First, for the two items on disagreement and equity, their zero-order correlations with the division of labor items (i.e., the task and time pies and the contributions of each member) will speak to the question of whether issues of conflict and equity are associated in any meaningful way with how much household work is undertaken, and with who does it. Second, it will be useful to ask whether the items on disagreement and equity systematically varied with the employment of wives. Addressing that question requires a look at households differentiated by wives' employment and the associations that resulted.

The first set of relationships to be considered are those centering on the differences of opinion that wives and husbands had about the apportionment of their household labors. These items were included only on the wives' questionnaires, so here one must depend solely on the wives' assessment of conflict over household work.

Disagreements over Who Should Do What

To begin, wives were asked, "How much difference of opinion is there in your household about who should do what household work?" and "When you differ with your husband about who should be doing what, who usually gives in, you or your husband?" These items followed a number of questions about how wives felt about the household work they did. The questions were intended to tap variation in affective response to the allocation of household labor. However, after seeing the relatively uniform patterns in who did what, one might expect that some respondents would rail against their arrangements, with the consequence of lots of "difference of opinion."

Table 7.1 contains the frequency distributions for the two question-

TABLE 7.1
Frequency Distribution for "Difference of Opinion"
about the Division of Household Labor[a]

"How much difference of opinion is there
about who should do what household work?"

	Frequency	Percentage
None	190	56.72
A little	60	17.91
Some	60	17.91
A lot	25	7.46
Total	335	100.00

"Who usually gives in when there is a difference
of opinion about who should do what?"

	Frequency	Percentage
Husband	56	16.72
50/50	158	47.16
Wife	121	36.12
Total	335	100.00

[a]$N = 335$.

naire items addressing the wives' responses about disagreement over the allocation of household work. To begin, we see that over half of the wives reported no difference of opinion over who should do what, with an additional 18% reporting only "a little" difference of opinion. Thus, the frequency distributions alone would lead one to conclude that there was little voiced concern about the patterns revealed earlier.[1] Moreover, when asked "who usually gives in" when there was a difference of opinion, 47% of the wives reported resolving the difference "50/50," and 36% reported themselves as "usually giving in" in such disagreements. Only 17% of the wives reported their husbands as "usually giving in."

We must still ask what association there is between the items that reflect the apportionment of work and the items that reflect conflict over it. For example, one expectation is that the more household work there is, the more likely it is that there will be disagreement over it. In other words, whether measured through the number of tasks required or the time it takes to complete them, the household labor pie would be positively associated with the degree of disagreement over who should do

---

[1]Nevertheless, as both silence and voiced dissent can constitute a difference of opinion, these findings should be treated with some caution.

what. Likewise, one might expect that the tasks and time of wives and husbands are associated with these items, but in different ways. It may be that in households where wives take on a relatively *greater* number of tasks (or spend more time on household labor), there is *less* likelihood of disagreement over it. The presumption is that the members of such households have perhaps made their peace with this issue, and that they experience little difference of opinion. Of course, the causal direction might well work the other way in a kind of "female submission" model: in households where there is little disagreement, wives may be acquiescing to greater amounts of labor. In contrast, one might expect that, in households where husbands take on a greater number of household tasks or devote greater amounts of time to them, there is ongoing disagreement over who should do what. This may seem a counterintuitive expectation, but it is based on the notion that, once the more traditional arrangements, guided by a clear normative structure (where wives do vastly greater amounts of work) are breached, differences of opinion not ordinarily tolerated at this work site materialize. In short, household "anomie" may breed dissension. I return to related considerations shortly, when the possibility for change is addressed directly. Still, for this relationship, too, the causal direction may work the other way: "differences of opinion" may prompt *husbands* to acquiesce to greater amounts of household labor.

With respect to the items about "who gives in," the expectations are even less clear. There may be little association between the division of household labor and how differences of opinion are resolved. How husbands and wives settle disagreements may be more a function of their particular style of interaction and may be less affected by, or contingent on, a specific issue.

Table 7.2 contains the 12 zero-order correlation coefficients addressing the association between the two new variables of interest and the prior household labor variables. It is not necessary to dwell on the obvious: there is virtually no relationship between the new items and who does what in the household. These data suggest that whatever the mechanism linking the division of household labor with disagreement over it, it does not emerge in a simple zero-order relationship. Neither the size of the household labor pie nor the work of wives and husbands seemed to be associated with differences of opinion or with how such differences were resolved. Moreover, only one coefficient proved statistically significant (.05 level); there is a slight suggestion that the greater the amount of time husbands spent on household labor, the greater the degree of dis-

TABLE 7.2
*Zero-Order Pearson Correlations between Household Labor
and "Difference-of-Opinion" Variables*[a]

Variable	How much difference of opinion?	Who gives in?
Total household work tasks	0.064	−0.048
Total household work time	0.042	0.023
Wives' household task contribution	0.020	0.056
Wives' household-work-time contribution	−0.077	0.001
Husbands' household-task contribution	0.013	−0.003
Husbands' household-work-time contribution	0.180*	0.038

[a]$N = 335$.
*$p < .05$ (two-tailed test).

agreement between wives and husbands over the allocation of household labor.

It may be that conflict over who does what household tasks surfaces only when some *external* pressures force the issue. After all, the data presented earlier suggested that the apportionment of household labor reflects a fairly well-established—even entrenched—set of cultural expectations. It seems reasonable to assume that there is a strong tug away from frequent conflict over such mundane and everyday matters as who will do what, when, for how long, and in what way. Perhaps it is only when household members face pressures that counter the pull toward consensus that disagreement will occur. And it may be that wives' market work—the only "legitimate" claim on their household time—would potentiate an association between husbands' increased household labor *and* differences of opinion about it. In short, under these fluctuating conditions, it may seem as if there is something to disagree *about*. The underlying model would therefore posit that greater differences of opinion over household labor result primarily when wives are employed. Thus, the correlation constructed to reflect the impact of employment allows us to ask the question, What is the association between who does what and disagreement over it, under the two "conditions" of wives' employment status?

It was expected that disagreement over the allocation of household labor would increase with greater household labor demands (either through task or time) or with greater contribution by the husbands *if* the wives were employed. There were no particular expectations about changes in who would "give in" in such disagreements, given wives' employment status, but these coefficients are also considered in Table 7.3.

Making sense of Table 7.3 is a straightforward proposition, as very little seems to be occurring. For either the "difference of opinion" or the "who gives in" variables, the wives' employment status did not seem to effect a new association with the division of labor. Only two relationships suggest something of substantive import. The first echoes the prior zero-order correlation in Table 7.2 between the husbands' household-work time and the degree to which wives and husbands differed about who should do what. There we saw a .18 correlation between the two. Here the association between the husbands' household-work time and the level of disagreement was greater (.214 vs. .167) when the wives' were employed, and these associations are the only ones that achieved statistical significance. It may be that the wives' employment provided the impetus to change (however slight), generating not only a difference of opinion about who should do what, but also an increase in the husbands' household-work time.

The only other suggestion of an effect is the change in the correlation between "who gives in" and the husbands' household-task contribution. It appears that the employed wives with husbands who took on more household tasks were much less likely to "give in" during household labor disagreements. Perhaps it is only under such conditions that a more traditional interactional style between wives and husbands is modified. It could also be the case that those wives who are most likely to be employed and to have husbands who engage in greater numbers of household tasks are also those wives less likely to "give in" in disagreements of *any* kind. Nevertheless, it should be pointed out that the overwhelming statistical and substantive message of Table 7.3 is that both the degree to which wives and husbands differ in their opinions about who should do what and the degree to which wives "give in" seem largely unaffected by how much household work is done, who does it, or whether wives are also employed outside the home. In other words, Tables 7.2 and 7.3 may describe a constant rather than a variable, where how people *interact* about who does what is as stable a phenomenon as the division of the work itself.

Although there is little that explains variation in the difference of opinion about the allocation of household labor, there remains the question of how the *equity* of the arrangements is perceived by husbands and wives.

TABLE 7.3
Zero-Order Pearson Correlations between
Household Labor and "Difference-of-Opinion"
Variables under Wife Employment/Unemployment Condition[a]

	How much difference of opinion?		Who gives in?	
Variable	Wife employed	Wife unemployed	Wife employed	Wife unemployed
Total household work tasks	0.045	0.126	−0.019	−0.043
Total household work time	0.123	0.052	0.034	0.038
Wives' household-task contribution	−0.017	0.086	−0.045	−0.044
Wives' household-work-time contribution	0.004	−0.064	0.010	0.025
Husbands' household-task contribution	−0.012	0.070	−0.117	0.052
Husbands' household-work-time contribution	0.214*	0.167*	0.046	0.033

[a]$N = 335$.
*$p < .05$ (two-tailed test).

Perceptions of Equity

Near the conclusion of their interviews, our respondent husbands and wives were asked somewhat different questions about the equity of their household-labor arrangements. The husbands were asked, "Now thinking about who does what around the house, do you think these arrangements are fair? That is, are they very fair, somewhat fair, somewhat unfair, or very unfair?" So that we could gather more detailed information, the wives were asked, "Thinking in terms of how *fair* these arrangements are, do you feel you should be doing a lot less housework compared to other members of your household, somewhat less housework compared to other members of your household, about the same as you do now compared to other members of your household, somewhat more housework compared to other members of your family, or a lot more?'' Table 7.4 shows the frequencies for both of these questionnaire items, and although the items were not worded identically, for present purposes the responses are nonetheless comparable.

One must conclude from Table 7.4 that, in general, the husbands and wives perceived their household labor arrangements to be equitable. For example, fully 94% of the husbands reported their arrangements to be ''somewhat fair'' or ''very fair.'' At nearly the same level, when ''thinking about how fair these arrangements are,'' about 70% of all the wives reported that they should be doing ''about the same'' amount of housework, with an additional 9% reporting that they should do ''somewhat more'' or ''a lot more.'' An interesting difference did emerge in the relative number of husbands who believed the arrangements to be ''very unfair'' or, in the case of the wives, the number who believed they should be doing less housework. Although only about 6% of the husbands reported inequity in their household labor arrangements, about 21% of the wives said that they should be doing ''somewhat less'' or ''a lot less.'' Thus, there was some variation here, and it could be explored much as the earlier items on differences of opinion were explored.

First, Table 7.5 shows the zero-order correlations between the items on equity and the endogenous variables of household labor. For the husbands' ''how fair'' variable, a positive association indicates greater contribution and greater perceived equity; for wives' variables a positive association indicates greater contribution and a judgment that, relative to others, the wives should do more. As with the prior variables, there is nothing particularly compelling about the association between perceptions of equity and who does what: With the exception of a general trend away from a perception of fairness when the tasks and time of the household or the members' contributions increased, there is very little happening here; in fact, only one correlation exceeds .10 and is statistically significant. The larger the household task pie, the less likely were the husbands to say that their household labor arrangements were equitable. Yet, very little is suggested by the same associations with the husbands' contributions alone.

Second, Table 7.6 addresses the same question posed earlier: What was the effect of the wives' employment status on the association between perceptions of equity and the division of household labor? Here, one might expect that, particularly for husbands, the wives' *unemployment* might foster a negative association between increases in what was to be

TABLE 7.4

Frequency Distribution for Perceptions of Equity in Division of Labor[a]

"Do you think these arrangements are fair?" (Husbands only)		
	Frequency	Percentage
Very unfair	2	0.60
Somewhat unfair	18	5.37
Somewhat fair	123	36.72
Very fair	192	57.31
Total	335	100.00

"Should you be doing more or less household work?" (Wives only)		
	Frequency	Percentage
A lot less	11	3.28
Somewhat less	60	17.91
About the same	234	69.85
Somewhat more	25	7.46
A lot more	5	1.49
Total	335	100.00

[a]$N = 335$.

done, or the members' own contributions, and the husbands' perceptions of how fair the arrangements were. Similarly, but for the alternative condition, one could expect a negative association between the household work variables, the wives' *employment,* and the wives' notions of whether they should be doing more or less household labor.

Table 7.6 indicates that, for both equity variables, the wives' employment status did not markedly change the nearly null association between household work arrangements and perceptions of equity. The suggestion

TABLE 7.5

Zero-Order Pearson Correlations between
Household Labor and "Equity" Variables[a]

Variable	(Husbands) "How fair"	(Wives) "More or less"
Total household work tasks	−0.127*	−0.089
Total household work time	−0.104	−0.076
Wives' household-task contribution	−0.081	−0.096
Wives' household-work-time contribution	−0.074	−0.039
Husbands' household-task contribution	0.045	−0.002
Husbands' household-work-time contribution	−0.077	−0.076

[a]$N = 335$.
*$p < .05$ (two-tailed test).

of an overall negative association first revealed in the marginals of Table 7.1 is reiterated here, but very little is added to the story. A hint that the wives' unemployment exerted an effect does appear for the husbands' "How fair?" variable. Under that employment condition, an increase in total household work time or the husbands' household-work time generated a relatively large shift toward the husbands' perception of inequity in the division of labor. These findings are inconclusive, and again, the causal direction can barely be guessed at. Yet, it is also the case that, earlier, the variables for household time—both total time and members' time—captured the most variance. Thus, this may reflect a genuine association between the husbands' household time, the wives' employment, and the husbands' sense of "how fair" their work arrangements were. At the same time, Table 7.6 suggests an interesting negative association between greater *wives'* contributions and their notions of equity. There is a hint here that both the husbands and the wives who devoted greater time to household labor in such "employed" households were especially likely to see such arrangements as unfair. Similarly, the wives in households with more work to be done or the wives who undertook greater numbers of tasks also thought that they should be doing less. In short, powerful normative assumptions about women's work operated most strongly when the wives' were unemployed.

With these last findings on worker perceptions of difference and equity added to the analysis, the picture of household labor and its division is complete; it becomes one in which the imperatives of the work itself collide with an existing normative structure and interact with what sense the workers make of both. Moreover, with the insights that even these scant data on perceived equity provide, it is possible to speculate about the astounding stability (some might call it intransigence) in the way in which Americans divide the work of the household and the prospects for change suggested by the analysis. These issues comprise the final considerations of this book.

THE STRUCTURES OF HOUSEHOLD LABOR

The analysis has made clear that how families come to allocate their household labors depends on a great deal more than the prior, simplistically conceived models suggest. Hardly a question simply of who has more time, or whose time is worth more, who has more skill, or who has

TABLE 7.6

Zero-Order Pearson Correlations between Household Labor and "Equity" Variables under Wife Employment/Unemployment Condition[a]

Variable	"How fair" (H)		"More or less" (W)	
	Wife employed	Wife unemployed	Wife employed	Wife unemployed
Total household work tasks	− 0.134	− 0.130*	− 0.040	− 0.144*
Total household work time	0.008	− 0.166*	− 0.156	− 0.068
Wives' household-task contribution	− 0.132	−0.062	− 0.041	− 0.151*
Wives' household-work-time contribution	− 0.097	− 0.066	− 0.136	− 0.025
Husbands' household-task contribution	0.070	0.033	0.087	− 0.043
Husbands' household-work-time contribution	0.172	− 0.193*	− 0.062	− 0.081

[a]N = 335.
*$p < .05$ (two-tailed test).

more power, it is clear that a complicated relation between the structure of work imperatives and the structure of normative expectations attached to the work as *gendered* determines the ultimate allocation of household members' time to work and home. That complex relation has been only roughly approximated here, but its presence in the findings is undeniable. Separately, these household labor "structures" determined the particulars of the results, and taken together, they articulate the complexity of these work relations.[2]

[2]For this concluding discussion, I focus primarily on the determinants of the division of household labor, and of necessity, I neglect the determinants of market time allocation. The relation between household members' allocation of time to home and market, however, remains crucial to an understanding of the work imperatives imposed on household members.

The Structure of Work Imperatives

This analysis rested on a presumption that the determinants of the tasks and the time of the household may be different from the determinants of their allocation. Analytic models were constructed to address the expectation that the market and household pie would impose its own influence on how work was apportioned among household members.

In Chapter 4, it was clear that a variety of factors independent of household member preferences affects the nature and amount of work to be undertaken. For example, children exert the greatest impact on the tasks and time of the household. Whether through the demands that come with their dependency or through the contributions that they make to the household as productive members, children leave their mark on this work site in profound ways. Any other influence exerted by characteristics of the home, characteristics of the members, or their preferences pales in comparison with the influence of children on the household and (indirectly) the market pie.

Such a conclusion would be of no interest if the household labor pie had little effect on the members' contributions to household labor. But, in fact, and to reiterate a bit from Chapter 5, by far the most important determinant of the wives' contributions to household tasks or time was the *total* tasks or time presented to the household unit. In addition, recall that these forces had no impact on the husbands' contributions.

Regardless of the asymmetry of the effects, the fact remains that what is to be done and the time it takes to do it constitute the context in which the allocation of household labor to all members occurs; this context imposes crucial constraints on the process by which household labor is divided. Indeed, there lies the variance to be explained. No matter what the work to be done, who does it or even how it must be allocated is in part a question not of what the members may wish, but of what the demands of people and tasks require. And it is in this context that any normative structure operates.

For example, even the *contemplation* of what is fair or unfair can be eclipsed by the sheer number of the tasks that constitute infant care.[3] Yet, patterns of work allocation established to respond to the demands of tasks during a *particular* period in the life cycle of a household may remain long after the relevant circumstances have changed. With the ar-

---

[3]As one young father of an infant said, "For the first six months, the question of fairness became a real problem— we were *both* doing more than was fair."

rival of a new baby, a wife may leave the workplace for a time and take primary responsibility for both infant care and the work of the household. After all, it is she who spends her days in this work environment, and in practice, it may be impossible to differentiate her work as strictly child care or strictly household labor.[4] Once she is back in employment, however, the logic of the arrangement that was so apparent earlier is gone; nevertheless, what "worked" before becomes the way-we've-always-done-it, and thus the way-we-do-it. Note, too, that when wives return to employment, it is only *their* circumstances that have changed. Thus, any change in the division of household labor in response to new circumstances would logically imply more household labor from the *husbands*. Old habits and routines die hard, precisely because change requires so much effort.

The Normative Structure of Household Labor

We have no direct evidence of how members' perceptions of who *should* do what affects who *does* do what. One can get an important sense of how our respondents felt about their work arrangements through the questionnaire items just discussed, and their implications are considered shortly. The actual mechanisms by which the normative structure of gender imposes itself on this work site can be discerned only indirectly, and not without some speculation. Yet, the circumstantial evidence surrounding the "gendered" nature of this work and its allocation is overwhelming.

In the specific instance of the normative orientations that might affect the division of household labor, some rationales ("being a good homemaker," "doing it the way it was done when the wife was growing up," and "getting it over with") made a significant difference in the wives' contributions. And, of course, as there was no significant relation between the wives' work and the husbands' work, such normative orientations had no indirect effect on how much the husbands contributed.

On a more general level, however, and over and above the obvious worker concerns of marginal productivity, the clear presumption existed

---

[4]Nevertheless, women sometimes express strong feelings about the difference between the two. Note these two examples: "I'm a mother and wife first. I'm a housewife last. There's a difference when I do things with the children"; "You have to understand—children are why we *do* housework. They are why we are in therapy; they are why we're not working; they are why we're here at *all.*"

that the wives were responsible for the work of the household. It is this overarching normative orientation that found its way into the few measures that tapped it, and that, more important, drove these patterns to their consistent asymmetry. This sort of normative structure—resting as it does on gender relations—lends a kind of solidity to the arrangement of work that, in principle, could be organized in many different ways or might be subject to substantial influence from pressures external to the household but is not.[5]

The normative structure that motivates these work patterns may provide some ballast for an otherwise problematic set of activities for household members. Yet, it is hardly the intention of this analysis to suggest that household labor could be accomplished *only* within this sort of normative structure. Indeed, one doesn't need a degree in the New Home Economics to build a strong case against workers' arranging production so that, regardless of the time commitments of the members, *one* member will invariably do the lion's share of the work. Simple logic argues otherwise. Therefore, one must wonder what it is that motivates a continued dependence on this way of organizing household labor. Any answers (or at least an approach to them) carry implications for the role of individual choice and possible change in our work lives. At the risk of overdrawing their positions (and exaggerating some obvious shortcomings), but as a useful starting point nonetheless, I will briefly return to traditional sociological and neoclassical economic perspectives.

MECHANISMS OF CHOICE AND CONSTRAINT

What might be a sociological account of the findings concerning the allocation of market and household labor? To begin, institutional and normative forces combine to limit severely the choices of all members of the household. To return to a prior example, the overwhelming demands of an infant child, the rigid organization of employment, and the clear cultural message that only a mother can truly satisfy a child's physiological and emotional needs provide little incentive to parents to elect full-time employment and to share the rearing of their child. The sociologi-

---

[5]Such normative notions also operate to hamper our ability to imagine other ways of organizing work. Sometimes, science fiction (e.g., LeGuin, 1974; Gilman, 1979) can help us to think "outlandish" thoughts about everyday life (see also Oakley, 1980, for a discussion).

cal world is "lumpy"; when movement occurs, it comes in discrete states: one is employed, or not; one is married, or not; one has children, or not. This (often binary) world is portrayed as imposing a set of impersonal forces on the individual who must negotiate her or his choices accordingly.

This perspective becomes most problematic when it tries to account for individual variation over time. Any form of social science explanation that presupposes a social world where individual human action is often incidental to it faces trouble when confronted with variation and change. Moreover, constraint is surely not the only dimension worth considering in the study of household work.

Another vantage point, which is no less a reality in the data, is that aspect of household labor best appreciated from the neoclassical economic standpoint. Here, the actors become the whole story, and social (or normative) structures are a relatively trivial feature of their functioning. Rather than being weak and ineffectual, individual experience and choices are crucial and continuous, constantly balancing all sorts of complicated opportunity costs within a single full-income constraint. For example, wives do not decide whether or not to get a job; they decide to work more or fewer hours per week. This more hydraulic model counters the "actorless" world of the sociologist, as individual choice operates to produce the everyday practices surrounding household labor. Yet, unlike explanations of the sociological variety, the economic models ignore the material and cultural context of choice and thus face trouble when they face data. In the case of the present analysis, one finds very little variation that might be introduced by individual choice, regardless of circumstance or biography. This story is one of constancy, not variation.

Quite obviously, neither traditional sociological nor economic explanations of the division of household and market labor make it easy to give formal attention to the two realities of choice *and* constraint. In their failure to handle the direct experience of work creatively, these perspectives reduce the mechanisms of the organization of household labor either to a social system that is fully constraining, or to one that knows only the individual (and therefore somewhat questionable) choices of institutionally unconstrained members.

How does one combine the two perspectives and thus improve on their ability to account for the workings of these social relations? Both sociology and the New Home Economics must be reintroduced to the complexities of the social systems that they wish to explain. The nature of the household production process itself must be reconceptualized, so that households become considerably more complicated than Becker's "small factory" metaphor would suggest. This reconceptualization would attend to both the work and the normative structures of household labor.

Rethinking Household Production

Let us return to a much-criticized assumption from the New Home Economics: households are "at the margin" in their organization of production, and thus, given a set of resources and an efficient "production function," resources are optimally allocated within the household. With this assumption, and the data, one is forced to contemplate how the members could rationally establish the arrangements that they do solely for the production of household goods and services. Moreover, even if such arrangements were optimal, why would the workers consider them fair? If only on the grounds of efficiency, might one not instead expect a greater effort by wives and husbands to equalize the division of household labor? One answer is that one might expect such effort if the division of labor were brought to bear only on efficient production, or if household goods and services were *all that were being produced.* In short, if we retain the assumption that the lopsided arrangements surrounding the allocation of household work are optimal for *some* production process, we must again ask the simple question, What is being produced?

At least metaphorically, the division of household labor facilitates *two* production processes: the production of goods and services and what we might call the production of gender. Simultaneously, household members "do" gender, as they "do" housework and child care, and what I have been calling the division of household labor provides for the joint production of household labor and gender; it is the mechanism by which both the material and the symbolic products of the household are realized.[6]

The Production of Gender

If we are to speak of the "production" of gender, the traditional and static notion of sex, or gender "role," with its rather vague behavioral

---

[6]Also produced are age relations, where parents and children "do" socialization, and instances of household labor can become "socialization-relevant." Although this is not the focus here, the active accomplishment of age relations and socialization would be critical to any full examination of children's labor within the household (for a related discussion, see Wittner, 1980).

referents must be abandoned. (For a discussion, see Hochschild, 1973; Tresemer, 1975; Thorne, 1976; Lopata and Thorne, 1978.) Increasingly, the concept of gender "role" as a set of learned and enacted sex-linked expectations has been slowly supplanted by a conception of gender as an active, behaviorally based, and demonstrable accomplishment, a "situationally accountable feature of sexually categorized human beings" (West and Zimmerman, 1984, p. 3).[7] To appreciate gender as an ongoing accomplishment, Goffman's concept of gender display (1977, 1979), as well as a recent (West and Zimmerman, 1984) critique and extension of it, is instructive.[8]

Goffman (1977) conceived of gender as constituted by a family of behavioral displays, or "sex-class-specific ways of appearing, acting, feeling" (p. 303) that serve to establish or reaffirm members' categorical identity and essential nature, and to "align" members to each other in social situations. As Goffman (1979) noted:

> If gender be defined as the culturally established correlates of sex (whether in consequence of biology or learning), then gender display refers to conventionalized portrayals of these correlates. (p. 1)

West and Zimmerman (1984) have elaborated on Goffman's notion of gender displays as "indicative" behaviors, in order to consider the mechanisms by which gender is accomplished normatively. They argued quite convincingly that the "doing" of gender does not simply mean that, through a set of behavioral displays (e.g., a husband "helps" his wife carry heavy grocery bags, and a wife "nags" her husband about cleaning the rain gutters), we affirm our *categorical* status as male or female. Instead, they maintained that

> Hence, gender displays pay homage to cultural conceptions of proper relationships between the sexes rather than as Goffman (1977: 71) notes, literally depicting them.... Gender display...must be understood then, as a stance toward the conventions applicable to it rather than a precise predictor of how an individual will act.... We argue that...accomplishing gender...refers to the ongoing task of rendering oneself *accountably* masculine or feminine. (pp. 12–16; emphasis in original)

---

[7] I do not suggest that socialization to gender-appropriate behavior is trivial or developmentally inconsequential. On the contrary, learning to "do" gender is crucial to achieving the identity and the status of a competent member of a social group. (For review and discussion, see Cahill, 1982.)

[8] A complete exegesis on the importance and the implications of this reconceptualization of gender cannot be presented here. The reader is directed to a number of instructive first statements (e.g., Henley, 1977; Lopata and Thorne, 1978; Cahill, 1982; West, 1982).

For West and Zimmerman, and as demanded by this analysis, the normative structures embedded in human activity (including household labor) become crucial because, as they (West and Zimmerman, 1984) noted:

> The task of "measuring up" to one's gender is faced again and again in different situations with respect to different particulars of conduct. The problem involved is to produce configurations of behavior *which can be seen* by others as normative gender behavior. (pp. 19–20; emphasis in original)

Thus, it can be argued that the allocation of household labor—implying as it does a fairly complicated process of coordinating work efforts—involves interactions that, in West and Zimmerman's terms (1984), "pose gender relevant issues" (p. 30). The production process itself is defined through the production of household commodities *and* through the production of gender. The combination of the two results in a new production function, as well as a set of household commodities bred from the fusion of household work and gender.[9] This may prove a way to reconceptualize the joint production of household goods and services and gender relations, but we must still question the *nature* of the gender relations produced through the allocation of household labor. West and Zimmerman (1984) directed us to an answer:

> Thus when talking about the relationship of categorical identity (male or female) to gender (accountable maleness or femaleness), it may be that the primary category-bound activities are, for men and women respectively, dominance and submission. The practical problem, then, for members who seek to render their activities accountable in such terms is to devise out of the stuff of mundane interplay situationally responsive means of doing dominance and submission. (p. 28)

Instances of "doing" dominance and submission are surely frequent in work settings other than the household and are obviously not necessarily tied to heterosexual gender relations (e.g., same-sex supervisor and worker). Likewise, not all household labor involves displays of dominance indicative of the doing of gender. For example, we know that both men and women sometimes speak of "how different" or "how easy" it was

---

[9]Of course, Becker (1981) might reply that here gender would simply represent one more household commodity produced through a single household-production function. Yet, this sort of response is vacuous and sidesteps the fact that it is the *joint* production of household work commodities and gender that is at issue. In the speculative model proposed here, joint production is not (as Becker might have it) an occasional theoretical inconvenience. Quite the opposite, the joint production of household work commodities and gender is fundamental and endemic to the production process; this model *rests* on joint production.

when, prior to marriage, they lived in same-sex roommate arrangements. One might argue that not only are the demands of work likely to be lighter in that sort of arrangement, but more important, the process by which the labor is divided is subject only to considerations of *the work itself,* as that is all that is being produced. The production of gender relations through the exercise of dominance and submission is largely irrelevant in such arrangements; as a result, the work of a "single" life seems so different, and so uncomplicated. Yet, it may be that, in households where the appropriation of *another's* labor is possible, in practice the expression of work and the expression of gender (dominance and submission) are inseparable.

When the production of household goods and services and the production of gender relations are combined in a single setting, the mechanisms by which their joint production is arranged may be problematic for the household members. After all, through the daily practice of household activities, the wife and husband face the constraints imposed by the demands of household labor and the situational exigencies posed by gender practices. From this dual production process emerges the variety of individual members' adaptations to household arrangements and the members' perceptions of choices made and contemplated. Gender ideals shape the way in which the production of gender will manifest itself in daily practice. Similarly, the particulars of the household production function affect how household work will unfold. Thus, child care (or laundry, or household repair, and so on) can become the occasion for producing commodities (e.g., clean children, clean laundry, and new light switches) and a reaffirmation of one's *gendered* relation to the work and to the world. In short, the "shoulds" of gender ideals are fused with the "musts" of efficient household production. The result may be something resembling a "gendered" household-production function. Here, it will be helpful to identify at least some rough reflections of a system where the division of household labor poses both work- and gender-relevant issues for the members. They are found in the daily concerns of household life.

Work and Gender: Some Illustrations

Thirty open-ended interviews conducted with the wives in an earlier phase of our project at least hint at how the division of household labor may involve the production of both work relations and gender relations.[10] These brief illustrations—by no means meant to be systematic nor intended to represent all the qualitative data from which they are drawn—are the responses of six women to the question "what household work does your husband do?"

First, the division of household labor became "gender-relevant," usually implicitly, but sometimes more obviously. Below are the responses of three women to the question:

> He puts dishes away, does the laundry, and in dire emergencies, he picks up toys, vacuums, mows the lawn. He usually only does those things if we're having company and I can't get to them. I'm also generally responsible for outside-the-house jobs. He just shovels snow on the outside.

> He helps out regularly. Twice a week he plays games with the kids. He helps [daughter] with her [multiplication] tables three times a week. He sleds with the kids and ice skates with them, too. My sister and I go to visit my mother in a nursing home every Sunday and he watches the kids. Sometimes he takes them bowling.

> Never. He never helps me. I suppose I should say "rarely." That's a better word to describe it. He hangs up his clothes once in a while. He puts his dirty socks down the laundry chute. In extreme circumstances, he makes the bed. He does nothing. He doesn't have to. It's not his job. People should do what they like.

Goffman (1977) described gender ideals as the essential source for maintaining gender differences, because they

> provide...a source of accounts that can be drawn on in a million ways to excuse, justify, explain, or disapprove the behavior of an individual or the arrangement under which he lives. (p. 303)

Thus, a more interesting and subtle process for household members is one where gender intervenes to influence directly the division of household labor. It may be argued that, because gender relations—the doing of dominance and submission—are an everyday proposition, then gender may serve as a warrant for household members' claiming particular relationships to, or stances toward, household labor. When the time comes to allocate the household members' labor, there are available a host of "good reasons" that husbands, *regardless* of other considerations,

[10]A more systematic treatment of these data may be found in Berheide *et al.* (1976) and in Berk and Berheide (1977).

should be market specialists, and wives either household specialists or modern-day generalists, devoting time to both work sites. Obvious examples emerge in the quotes to follow, where the wives' acceptance of their husbands' claims to incompetence in (or obliviousness to) household labor is striking:

> He doesn't do much. I get irritated at him at times. He's unaware that there are things for him to do. . . . He'd leave the paper on the couch, but now he picks it up. He does this for a month, forgets, and then I have to remind him.

> He tries to be helpful. He tries. He's a brilliant and successful lawyer. It's incredible how he smiles after he sponges off the table and there are still crumbs all over.

The imperatives posed by the production of gender relations mean that the division of household labor not only is concerned with the rational sorting and optimal matching of tasks and time to household members, but is also centered on the symbolic affirmation of the members or their "alignment" with each other as husband and wife, man and woman, brother and sister. Nevertheless, how much is gender, and how much is work is hardly the question. Instead, it is clear that, as gender and work are "done," already-existing patterns of both are ratified by household members. The way household labor is divided is brought into line with an image of how it *should* be divided:

> If my son is dirty and needs his diaper changed, my husband says, "Honey, you do it." It's like he has dibs on not doing it.

Having "dibs" depends, of course, on an active acceptance of a particular gendered relationship to the world of work. And although it perplexed the young mother above, she nevertheless perceived her husband's claim as legitimate. Ultimately, then, and from day to day, work and gender combine, and the division of household labor becomes the activity around which the two can determine and capacitate each other.

Thus, if we return to the problem of household decision-making, we can see more clearly that questions of how to allocate the time and tasks of the household members (between home and market and among the members) must attend to the demands of this hybrid production process. In practice, this means that the rationales taken as legitimate, and the considerations defined as pertinent to decision-making involve issues of both gender and work.

The mechanism by which such decisions are made in this work environment may constitute a real—and more complicated—process barely hinted at by the New Home Economics. In addition to seeking the combined optimal allocation of resources, under the dual constraints of time and income, household members' time and task contributions are apportioned as well to "align" what is happening in the situation with normative notions of what *should* be happening in the situation. In short, how household and market work *should* be allocated (according to the dictates of gender and work ideals) is brought to bear on how the work *can* be allocated (subject to the constraints of income and time). The joint production of work and gender represents a maximization process with a *new* mix of incentives, tasks, and perceptions of opportunity costs. It is this maximization process, with its complicated agendas involving work and gender—the material and the symbolic—that effectively guarantees the asymmetric patterns found so often in studies of the division of household labor. And ultimately, it is within these two interwoven structures that household members make their choices and get the business of living done.

It is no surprise that all this goes on without much notice being taken. As one respondent noted in her diary:

> Some things are done so many times a day and for so many years that it is difficult to assess my true reaction to having to do them. They are taken for granted and done without thinking about them.

The taken-for-granted quality of these work arrangements clearly extends to a lack of voiced concern about their equity. Notions underlying equity theory would have it that the perceived "fairness" of the division of labor results from an evaluation of the fit between the contributions made and the benefits received. (For a more extensive discussion, see Walster, Walster, and Traupmann, 1978.) Earlier, it was somewhat perplexing to learn that, despite some real lopsidedness in household contribution, most wives and almost all husbands thought the division of labor in their households fair. This finding proves to be consistent with what little empirical research there is on couples' assessments of the equity of various aspects of their marriages. For example, Schafer and Keith (1981) found that wives were more likely than husbands to report inequity in the performance of household roles, but that, in the main (and increasing over the course of the relationship), couples reported high levels of marital equity. These simple findings notwithstanding, the prior discussion would suggest that there is more to marital equity than the "pop bottle" calculus of whether one gets a return on one's deposits.

Quite obviously, whether one perceives a work arrangement to be fair depends fundamentally on what alternatives are conceivable and are judged viable. After all, if no alternative arrangement is thought possible, then an acknowledgment of inequity may be psychologically untenable. Nevertheless, any perceptions of equity in the division of household labor are obviously structured by and prove conditional on the experience of both the production of gender and the production of household goods and services. In this case, the fusion of the two militates against alternative ways of allocating the work. If the "doing" of gender provides a framework by which husbands and wives reaffirm their relation to each other and to work, as competent members, then departures from these normatively circumscribed ideals are ruled out. After all, "doing" gender serves to guide and thus limit the members, not to expand on already-complicated human affairs. A "gendered" household-production function may be efficient, free of the risk of even implicit social sanction, safe, and certainly familiar. It can serve as a refuge for almost all of us—the cowardly or the simply tired. Yet, with this comes the reiteration of the status quo and thus a more limited vision of alternatives. Once alternative ways of arranging household labor are ruled out, the probability that inequity will be perceived and acknowledged is lowered. Goffman's (1979) remarks are instructive once more. Of gender display, he wrote:

> The expression of subordination and domination through this swarm of situational means is more than a mere tracing of symbol or ritualistic affirmation of the social hierarchy. These expressions considerably constitute the hierarchy; they are the shadow *and* the substance. (p. 6; emphasis in original)

Thus, perhaps, it is only researchers who are preoccupied with the question of "how fair" household work arrangements are. Such questions are rarely contemplated by household members, and when they are, the constraints posed by the way in which the work and gender are accomplished day to day determine the perceived viability of the alternatives.

A FINAL NOTE ON CHANGE

Although exhibiting near-uniform patterns, the prior chapters imply that how members allocate their efforts to home and market are nevertheless subject to change. Yet, even the rough sketch of the work–gender production process offered here suggests that impetus for change is unlikely to come from within. Again, the nature of production itself imposes critical constraints on the ability of household members to effect fundamental change. The production of household goods and services—and with it, the production of gender—may serve to thwart the efforts of any member to transform her or his household-work life. It is especially difficult when, as is often the case, a lone voice calls for change. As one mother wrote in her household diary:

> I wish there were some accurate way to record and describe how much work it is to get others to do their work—children dressing for school, or putting away toys, for example.

Rather, a reorganization of household production is more likely to find its origins in forces outside the household. That is, demands emanating from extrahousehold commitments will, in "collision" with household production demands, promote change in the organization of that production.[11] Indeed, in earlier chapters, it was suggested that market demands can directly affect total household labor time, and that the introduction of children into the household can significantly increase household labor tasks and time. Nevertheless, although these exogenous forces clearly affect the size of the household and market pie, they do little to transform who does what and how much.

Our cross-sectional sample of 335 couples was certainly not of sufficient size to allow us to address the question of change adequately, but some unsystematic observations may prove provocative. A search for those husbands who were household labor "outliers" unearthed some interesting characteristics. The criterion employed for the definition and selection of the "outlier" husbands (referred to by some on the project as *Ted Kramers*) was a level equivalent to the *mean* household-task or household-time contribution of the sample wives. When that criterion was applied, roughly 10% of the sample of husbands was selected.

These husbands and their households did indeed differ in important respects from the larger sample. First, they had greater numbers of children—especially small children—so that they were slightly younger (and poorer) than the larger sample of husbands. Second, and more important perhaps, over half the outlier husbands had wives who were em-

---

[11]For a similarly underdeveloped argument concerning these catalysts of change, see Eisenstein (1981, pp. 201–214).

ployed full time. Thus, a majority of these men had preschool children *and* full-time employed wives. These husbands lived in what might be called labor-intensive households; they did more, there was more to be done, and along with their wives, they had little choice in the matter.[12]

What this may indicate is that, subject to new constraints imposed from *outside* the household, or external to the members' preferences (e.g., increased employment, more children, and illness), the particular production function of the "gendered" household may change. Whether the everyday enactment of gender dominance and submission will continue is not at issue. Just as household work will go on, so, too, will the production of gender. Under some circumstances, however, exogenous pressures could force a change in the gender "production function," where, for some harassed couples, "doing" gender in traditional ways becomes a luxury. Or for others, a greater number of household goods and services may be purchased outside the household, partially severing the close connection between the production of household commodities and the doing of gender. Thus, depending on class position, household members may face either an insurmountable budget constraint or the resources to opt out of household production. In either case (perhaps for the very poor or the very rich), a change would result in the number of "gender-relevant" occasions posed by household labor. Where this leaves the *middle*-class household, where production is neither as economically constrained nor as easily marketized, is less clear. But it may be that, in the future, husbands and wives will have no chioice but to shift the locus for the doing of gender away from the allocation of household members' labors, or to deemphasize one production process in the interests of the other. Still, such speculations on the "degendering" of household work raise serious and unresolved questions about the intractability of the dominance and submission orchestrated around gender and about the precise interplay between work and gender relations among family members. Moreover, although analytically separable, such convenient distinctions between the accomplishment of gender, dominance and submission, and the organization of society's work obscure actual experience. A more rigorous articulation of these issues remains a crucial research agenda.

Even were change likely, it would be a dangerous distortion of reality to suggest that men and women experience household and market

---

[12]It is perhaps unnecessary to point out that the *relative* position of the wives and husbands in labor-intensive households remained similar to that of the larger sample; both the wives and the the husbands did more, with husbands contributing a significant but nevertheless small fraction of the total work done.

production in the same way. Halfhearted protestations to the contrary, men benefit directly from the labors of women, and from the system of male dominance within which those labors occur. Thus, whatever change does result will come from the new bargains struck between those who stand to gain and those who face no better deal (Goode, 1982). Only then will the production of household well-being become more complicated, more uncertain, and more equitable.

References

Amsden, A. Introduction. In A. Amsden (ed.), *The Economics of Women and Work.* New York: St. Martin's Press, 1980.

Angrist, S. S., Lave, J. R., and Mickelsen, R. How working mothers manage: Socioeconomic differences in work, child care and household tasks. *Social Science Quarterly,* 1976, *56,* 631–637.

Arvey, R., and Gross, R. Satisfaction levels and correlates of satisfaction in the homemaker job. *Journal of Vocational Behavior,* 1977, *10,* 13–24.

Bahr, S. Effects on power and division of labor. In L. Hoffman and F. I. Nye (Eds.), *Working Mothers.* San Francisco: Jossey-Bass, 1974.

Becker, G. S. A theory of marriage. In T. W. Schultz (Ed.), *Economics of the Family.* Chicago: University of Chicago Press, 1974.

Becker, G. S. *Human Capital.* Chicago: University of Chicago Press, 1975.

Becker, G. S. The economic approach to human behavior. In G. S. Becker (Ed.), *The Economic Approach to Human Behavior.* Chicago: University of Chicago Press, 1976a.

Becker, G. S. A theory of the allocation of time. In G. S. Becker (Ed.), *The Economic Approach to Human Behavior.* Chicago: University of Chicago Press, 1976b.

Becker, G. S. *A Treatise on the Family.* Cambridge: Harvard University Press, 1981.

Ben-Porath, Y. Economics and the family—Match or mismatch? A review of Becker's "A Treatise on the Family." *Journal of Economic Literature,* 1982, *20,* 52–63.

Benston, M. The political economy of women's liberation. *Monthly Review,* 1969, *4,* 13–27.

Berheide, C., Berk, S. F., and Berk, R. A. Household work in the suburbs: The job and its participants. *Pacific Sociological Review,* 1976, *19,* 491–517.

Berk, R. A. The new home economics: An agenda for sociological research. In S. F. Berk (Ed.), *Women and Household Labor.* Beverly Hills, Calif.: Sage Publications, 1980.

Berk, R. A., and Berk, S. F. A simultaneous equation model for the division of household labor. *Sociological Methods and Research,* 1978, *6,* 431–468.

Berk, R. A., and Berk, S. F., *Labor and Leisure at Home: Content and Organization of the Household Day.* Beverly Hills, Calif.: Sage Publications, 1979.

Berk, R. A., and Berk, S. F. Supply-side sociology of the family: The challenge of the new home economics. *Annual Review of Sociology,* 1983, *9,* 375–395.

213

Berk, S. F. *The Division of Household Labor: Patterns and Determinants.* Doctoral dissertation, Northwestern University, 1976.

Berk, S. F. Husbands at home: The organization of the husbands' household day. In K. W. Feinstein (Ed.), *Working Women and Families.* Beverly Hills, Calif.: Sage Publications, 1979.

Berk, S. F. Some behavioral consequences of women's labors: A nonrecursive model. In I. H. Simpson and R. Simpson (Eds.), *Research in the Sociology of Work,* Vol. 2. Greenwich: Jai Press, 1983.

Berk, S. F., and Berheide, C. W. Going backstage: Gaining access to observe household work. *Sociology of Work and Occupations,* 1977, *4,* 27–48.

Berk, S. F., and Berheide, C. W. *The Measurement of Household Work: An Examination of Ambiguities.* University of California, Santa Barbara, unpublished manuscript, 1978.

Berk, S. F., and Shih, A. Contributions to household labor: Comparing wives' and husbands' reports. In S. F. Berk (Ed.), Women and Household Labor. Beverly Hills, Calif.: Sage Publications, 1980.

Bernard, J. My four revolutions: An autobiographical history of the ASA. *American Journal of Sociology,* 1973, *73,* 773–791.

Blaug, M. *The Methodology of Economics.* Cambridge: Cambridge University Press, 1980.

Blood R. O., Jr., and Wolfe, D. M. *Husbands and Wives: The Dynamics of Married Living.* Glencoe, Ill.: Free Press, 1960.

Booth, A., and Welch, S. Spousal consensus and its correlates: A reassessment. *Journal of Marriage and the Family,* 1978, *40,* 23–32.

Bott, E. *Family and Social Network.* London: Tavistock, 1957.

Boulding, E. *Children's Rights and the Wheel of Life.* New Brunswick, N.J.: Transaction Books, 1979.

Bowen, W., and Finegan, T. A. *The Economics of Labor Force Participation.* Princeton, N.J.: Princeton University Press, 1969.

Bridges, W. P., and Berk, R. A. Determinants of white collar income—An evaluation of equal pay for equal work. *Social Science Research,* 1974, *3,* 211–233.

Brown, C. V. Home production for use in a market economy. In B. Thorne and M. Yalom (Eds.), *Rethinking the Family.* New York: Longman, 1982.

Brown, G. W., and Rutter, M. The measurement of family activities and relationships. *Human Relations,* 1966, *19,* 241–263.

Brownmiller, S. *Against Our Will: Men, Women and Rape.* New York: Simon and Schuster, 1975.

Buric, O., and Zecevic, A. Family authority, marital satisfaction and the social network in Yugoslavia. *Journal of Marriage and the Family,* 1967, *29,* 325–336.

Burr, W. R. *Theory Construction and the Sociology of the Family.* New York: Wiley, 1973.

Burris, V. *The Dialectic of Women's Oppression: Notes on the Relation between Capitalism and Patriarchy.* University of Oregon, unpublished manuscript, 1980.

Cahill, S. E. *Becoming Boys and Girls.* Doctoral dissertation, University of California, Santa Barbara, 1982.

Cain, G. C. *Married Women in the Labor Force: An Economic Analysis.* Chicago:

University of Chicago Press, 1966.

Cannon, R. L. *The Private Sphere: How Women Feel about the Work They Do.* University of California, Santa Barbara, unpublished manuscript, 1978.

Chapin, F. S., Jr. *Human Activity Patterns in the City.* New York: Wiley, 1974.

Chesler, P. *Women and Madness.* New York: Doubleday, 1972.

Chiswick, C. U. The value of a housewife's time. *Journal of Human Resources,* 1982, *17,* 413–425.

Cogle, F. L., and Tasker, G. E. Children and housework. *Family Relations,* 1982, *31,* 395–399.

Condran, J. G., and Bode, J. G. Rashomon, working wives, and family division of labor: Middletown, 1980. *Journal of Marriage and the Family,* 1982, *44,* 421–426.

Corrales, R. G. Power and satisfaction in early marriage. In R.E. Cromwell and D. H. Olson (Eds.), *Power in Families.* New York: Wiley, 1975.

Coulson, M., Magas, B., and Wainwright, H. The housewife and her labour under capitalism—A critique. *New Left Review,* 1975, *89, 59–71.*

Cowan, R. S. The Industrial Revolution in the home: Household technology and social change in the 20th century. *Technology and Culture,* 1976a, *17,* 1–23.

Cowan, R. S. Two washes in the morning and a bridge party at night: The American housewife between the wars. *Women's Studies,* 1976b, *3,* 147–172.

Cowan, R. S. *More Work for Mother.* New York: Basic Books, 1983.

Cowles, M. L., and Dietz, R. P. Time spent in homemaking activities by a selected group of Wisconsin farm homemakers. *Journal of Home Economics,* 1956, *48,* 29–35.

Cromwell, R. E., and Olson, D. H. Multidisciplinary perspectives of power. In R. E. Cromwell and D. H. Olson (Eds.), *Power in Families.* New York: Wiley, 1975a.

Cromwell, R. E., and Olson, D. H. (Eds.). *Power in Families.* New York: Wiley, 1975b.

Dalla Costa, M. Women and the subversion of the community. *Radical America,* 1972, *6,* 67–102.

Douglas, S. P., and Wind, Y. Examining family role and authority: Two methodological issues. *Journal of Marriage and the Family,* 1978, *40,* 35–47.

Duncan, O. D. Comment. In T. W. Schultz (Ed.), *Economics of the Family.* Chicago: University of Chicago Press, 1974.

Ehrenreich, B. Life without father: Reconsidering socialist-feminist theory. *Socialist Review,* 1984, *14,* 48–57.

Ehrenreich, B., and English, D. The manufacture of housework. *Socialist Revolution,* 1975, *4,* 5–40.

Ehrenreich, B., and English, D. *For Her Own Good: 150 Years of the Experts' Advice to Women.* New York: Anchor Press, 1978.

Eisenstein, Z. (Ed.). *Capitalist Patriarchy and the Case for Socialist Feminism.* New York: Monthly Review Press, 1979.

Eisenstein, Z. *The Radical Future of Liberal Feminism.* New York: Longman, 1981.

Engels, F. *The Origin of the Family, Private Property and the State.* New York: Pathfinder Press, 1972.

Epstein, C. *Woman's Place.* Berkeley: University of California Press, 1971.

Ericksen, J., Yancey, W., and Ericksen, E. The division of family roles. *Journal of Marriage and the Family*, 1979, *41*, 301–313.

Farkas, G. Education, wage rates, and the division of labor between husband and wife. *Journal of Marriage and the Family*, 1976, *3*, 473–484.

Fee, T. Domestic labor: An analysis of housework and its relation to the production process. *Review of Radical Political Economics*, 1976, *8*, 1–8.

Ferber, M. A., and Birnbaum, B. G. Rejoinder. *Journal of Consumer Research, 1977*, *4*, 183–184.

Ferguson, A., and Folbre, N. The unhappy marriage of patriarchy and capitalism. In L. Sargent (Ed.), *Women and Revolution*. Boston: South End Press, 1981.

Ferree, M. M. Working-class jobs: Housework and paid work as sources of satisfaction. *Social Problems*, 1976, *23*, 431–441.

Ferree, M. M. Satisfaction with housework: The social context. In S. F. Berk (Ed.), *Women and Household Labor*. Beverly Hills, Calif.: Sage Publications, 1980.

Fishman, P. M. Interaction: The work women do. *Social Problems*, 1978, *25*, 397–406.

Folbre, N. Exploitation comes home: A critique of the Marxian theory of family labour. *Cambridge Journal of Economics*, 1982, *6*, 317–329.

Foote, N. (Ed.). *Household Decision-Making*. New York: New York University Press, 1961.

Freidan, B. *The Feminine Mystique*. Toronto: George J. Mcleod, 1963.

Gardiner, J. Women's domestic labour. *New Left Review*, 1975, *89*, 47–58.

Garland, T. N. The better half: The male in the dual professional family. In C. Safilios-Rothschild (Ed.), *Toward a Sociology of Women*. Lexington, Mass.: Xerox College Publishing, 1972.

Gauger, W. Household work: Can we add it to the GNP? *Journal of Home Economics*, 1973, *65*, 12–15.

Gavron, H. *The Captive Wife*. Harmondsworth, England: Penguin, 1966.

Geerken, M., and Gove, W. R. *At Home and at Work: The Family's Allocation of Labor*. Beverly Hills, Calif.: Sage Publications, 1983.

Gerstein, I. Domestic work and capitalism. *Radical America*, 1973, *7*, 100–128.

Gilman, C. P. *Herland*. New York: Pantheon, 1979.

Glazer, N. Everyone needs three hands: Doing unpaid work. In S. F. Berk (Ed.), *Women and Household Labor*. Beverly Hills, Calif.: Sage Publications, 1980.

Goffman, E. The arrangement between the sexes. *Theory and Society*, 1977, *4*, 301–331.

Goffman, E. *Gender Advertisements*. New York: Harper and Row, 1979.

Goode, W. J. Why men resist. In B. Thorne and M. Yalom (Eds.), *Rethinking the Family*. New York: Longman, 1982.

Gough, I. Productive and unproductive labour in Marx. *New Left Review*, 1972, *92*, 47–72.

Granbois, D. H., and Willett, R. P. Equivalence of family role measures based on husband and wife data. *Journal of Marriage and the Family*, 1970, *32*, 68–72.

Griffin, S. *Rape, the Power of Consciousness*. San Francisco: Harper and Row, 1979.

Griliches, Z. Comment. In T. W. Schultz (Ed.), *Economics of the Family*. Chicago: University of Chicago Press, 1974.

Gronau, R. The effect of children on the housewife's value of time. In T. W.

Schultz (Ed.), *Economics of the Family.* Chicago: Chicago University Press, 1974.

Gronau, R. Leisure, home production, and work: The theory of the allocation of time revisited. *Journal of Political Economy,* 1977, *4,* 1099–1124.

Gross, E. Plus ça change . . . the sexual structure of occupations over time. *Social Problems,* 1968, *16,* 198–208.

Hacker, S. Farming out the home: Women and agribusiness. *The Second Wave,* 1977, *5,* 38–49.

Hallenbeck, P. An analysis of power dynamics in marriage. *Journal of Marriage and the Family,* 1966, *28,* 200–203.

Hamilton, R. *The Liberation of Women: A Study of Patriarchy and Capitalism.* London: George Allen and Unwin, 1978.

Hannan, M. T. Families, markets, and social structures: An essay on Becker's "A treatise on the family." *Journal of Economic Literature,* 1982, *20,* 65–72.

Harrison, J. The political economy of housework. *Bulletin of the Conference of Socialist Economists,* 1973, *4.*

Hartmann, H. The family as the locus of gender, class and political struggle: The example of housework. *Signs,* 1981a, *6,* 366–394.

Hartmann, H. The unhappy marriage of Marxism and feminism: Toward a more progressive union. In L. Sargent (Ed.), *Women and Revolution.* Boston: South End Press, 1981b.

Hartsock, N. C. The feminist standpoint: Developing the ground for a specifically feminist historical materialism. In S. Harding and M. B. Hintikka (Eds.), *Discovering Reality: Feminist Perspectives on Epistemology, Metaphysics, Methodology, and Philosophy of Science.* Holland: D. Reidel Publishing, 1983.

Hawrylyshyn, O. *Toward a Definition of Non-Market Activities.* Institute of Economic Research, Discussion Paper 214, Queen's University, Ontario, Canada. 1976.

Heckman, J. J. Sample selection bias as a specification error with an application to the estimation of labor supply functions. In J. P. Smith (Ed.), *Female Labor Supply: Theory and Estimation.* Princeton, N.J.: Princeton University Press, 1980.

Hedges, J. N., and Barnett, J. K. Working women and the division of household tasks. *Monthly Labor Review,* 1972, *95,* 9–13.

Heer, D. M. The measurement and bases of family power: An overview. *Marriage and Family Living,* 1963, *25,* 133–138.

Henderson, J. M., and Quandt, R. E. *Microeconomic Theory.* New York: McGraw-Hill, 1971.

Henley, N. M. *Body Politics: Power, Sex, and Nonverbal Communication.* Englewood Cliffs, N.J.: Prentice Hall, 1977.

Himmelweit, S., and Mohun, S. Domestic labour and capital. *Cambridge Journal of Economics,* 1977, *1,* 15-31.

Hochschild, A. R. A review of sex role research. *American Journal of Sociology,* 1973, *78,* 1011–1029.

Hoffman, L. Parental power relations and the division of household tasks. In F. I. Nye and L. Hoffman (Eds.), *The Employed Mother in America.* Chicago: Rand McNally, 1963.

Holmstrom, L. L. *The Two-Career Family.* Cambridge, Mass.: Schenkman, 1972.

Humphries, J. Class struggle and the persistence of the working-class family. Cambridge Journal of Economics, 1977, *1*, 241–258.

Johnson, S. B. The impact of women's liberation on marriage, divorce, and family life-style. In C. B. Lloyd (Ed.), *Sex Discrimination and the Division of Labor*. New York: Columbia University Press, 1975.

Kenkel, W. F. Influence differentiation in family decision-making. *Sociology and Social Research*, 1957, *42*, 18–25.

Kmenta, S. *Elements of Econometrics*. New York: Macmillan, 1971.

Komarovsky, M. *Blue-collar Marriage*. New York: Random House, 1962.

Kuhn, A., and Wolpe, A. Feminism and materialism. In A. Kuhn and A. Wolpe (Eds.), *Feminism and Materialism: Women and Modes of Production*. London: Routledge and Kegan Paul, 1978a.

Kuhn, A., and Wolpe, A. (Eds.). *Feminism and Materialism: Women and Modes of Production*. London: Routledge and Kegan Paul, 1978b.

Lamouse, A. Family roles of women: A German example. *Journal of Marriage and the Family*, 1969, *31*, 145–153.

Lancaster, K. J. A new approach to consumer theory. *Journal of Political Economy*, 1966, *74*, 132–157.

Larson, L. E. System and subsystem perception of family roles. *Journal of Marriage and the Family*, 1974, *36*, 125–138.

LeGuin, U. *The Dispossessed*. New York: Avon, 1974.

Lehrer, E., and Nerlove, M. Women's life-cycle time allocation: An econometric analysis. In S. F. Berk (Ed.), *Women and Household Labor*. Beverly Hills, Calif.: Sage Publications, 1980.

Leibowitz, A. Women's work in the home. In C. B. Lloyd (Ed.), *Sex Discrimination and the Division of Labor*. New York: Columbia University Press, 1975.

Lesourne, J. *A Theory of the Individual for Economic Analysis*. New York: North Holland, 1977.

Liu, W. T., Hutchinson, I. W., and Hong, L. K. Conjugal power and decision-making: A methodological note on cross cultural study of the family. *American Journal of Sociology*, 1972, *79*, 84–98.

Lloyd, C. B. The division of labor between the sexes: A review. In C. B. Lloyd (Ed.), *Sex Discrimination and the Division of Labor*. New York: Columbia University Press, 1975.

Lloyd, C. B., and Niemi, B. T. *The Economics of Sex Discrimination*. New York: Columbia University Press, 1979.

Lloyd, C. B., Andrews, E. S., and Gilroy, C. L. (Eds.). *Women in the Labor Market*. New York: Columbia University Press, 1979.

Lopata, H. Z. *Occupation: Housewife*. London: Oxford University Press, 1971.

Lopata, H. Z., and Thorne, B. On the term "sex roles." *Signs*, 1978, *3*, 718–721.

Mahoney, T. A. Influences on labor force participation of married women. In N. N. Foote (Ed.), *Household Decision-Making*. New York: New York University Press, 1961.

Malos, E. Housework and the politics of women's liberation. *Socialist Review*, 1978, *37*, 41–71.

Malos, E. (Ed.). *The Politics of Housework*. London: Allison and Busby, 1980.

Manser, M., and Brown, M. Marriage and household decision-making: A bargaining analysis. *International Economic Review*, 1980, *21*, 31–44.

Marx, K. *Capital, Vol. 1.* (Trans. B. Fowkes). New York: Random House, 1977.

McDonald, G. W. Family power: The Assessment of a decade of theory and research, 1970–1979. *Journal of Marriage and the Family*, 1980, *42*, 841–854.

McDonough, R., and Harrison, R. Patriarchy and relations of production. In A. Kuhn and A. Wolpe (Eds.), *Feminism and Materialism: Women and Modes of Production.* London: Routledge and Kegan Paul, 1978.

Meissner, M. Sexual division of labour and inequality: Labour and leisure. In M. Stephenson (Ed.), *Women in Canada.* Toronto: The Women's Educational Press, 1977.

Meissner, M. *The Domestic Economy: Now You See It, Now You Don't.* University of British Columbia, unpublished manuscript, 1980.

Meissner, M., Humphreys, E. W., Meis, S. M., and Sheu, W. J. No exit for wives: Sexual division of labour and the cumulation of household demands. *Canadian Review of Sociology and Anthropology*, 1975, *12*, 424–439.

Michael, R. T., and Becker, G. S. On the new theory of consumer behavior. In G. S. Becker (Ed.), *The Economic Approach to Human Behavior.* Chicago: Chicago University Press, 1976.

Millett, K. *Sexual Politics.* New York: Hearst Corporation, 1970.

Mincer, J. Labor force participation of married women: A study of labor supply. In H. G. Lewis (Ed.), *Aspects of Labor Economics.* Princeton, N.J.: Princeton University Press, 1962.

Mitchell, J. *Woman's Estate.* New York: Random House, 1971.

Model, S. Housework by husbands: Determinants and implications. In J. Aldous (Ed.), *Two Paychecks in Dual-Earner Families.* Beverly Hills, Calif.: Sage Publications, 1982.

Molyneux, M. Beyond the domestic labor debate. *New Left Review*, 1979, *116*, 3–27.

Morgan, J. M., Sirageldin, I. A., and Baerwaldt, N. *Productive Americans.* Ann Arbor: Institute for Social Research, University of Michigan, 1966.

Morton, P. A woman's work is never done. In E. H. Altbach (Ed.), *From Feminism to Liberation.* Cambridge, Mass.: Schenkman Publishing, 1971.

Nerlove, M. Toward a theory of population and economic growth. In T. W. Schultz (Ed.), *Economics of the Family.* Chicago: University of Chicago Press, 1974.

Nickols, S. *Work and Housework: Family Roles in Productive Activity.* Paper presented at the annual meeting of the National Council on Family Relations, October 1976, New York.

Nye, I. F. Is choice and exchange theory the key? *Journal of Marriage and the Family*, 1978, *40*, 219–233.

Nye, I. F. Choice, exchange, and the family. In W. R. Burr, R. Hill, F. I. Nye, and I. L. Reiss (Eds.), *Contemporary Theories about the Family*, Vol. 2. New York: Free Press, 1979.

Nye, F. I. Family mini theories as special instances of choice and exchange theory. *Journal of Marriage and the Family*, 1980, *42*, 479–490.

Oakley, A. *The Sociology of Housework.* New York: Pantheon, 1974.

Oakley, A. Reflections on the study of household labor. In S. F. Berk (Ed.), *Women and Household Labor.* Beverly Hills, Calif.: Sage Publications, 1980.

Olson, J. T. Role conflict between housework and childcare. *Sociology of Work and Occupations,* 1979, *6,* 430–456.

Olson, J. T. The impact of housework on childcare in the home. *Family Relations,* 1981, *30,* 75–81.

Parsons, T., and Bales, R. F. *Family: Sociology and Interaction Process.* London: Routledge and Kegan Paul, 1956.

Perruci, C. C., Potter, H. R., and Rhoads, D. L. Determinants of male family-role performance. *Psychology of Women Quarterly,* 1978, *3,* 53–66.

Pleck, J. H. The work-family role system. *Social Problems,* 1977, *24,* 417–427.

Pleck, J. H. Men's family work: Three perspectives and some new data. *The Family Coordinator,* 1979, *28,* 481–488.

Pleck, J. H. Husbands' paid work and family roles: Current research issues. In H. Lopata and J. H. Pleck (Eds.), *Research in the Interweave of Social Roles: Vol. 3. Families and Jobs.* Greenwich, Conn.: JAI Press, 1983.

Pleck, J. H., and Rustad, M. *Wives, Employment, Role Demands, and Adjustment: Final Report.* Wellesley College Center for Research on Women, unpublished manuscript, 1980.

Pleck, J. H., and Staines, G. L. Work schedules and work-related family conflict in two-earner couples. In J. Aldous (Ed.), *Two Paychecks in Dual-Earner Families.* Beverly Hills, Calif.: Sage Publications, 1982.

Pleck, J. H., Staines, G., and Lang, L. Conflicts between work and family life. *Monthly Labor Review,* 1980, *103,* 29–31.

Pollack, R. A., and Wachter, M. L. The relevance of the household production function and its implications for the allocation of time. *Journal of Political Economy,* 1975, *83,* 255–277.

Presser, H. B., and Baldwin, W. Child care as a constraint on employment: Prevalence correlates, and bearing on the work and fertility nexus. *American Journal of Sociology,* 1980, *86,* 1202–1213.

Rapoport, R., and Rapoport, R. *Dual-Career Families.* Harmondsworth, England: Penguin, 1971.

Rapoport, R., and Rapoport, R. *Dual-Career Families Re-examined.* New York: Harper and Row, 1976.

Rapoport, R., and Rapoport, R. *Working Couples.* New York: Harper and Row, 1978.

Rapp, R. Family and class in contemporary America: Notes toward an understanding of ideology. *Science and Society,* 1978, *42,* 257–277.

Reid, M. G. *Economics of Household Production.* New York: Wiley, 1934.

Reid, M. G. Comment. In T. W. Schultz (Ed.), *Economics of the Family.* Chicago: Chicago University Press, 1974.

Reid, M. G. How new is the "new home economics"? *Journal of Consumer Research,* 1977, *4,* 181–183.

Robinson, J. P. *How Americans Use Time: A Social-Psychological Analysis.* New York: Praeger, 1977a.

Robinson, J. P. The "new home economics": Sexist, unrealistic, or simply irrelevant? *Journal of Consumer Research,* 1977b, *4,* 178–181.

Robinson, J. P. Housework technology and household work. In S. F. Berk (Ed.), *Women and Household Labor.* Beverly Hills, Calif.: Sage Publications, 1980.

Robinson, J. P., Converse, P., and Szalai, A. Everyday life in the twelve countries. In A. Szalai *et al.* (Eds.), *The Use of Time.* The Hague: Mouton, 1972.

Rodman, H. Marital power in France, Greece, Yugoslavia, and the United States: A cross-national discussion. *Journal of Marriage and the Family,* 1967 (May), 320–324.

Rosenweig, M. R. Farm-family schooling decisions: Determinants of quantity and quality of education in agricultural populations. *Journal of Human Resources,* 1977, *12,* 71–91.

Rowbotham, S. *Woman's Consciousness, Man's World.* Harmondsworth, England: Penguin Books, 1973.

Rowntree, M., and Rowntree, J. More on the political economy of women's liberation. *Monthly Review,* 1970, *21,* 26–31.

Rubin, G. The traffic in women: Notes on the "political economy" of sex. In R. Reiter (Ed.), *Toward an Anthropology of Women.* New York: Monthly Review Press, 1975.

Ryder, N. B. Comment. In T. W. Schultz (Ed.), *Economics of the Family.* Chicago: Chicago University Press, 1974.

Safilios-Rothschild, C. A comparison of power structure and marital satisfaction in urban Greek and French families. *Journal of Marriage and the Family,* 1967, *29,* 345–352.

Safilios-Rothschild, C. Family sociology or wives' family sociology? A cross-cultural examination of decision-making. *Journal of Marriage and the Family,* 1969, *31,* 290–304.

Safilios-Rothschild, C. The study of family power structure: A review. *Journal of Marriage and the Family,* 1970, *32,* 539–552.

Safilios-Rothschild, C. A macro- and micro-examination of family power and love: An exchange model. *Journal of Marriage and the Family,* 1976, *38,* 355–361.

Sargent, L. (Ed.). *Women and Revolution.* Boston: South End Press, 1980.

Sawhill, I. Economic perspectives on the family. In A. Amsden (Ed.), *The Economics of Women and Work.* New York: St. Martin's Press, 1980.

Scanzoni, J. H. *Opportunity and the Family.* New York: Free Press, 1970.

Scanzoni, J. H. *Sexual Bargaining: Power Politics in the American Marriage.* Englewood Cliffs, N.J.: Prentice-Hall, 1972.

Scanzoni, J. H. *Men, Women, and Change.* New York: McGraw-Hill, 1976.

Scanzoni, J. H. *Sex Roles, Women's Work and Marital Conflict—A Study of Family Change.* Lexington, Mass.: Lexington Books, 1978.

Scanzoni, J. Social processes and power in families. In W. R. Burr, R. Hill, F. I. Nye, and I. L. Reiss (Eds.), *Contemporary Theories about the Family, Vol. 1.* New York: Free Press, 1979.

Scanzoni, J., and Szinovacz, M. *Family Decision-Making, Vol. 3.* Sage Library of Social Research. Beverly Hills, Calif.: Sage Publications, 1980.

Schafer, R. B., and Keith, P. M. Equity in marital roles across the family life cycle. *Journal of Marriage and the Family*, 1981, *43*, 359–367.

Schnaiberg, A. S., and Goldenberg, S. Closing the circle: The impact of children on parental status. *Journal of Marriage and the Family*, 1975, *37*, 937–953.

Schultz, T. W. (Ed.). *Investment in Education: The Equity Efficiency Quandary*. Chicago: Chicago University Press, 1972.

Schultz, T. W. Fertility and economic values. In T. W. Schultz (Ed.), *Economics of the Family*. Chicago: Chicago University Press, 1974.

Secombe, W. The housewife and her labour under capitalism. *New Left Review*, 1974, *83*, 3–24.

Secombe, W. Domestic labour: A reply to critics. *New Left Review*, 1975, *94*, 85–96.

Silverman, W., and Hill, R. Task allocation in marriage in the United States and Belgium. *Journal of Marriage and the Family*, 1967, *29*, 353–359.

Smith, D. E. *On Sociological Description: A Method from Marx*. Ontario Institute for Studies in Education, unpublished manuscript, 1978.

Smith, D. E. A sociology for women. In J. A. Sherman and E. T. Beck (Eds.), *The Prism of Sex*. Madison: University of Wisconsin Press, 1979.

Smith, D. E., and David, S. (Eds.). *Women Look at Psychiatry*. Vancouver, Canada: Press Gang, 1975.

Smith, J. P. *Female Labor Supply Theory and Estimation*. Princeton, N.J.: Princeton University Press, 1980.

Smith, P. Domestic labour and Marx's theory of value. In A. Kuhn and A. Wolpe (Eds.), *Feminism and Materialism: Women and Modes of Production*. London: Routledge and Kegan Paul, 1978.

Sokoloff, N. J. *Between Money and Love*. New York: Praeger, 1980.

Sprey, J. The family as a system in conflict. *Journal of Marriage and the Family*, 1969, *31*, 699–706.

Sprey, J. Family power and process: Toward a conceptual integration. In R. E. Cromwell and D. H. Olson (Eds.), *Power in Families*. New York: Wiley, 1975.

Sprey, J. Conflict theory and the study of marriage and the family. In W. R. Burr, R. Hill, I. L. Reiss, and F. I. Nye (Eds.), *Contemporary Theories about the Family*, Vol. 2. New York: Free Press, 1979.

Stafford, F. P. Women's use of time converging with men's. *Monthly Labor Review*, 1980, *103*, 57–59.

Stafford, F. P., and Duncan, G. S. The use of time and technology by households in the United States. In R. G. Ehrenberg (Ed.), *Research in Labor Economics: A Research Annual*, Vol. 3. New York: Wiley, 1980.

Stafford, F. P., Backman, E., and Dibona P. The division of labor among cohabitating and married couples. *Journal of Marriage and the Family*, 1977, *39*, 43–57.

Strasser, S. *Never Done: A History of American Housework*. New York: Pantheon Books, 1982.

Szalai, A., Converse, P. E., Feldheim, P., Scheuch, E. K., and Stone, P. F. (Eds.). *The Use of Time: Daily Activities of Urban and Suburban Populations in Twelve Countries*. The Hague: Mouton, 1972.

Thorne, B. Is our field misnamed? Towards a rethinking of the concept "sex roles." *Newsletter*, American Sociological Association, 1976, *4*, 4–5.

Toomey, D. M. Conjugal roles and social networks in an urban working class sample. *Human Relations,* 1971, *24,* 417–431.

Tresemer, D. Assumptions made about gender roles. In M. Millman and R. M. Kanter (Eds.), *Another Voice: Feminist Perspectives on Social Life and Social Science.* New York: Doubleday, 1975.

Vanek, J. Time spent in housework. *Scientific American,* 1974, *231,* 116–120.

Vanek, J. Household work, wage work, and sexual inequality. In S. F. Berk (Ed.), *Women and Household Labor.* Beverly Hills, Calif.: Sage Publications, 1980.

Vogel, L. The earthly family. *Radical America,* 1973, *7,* 9–49.

Waite, L. J. Working wives and family life cycle. *American Journal of Sociology,* 1980, *85,* 272–294.

Wales, T. J., and Woodland, A. D. Estimation of the allocation of time for work, leisure and housework. *Econometrica,* 1977, *1,* 115–132.

Walker, K. E. Homemaking still takes time. *Journal of Home Economics,* 1969, *61,* 621–624.

Walker, K. E. Household work time: Its implication for family decisions. *Journal of Home Economics,* 1973, *65,* 7–11.

Walker, K. E., and Gauger, W. H. Time and its dollar value in household work. *Family Economic Review,* 1973, *7,* 8–13.

Walker, K. E., and Woods, M. *Time Use: A Measure of Household Production of Goods and Services.* Washington, D.C.: American Home Economics Association, 1976.

Walker, L. *The Battered Woman.* New York: Harper and Row, 1979.

Walster, E. G., Walster, W., and Traupmann, S. *Equity Theory and Research.* Boston: Allyn and Bacon, 1978.

Weinbaum, B. *The Curious Courtship of Women's Liberation and Socialism.* Boston: South End Press, 1978.

Weinbaum, B., and Bridges, A. The other side of the paycheck: Monopoly capital and the structure of consumption. *Monthly Review,* 1976, *28,* 88–103.

West, C. Why can't a woman be more like a man? *Work and Occupations,* 1982, *9,* 5–29.

West, C., and Zimmerman, D. *Doing Gender.* University of California, Santa Cruz, unpublished manuscript, 1984.

White, L. K., and Brinkerhoff, D. B. Children's work in the family: Its significance and meaning. *Journal of Marriage and the Family,* 1981, *43,* 789–798.

Willis, R. J. Economic theory of fertility behavior. In T. W. Schultz (Ed.), *Economics of the Family.* Chicago: Chicago University Press, 1974.

Wittner, J. G. Domestic labor as work discipline: The struggle over housework in foster homes. In S. F. Berk (Ed.), *Women and Household Labor.* Beverly Hills, Calif.: Sage Publications, 1980.

Wolfe, D. Power and authority in the family. In D. Cartwright (Ed.), *Studies in Social Power.* Ann Arbor: University of Michigan Press, 1959.

Wright, J. Are working women really more satisfied? Evidence from several national surveys. *Journal of Marriage and the Family,* 1978, *40,* 301–313.

Young, I. Socialist feminism and the limits of dual systems theory. Socialist Review, 1980, *10,* 169–188.

Young, I. Beyond the unhappy marriage: A critique of dual systems theory. In L. Sargent (Ed.), *Women and Revolution.* Boston: South End Press, 1981.

Young, M., and Wilmott, P. *The Symmetrical Family.* New York: Pantheon, 1973.

Zaretsky, E. *Capitalism, the Family, and Personal Life.* London: Pluto, 1976.

Zimmerman, D., and West, C. Sex roles, interruptions, and silences in conversation. In B. Thorne and N. Henley (Eds.), *Language and Sex: Difference and Dominance.* Rowley, Mass.: Newbury House, 1975.

Diary Instructions

The purpose of the diary is to record in great detail *all* the things you do in *one 24-hour period.* If you take a look at the blank diary sheets provided, you will find empty lines to be filled in with all the things you may do—making beds, getting dressed in the morning, making coffee, reading, writing a brief note, etc.—*each* followed by a series of questions.

The first question asks what time you started the particular activity that you have just listed. Try to be as accurate as possible—9:43 A.M., for example.

The second question asks for the time the activity ended. Again, try to be as accurate as possible.

When more than one activity is going on at the same time, a common time period should be shown.

The third question asks if you would call this particular activity "work, leisure, both, or neither." There is, of course, no right answer; just circle the one answer that best describes the household activity you have just written in.

The fourth question asks, "Who, if anyone, is with you?" when this activity was going on. You'll find a list of names; just circle all the people who were at home with you. In other words, you may circle more than one, for example, your husband and a neighbor.

The fifth question is "Who, if anyone, is helping you with this?" Again, you will find a list of people, and all you have to do is circle all that apply.

The sixth question asks, "Who, if anyone, is there just keeping you company?" Again, you'll find a list of people; circle all that apply.

The seventh question is a bit different and asks whether you are "watching or listening to any of the following" while doing the task you just listed. Here you are to circle any or all of the following: TV, radio, record player, tape player, or CB radio.

The final question asks for your feelings about the activity that you have just listed. All you have to do is read over a short list of words (*pleasant, tiring, difficult,* and so on) and circle all the words that best describe the activity.

You will see that there is room for any additional comments, and you should feel free to write in any other things you wish in that space.

You will see that we have also provided a brief sample diary listing various activities and starting and ending times. However, we have *not* filled in any of the answers to the other questions in the sample diary because we do not want to influence you in any way.

Please fill out the *24-hour* diary for the day written on the cover of your diary. We are trying to make sure that people who participate in the study provide us with a good cross section of days. If you cannot fill out the diary for the day listed, fill it out for the next day.

If you go out of your home on the day that you do the diary (to a job, to run errands, to visit a friend, and so on), just record that trip (e.g., "went to the drug store") and its starting and ending times, and answer the questions. It is not necessary to specify all the things that you did when you were out of the house.

Also, don't forget to include things like conversations with people (e.g., talked to plumber, scolded children, joked with neighbor, got phone call from grocery, wrote a letter or a note, read), as they are as important as other household activities. That is, we want to know everything you do in your household even if it seems ordinary to you.

Finally, please try to record your activities *as they occur* throughout the day; otherwise, it is very easy to forget exactly what you have done.

SAMPLE DIARY

Activity	Time started	Time ended
	A.M./P.M.	A.M./P.M.
Got up	7:15 A.M.	7:16 A.M.
Fixed coffee	7:16 A.M.	7:20 A.M.
Set breakfast table	7:20 A.M.	7:23 A.M.
Got dressed	7:23 A.M.	7:28 A.M.
Put make-up on	7:28 A.M.	7:35 A.M.
Made our bed	7:35 A.M.	7:36 A.M.
Straightened bedroom	7:36 A.M.	7:40 A.M.
Woke children	7:40 A.M.	7:42 A.M.
Put load in clothes washer	7:42 A.M.	7:45 A.M.
Helped daughter dress	7:45 A.M.	7:47 A.M.
Fixed breakfast	7:47 A.M.	8:00 A.M.
Helped son feed dog	7:49 A.M.	7:50 A.M.
Read newspaper	7:50 A.M.	7:59 A.M.
Served breakfast	8:00 A.M.	8:01 A.M.
Ate breakfast	8:01 A.M.	8:15 A.M.
Talked with family about the day to come	8:01 A.M.	8:15 A.M.
Wrote note to teacher excusing son from school	8:10 A.M.	8:15 A.M.
Cleaned up daughter's spilled milk	8:10 A.M.	8:12 A.M.
Said good-bye to husband	8:15 A.M.	8:16 A.M.
Settled argument between kids	8:15 A.M.	8:17 A.M.
Made sure children had schoolbooks	8:20 A.M.	8:25 A.M.

SAMPLE DIARY (*Continued*)

Activity	Time started	Time ended
Kissed children good-bye	8:25 A.M.	8:27 A.M.
Had coffee	8:27 A.M.	8:40 A.M.
Watched TV	8:27 A.M.	9:00 A.M.
Receive phone call from friend	8:30 A.M.	8:43 A.M.
Cleared table	8:31 A.M.	8:32 A.M.
Put away food	8:32 A.M.	8:33 A.M.
Wiped table	8:33 A.M.	8:34 A.M.
Loaded dishwasher	8:34 A.M.	8:40 A.M.
Wiped counter	8:40 A.M.	8:41 A.M.
Wiped stove top	8:41 A.M.	8:42 A.M.
Emptied garbage	8:43 A.M.	8:48 A.M.
Watered plants	8:48 A.M.	8:52 A.M.
Wrote out check for electric bill and envelope	8:52 A.M.	8:55 A.M.
Finished shopping list	8:55 A.M.	9:00 A.M.
Put son's bike away in garage	9:00 A.M.	9:02 A.M.
Drove to grocery store	9:02 A.M.	9:10 A.M.
Shopped for food	9:10 A.M.	9:40 A.M.
Stopped at post office	9:40 A.M.	9:50 A.M.
Wrote out birthday card for mailing	9:41 A.M.	9:43 A.M.
Drove home	9:50 A.M.	10:00 A.M.
Carried groceries in	10:00 A.M.	10:05 A.M.
Put groceries away	10:05 A.M.	10:15 A.M.
Wrote note to son	10:09 A.M.	10:11 A.M.
Went to bathroom	10:15 A.M.	10:20 A.M.
Drove to work	10:20 A.M.	10:30 A.M.
At work	10:30 A.M.	4:30 P.M.
And so on		

Household Work Study

Diary

Audits & Surveys, Inc.   Project # 4736

One Park Avenue   May, 1976
New York, New York 10016

Household Work Study: Diary

Interviewer's name _____

Interviewer's number _____

Respondent's name _____

Respondent's address _____

_____

This diary is to be kept for one day starting from when you got up
on _____ (day), _____ (date),
and ending when you get up the next morning.

1-4	(17- 20)	(21- 24)	(25)	(26-35)	(36-45)
3-9 / 6-8 / (7-13) / (14-16)				Who, if anyone, is with you? NO. No one H. Husband SO. Son D. Daughter SE. Servant R. Relative N. Neighbor F. Friend CHF. Children's friends DN. Does not apply	Who, if anyone, is *helping* you with this? NO. No one H. Husband SO. Son D. Daughter SE. Servant R. Relative N. Neighbor F. Friend CHF. Children's friends DN. Does not apply
			Would you call this particular activity . . . W. Work? L. Leisure? B. Both N. Neither		
Activity	Time started A.M./P.M.	Time ended A.M./P.M.	(Circle letter that applies)	Circle all letters that apply)	(Circle all letters that apply)
(001) Got up			W L B N	NO H SO D SE R N F CHF DN	NO H SO D SE R N F CHF DN
(002)			W L B N	NO H SO D SE R N F CHF DN	NO H SO D SF R N F CHF DN
(003)			W L B N	NO H SO D SE R N F CHF DN	NO H SO D SE R N F CHF DN
(004)			W L B N	NO H SO D SF R N F CHF DN	NO H SO D SE R N F CHF DN
(005)			W L B N	NO H SO D SF R N F CHF DN	NO H SO D SE R N F CHF DN
(006)			W L B N	NO H SO D SF R N F CHF DN	NO H SO D SE R N F CHF DN
(007)			W L B N	NO H SO D SF R N F CHF DN	NO H SO D SE R N F CHF DN
(008)			W L B N	NO H SO D SF R N F CHF DN	NO H SO D SE R N F CHF DN
(009)			W L B N	NO H SO D SF R N F CHF DN	NO H SO D SE R N F CHF DN
(010)			W L B N	NO H SO D SF R N F CHF DN	NO H SO D SE R N F CHF DN

(46–55)	(56–61)	(62–69)	
Who, if anyone, is there just keeping you company? NO. No one H. Husband SO. Son D. Daughter SE. Servant R. Relative N. Neighbor F. Friend CHF. Children's friends DN. Does not apply (Circle all letters that apply)	Are you also *watching or listening* to any of the following? TV. Television R. Radio RP. Record player TP. Tape player CBR. CB radio N. None (Circle all letters that apply)	Do you feel this household activity is. . . P. Pleasant? T. Tiring? B. Boring? S. Satisfying? D. Difficult? U. Unpleasant? F. Frustrating? NOF. No feeling, one way or another (Circle all letters that apply)	Your comments
NO H SO D SE R N F CHF DN	TV R RP TP CBR N	P T B S D U F NOF	
NO H SO D SE R N F CHF DN	TV R RP TP CBR N	P T B S D U F NOF	
NO H SO D SE R N F CHF DN	TV R RP TP CBR N	P T B S D U F NOF	
NO H SO D SE R N F CHF DN	TV R RP TP CBR N	P T B S D U F NOF	
NO H SO D SE R N F CHF DN	TV R RP TP CBR N	P T B S D U F NOF	
NO H SO D SE R N F CHF DN	TV R RP TP CBR N	P T B S D U F NOF	
NO H SO D SE R N F CHF DN	TV R RP TP CBR N	P T B S D U F NOF	
NO H SO D SE R N F CHF DN	TV R RP TP CBR N	P T B S D U F NOF	
NO H SO D SE R N F CHF DN	TV R RP TP CBR N	P T B S D U F NOF	
NO H SO D SE R N F CHF DN	TV R RP TP CBR N	P T B S D U F NOF	
NO H SO D SE R N F CHF DN	TV R RP TP CBR N	P T B S D U F NOF	

APPENDIX C

Contents of Household
Work–Task Codes

Nonhousehold Work Activities—Work
(0110–0180)
- 0110   Paid work
- 0120   Get ready for work
- 0130   To and from work
- 0140   Talk with other workers
- 0150   Business phone calls
- 0160   Meetings (including preparation)
- 0170   Seeking employment
- 0180   Volunteer work

School (0210–0240)
- 0210   At school
- 0220   Get ready for school
- 0230   To and from school
- 0240   Studying

Church (0300)
- 0300   Church

Diary (0400)
- 0400   Diary

Clean house—Whole process
(1000–1006)
- 1000   Whole process
- 1001   Dust house
- 1002   Vacuum house
- 1003   Clean upstairs
- 1004   Dust upstairs
- 1005   Clean downstairs
- 1006   Dust downstairs

Furniture (1010–1015)
- 1010   Clean furniture
- 1011   Dust furniture
- 1012   Polish furniture
- 1013   Straighten furniture
- 1014   Move furniture
- 1015   Fluff pillows

Windows, mirrors, pictures, lights
(1020–1029)
- 1020   Clean windows—Whole process
- 1021   Dust windows
- 1022   Clean window sill, ledges
- 1023   Clean blinds
- 1024   Clean draperies, curtains
- 1025   Open/shut draperies, curtains
- 1026   Clean mirrors
- 1027   Clean pictures
- 1028   Dust pictures
- 1029   Polish light fixtures

Floors, rugs, ceiling, baseboards,
surfaces, woodwork (1031–1039)
- 1031   Dust floors
- 1032   Sweep floors
- 1033   Scrub floors
- 1034   Vacuum floors

1035 Clean rugs
1036 Vacuum rugs
1037 Vacuum ceil-
      ings/baseboards
1038 Dust walls/woodwork
1039 Clean surfaces

Toys (1040)
1040 Clean up toys

Books, papers, magazines
(1051–1054)
1051 Clean up books
1052 Newspapers
1053 Papers
1054 Magazines

Glasses, dishes (1060)
1060 Clean glasses, dishes

Odds and ends (1070–1075)
1070 Clean odds and ends
1071 Dust odds and ends
1072 Clean ashtrays
1073 Clothes
1074 Decorative arranging
1075 Searching for things

Other's damage (1080)
1080 Clean house—Other's
      damage

Handling tools (1090–1092)
1090 Getting out/putting away

Cleaning tools
1091 Vacuuming maintenance
1092 Other appliance main-
      tenance

Kitchen—Whole process
(1100–1102)
1100 Whole process
1101 Dust kitchen
1102 Put things away

Kitchen—Oven (1111–1114)
1111 Clean oven
1112 Wash all stove
1113 Parts of stove
1114 Stove tops

Kitchen—Refrigerator (1120–1127)
1120 Whole process
1121 Defrost
1122 Outside
1123 Inside
1124 Vegetable bins
1125 Disposing of food
1126 Contents
1127 Make ice

Kitchen—Other appliances (1130)
1130 Other appliances

Kitchen—Floors, woodwork
(1141–1144)
1141 Sweep floors
1142 Wash floors
1143 Vacuum floors
1144 Clean woodwork

Kitchen—Furniture (1150–1151)
1150 Furniture
1151 Highchairs

Kitchen sinks (1160)
1160 Sinks

Kitchen—Counters, cabinets, shelves
(1171–1173)
1171 Counters
1172 Cabinets
1173 Dust pantry shelves

Kitchen—Curtains, windows (1180)
1180 Curtains, windows

Kitchen—Other's damage (1190)
1190 Other's damage

Bathroom—Whole process (1200)
1200 Whole process

Bathroom—Floors, walls, doors
(1211–1213)
1211 Floor (Clean)
1212 Vacuum floor
1213 Clean walls, doors

Bathroom—Sink (1220)
1220 Clean sink

Bathroom—Toilet (1230)
   1230 Clean toilet

Bathroom—Bowl (1240)
   1240 Clean bowl (Unspecified)

Bathroom—Showers, tubs
(1251–1252)
   1251 Showers
   1252 Tubs

Bathroom—Towels and other
Changeable items (1261–1262)
   1261 Towels
   1262 Put out new/clean items

Bathroom—Clean specific items
(1270)
   1270 Clean specific items

Bathrooms—Windows, glass (1280)
   1280 Clean windows, glass

Bathroom—Tile (1290)
   1290 Tile

Bedroom—Whole process
(1300–1301)
   1300 Whole process
   1301 Dust bedroom

Bedroom—Furniture (1310–1312)
   1310 Furniture
   1311 Dust furniture
   1312 Dressers

Bedroom—Beds (1321–1326)
   1321 Make beds
   1322 Remake beds
   1323 Fresh linen
   1324 Bedding
   1325 Strip beds
   1326 Prepare beds for sleep

Bedroom—Floor (1330–1332)
   1330 Floor
   1331 Dust floor
   1332 Vacuum floor

Bedroom—Clothes (1340)
   1340 Clothes

Bedroom—Toys (1350)
   1350 Toys

Bedroom—Dishes (1360)
   1360 Dishes

Bedroom—Other's damage (1370)
   1370 Other's Damage

Living room—Whole process
(1400–1401)
   1400 Whole process
   1401 Dust

Living room—Floors (1411–1412)
   1411 Vacuum floors
   1412 Dust floors

Living room—Furniture (1420–1421)
   1420 Furniture
   1421 Dust furniture

Living room—Objects (1431–1434)
   1431 Ashtrays
   1432 Dishes, glasses
   1433 Toys
   1434 Clothes, towels

Living room—Windows (1440)
   1440 Windows

Dining room—Whole process
(1450–1451)
   1450 Whole process
   1451 Dusting

Dining room—Floors (1460–1462)
   1460 Floors
   1461 Dust floors
   1462 Vacuum floors

Dining room—Furniture (1470)
   1470 Furniture

Dining room—Pictures (1480)
   1480 Pictures

Breakfast room—Floors (1490–1491)
   1490 Floors
   1491 Vacuum floors

Family, TV, rec. room, and den
(1500–1590)

1500 Family, rec., TV—Whole process
1510 Dust family, rec., TV room
1520 Vacuum family, rec., TV room
1530 Family, rec., TV—Toys
1540 Den—Whole process
1550 Den—Floors
1560 Vacuum den
1570 Dust den
1580 Den—Windows
1590 Den—Furniture

Hall, foyer—Whole process (1600)
1600 Whole process

Hall, foyer—Floors (1610–1612)
1610 Floors
1611 Dust floors
1612 Vacuum floors

Porch—Floors (1620)
1620 Floors

Porch—Dishes (1630)
1630 Dishes

Closets—Whole process (1640)
1640 Whole process

Closets—Floors (1650–1651)
1650 Floors
1651 Vacuum floors

Closet—Clothes (1660)
1660 Clothes

Basement—Whole process (1670)
1670 Whole process

Basement—Floor (1680–1681)
1680 Floor
1681 Vacuum floor

Basement—Objects (1690–1691)
1690 Specific objects
1691 Moving things around

Home and vehicle maintenance (1710–1790)
1710 Home repair/redecoration—Minor

1720 Home repair/redecoration—Carpentry
1730 Home repair/redecoration—Paint, wallpaper
1740 Drains
1750 Home security—Check, investigate
1760 Home security—Lights, heat
1770 Home security—Lock up
1780 Car maintenance
1790 Bike maintenance

Garbage (1810–1870)
1810 Collecting
1820 Bagging
1830 Carrying out
1840 Specific
1850 Running garbage/trash disposal
1860 Replacing can liners
1970 Cleaning cans/wastebaskets

Yard work (1900–1990)
1900 General
1910 Weeding
1920 Raking
1930 Mowing, trimming
1940 Picking
1950 Watering
1960 Digging
1970 Planting
1980 Check garden
1990 Clean immediate outside area

Meal preparation—Plan menus (2000–2040)
2000 Plan menus
2010 Plan menus—Today
2020 Plan menus—Future
2030 Consult cookbooks, recipes
2040 Copy recipes

Make meal (2100–2109)
2100 Whole process
2101 Partial process
2102 Coffee, tea

2103 Soft drinks
2104 Alcohol
2105 Mix milk
2106 Bottle—Baby
2107 Solids—Baby
2108 Fruit
2109 Soup

Make breakfast (2110–2112)
2110 Whole process
2111 Liquids
2112 Solids

Make dinner (2120–2141)
2120 Whole process
2121 Partial process
2122 Food—Defrost, out of refrigerator
2123 Assemble food
2124 Utensils
2125 Wash, clean food
2126 Slice, cut food
2127 Measuring
2128 Boiling water
2129 Grill
2130 Main dish—Whole process
2131 Main dish—Partial process
2132 Main dish—Put in, take out
2133 Main dish—Additional steps
2134 Vegetables—Whole process
2135 Vegetables—Partial process
2136 Salad—Whole process
2137 Salad—Partial process
2138 Salad—Dressing
2139 Bread, Rolls—Whole process
2140 Dessert—Whole process
2141 Freeze, store prepared foods

Make lunch (2150–2155)
2150 Whole process
2151 Partial process
2152 Sack—Whole process
2153 Sack—Partial process
2154 Sandwiches—Whole process

2155 Sandwiches—Partial process

Make snack (2160–2161)
2160 Whole process
2161 Solids

Outdoor cooking (2200)
2200 Outdoor cooking

Baking (2300–2310)
2300 Whole process
2310 Partial process

Set table (2400–2440)
2400 General
2410 General—Breakfast
2420 General—Dinner
2430 Specific
2440 Help other, supervise

Serve Meal (2500–2580)
2500 General
2510 Breakfast
2520 Dinner
2530 Lunch
2540 Desserts
2550 Bring out food
2560 Beverages
2570 Beverages—Pour
2580 Food on plates

Eating—General (2600)
2600 General

Eating—Breakfast (2610)
2610 Breakfast

Eating—Dinner (2620)
2620 Dinner

Eating—Lunch (2630)
2630 Lunch

Eating—Dessert (2640)
2640 Dessert

Eating—Snack (2650)
2650 Snack

Eating—Drink (2660–2663)
2660 General

2661 Soft
2662 Alcohol
2663 Coffee, tea

Eating—Solids (2670)
2670 Solids

Eating—Out (2680)
2680 Out

Eating—Cigarette (2690)
2690 Cigarette

Clean up after meals—Whole process (2700)
2700 Whole process

Clean up after meals—Put away food (2710)
2710 Put away food

Clean up after meals—Clear table (2720)
2720 Clear table

Clean up after meals—Wiping (2730)
2730 Wiping

Clean up after meals—Other's damage (2740)
2740 Other's damage

Clean up after meals—Breakfast (2750–2752)
2750 Whole process
2751 Put away food
2752 Clear table

Clean up after meals—Dinner (2760–2762)
2760 Whole process
2761 Put away food
2762 Clear table

Clean up after meals—Lunch (2770–2772)
2770 Whole process
2771 Put away unspecified things
2772 Clear table

Wipe table (2800–2810)
2800 Wipe table

2810 Wipe placemats—
       Tablecloth

Wash dishes—Whole process (2900–2905)
2900 All—Whole process
2901 Part—Whole process
2902 Glasses, cups, bottles—
       Whole process
2903 Pans—Whole process
2904 Utensils—Whole process
2905 Help someone—Whole
       process

Wash dishes—Dishwasher (2911–2914)
2911 Prepare dishes for dish-
       washer
2912 Load dishwasher
2913 Unload dishwasher
2914 On-off

Wash dishes—Before washing tasks (2921–2926)
2921 Stack
2922 Scrape
2923 Put in sink
2924 Soak
2925 Rinse
2926 Rinse glasses, cups

Wash dishes—After washing tasks (2931–2932)
2931 Dry
2932 Put away

Wash dishes—Polish silver (2940)
2940 Polish silver

Wash dishes—Wash appliances (2950)
2950 Wash appliances

Wash dishes—Breakfast (2960–2966)
2960 Whole process
2961 Load dishwasher
2962 Stack
2963 Put in sink
2964 Rinse
2965 Dry

2966   Put away

Wash dishes—Dinner (2970–2971)
2970   Whole process
2971 Put away

Wash dishes—Lunch (2980–2983)
2980   Whole process
2981   Load dishwasher
2982   Rinse
2983   Put away

Wash dishes—Snack (2990–2992)
2990   Whole process
2991   Load dishwasher
2992   Rinse

Care of clothes—Sewing
(3000–3060)
3000   Whole process
3010   Cut out
3020   Pinning
3030   Planning
3040   Mending
3050   Needlepoint, embroidery,
hooking
3060   Knit, crochet

Laundry (3100–3400)
3100   Whole process
3110   Beginning whole process
3120   Continue whole process
3130   Gather
3140   Hampers/chutes
3150   Pick up
3160   Sort dirty clothes
3170   Sort before drying
3180   Sort clean clothes
3190   Checking
3200   Planning
3210   Presoak
3220   Soap/bleach
3230   Fabric softner
3240   Washing—General
3250   Putting wash in
3260   Turning washer on
3270   Unload washer
3280   Change loads
3290   Drying—General

3300   Dryer—Putting clothes in
3310   Empty dryer
3320   Hang to dry
3330   Take down/put up line
3340   Take down lanudry
(hanging)
3350   Fold clothes
3360   Put away clean clothes
3370   Maintain laundry room/ap-
pliances
3380   Going down to laundry
3390   Bring up/in from laundry
3400   Laundromat

Hand laundry (3500–3510)
3500   Whole process
3510   Rinsed

Ironing (3600–3620)
3600   Whole process
3610   Support tasks
3620   Put clothes away

Hanging clothes (3700)
3700   Hanging clothes

Pack/unpack (3800)
3800   Pack/unpack

Shoe care (3900)
3900   Shoe care

Shopping—Groceries (4100–4160)
4100   General shopping
4110   Checking supplies
4120   Ads/coupons
4130   Lists
4140   Unload/carry in
4150   Washing/wrapping
4160   Put away

Errands (4200–4340)
4200   General
4210   Shopping
4220   Specific shopping
4230   Drug store
4240   Gas station
4250   Hardware
4260   Cleaners
4270   Newspaper

4280   Dentist
4290   Library
4300   Bank
4310   Post office
4320   By mail
4330   List making
4340   Unload/organize

Care of family—Wake family (5010)
5010   Wake family

Family medical (5021–5022)
5021   First aid
5022   Dispensing medicines

Gathering (5031)
5031   Finding
5032   Calling in

Ready to go (5040)
5040   Family ready to go

Family outings (5050–5051)
5050   General
5051   Specific

Biking (5060)
5060   Biking with family

Visit (5070)
5070   Visit family

Talk (5080)
5080   Talk with family

Written communication with family (5090)
5090   Written communication with family

Husband—Wake (5110)
5110   Wake

Husband—Chauffeur (5120–5123)
5120   General
5121   To/from train
5123   To/from work

Husband—Help (5130)
5130   Helping husband with work

Husband—Talk (5140–5141)
5140   Talk with husband

5141   Talk with husband and friend

Husband—Phone (5150)
5150   Phone calls

Husband—Visit (5160)
5160   Visit with husband

Husband/wife relations (5171–5173)
5171   Manage husband's possessions
5172   Recreation
5173   Affective care

Feed kids (5210–5219)
5210   General
5211   Breakfast
5212   Dinner
5213   Lunch
5214   Snack
5215   Liquids
5216   Solids
5217   Breast-feed
5218   Baby's bottle
5219   Solids to baby

Dress children (5220–5228)
5220   Whole process
5221   Pajamas
5222   Change of clothes
5223   Undress
5224   Lay out clothes
5225   Shoes
5226   Coats
5227   Shoes and coats
5228   Assist, supervise

Diapers (5230)
5230   Diapers

Wake children (5240)
5240   Wake children

Putting children to bed (5250–5254)
5250   Whole process
5251   Getting ready
5252   Tuck in
5253   Good night
5254   Special comfort

Children's naps (5261-5262)
5261 Putting down for
5262 Getting up from

Supervise children (5300-5390)
5300 Supervise children—Meals
5310 Supervise children—At play
5320 Supervise children—Nag
5330 Supervise children—Chores
5340 Supervise children—Discipline
5350 Intervening in children's fights
5360 Check children
5370 Watch children
5380 Arrange for baby-sitter
5390 Babbysitter—Take to or from

Taking children places (5410-5490)
5410 Escorting
5420 Carrying
5430 Chauffeur—General
5440 Chauffeur—To/from school
5450 Chauffeur—To/from nursery school
5460 Chauffeur—To/from lessons
5470 Chauffeur—To/from someone's house
5480 Chauffeur—To/from work
5490 Chauffeur—To/from professional services

Instructional aid for children 5500-5508)
5500 General help
5501 School
5502 Nonschool
5503 General play
5504 Read to/with
5505 Specific play
5506 Getting things out
5507 Being audience
5508 General attention

Instructional aid for children—Outings (5510)
5510 Family outings for children

Instructional aid for children—Walks (5520)
5520 Walk with children

Instructional aid for children—TV 5530)
5530 Watch children's TV shows

Instructional aid for children—Managing (5540)
Managing children's possessions

Interaction with children (5610-5680)
5610 Comfort children—Whole process
5620 Comfort children—Hold
5630 Talk with children—General
5640 Talk with children—About past/next day
5650 Talk with children—Listen
5660 Talk with children—Hello-good-bye
5670 Phone calls—Children
5680 Visit children

Clean children—Hygiene (5711-5719)
5711 Wash—Kids
5712 Wash—Baby
5713 Face, hands, feet
5714 Hair care
5715 Teeth care
5716 Checking
5717 Cut nails
5718 Toilet—Whole process
5719 Toilet—Specific

Clean Children—Bathe (5721-5725)
5721 Whole process
5722 Children in/out tub
5723 Preparing tub
5724 Tasks after bath
5725 Supervision

Self-waking (5810-5812)
5810 General
5811 Alarm
5812 Someone intrudes

Self-grooming (5820-5828)

5820   General
5821   Go to toilet
5822   Face/hands/teeth
5823   Shower/bath
5824   Comb/brush hair
5825   Wash hair
5826   Dry/set hair
5827   Wash hair tools
5828   Cosmetics

Self-dressing (5830–5834)
5830   Whole process
5831   Undress
5832   Partial process
5833   Assemble/select
5834   New clothes

Self-ready to go (5840)
5840   Ready to go

Self-medical (5850)
5850   Family medical—Self

Self-going to bed (5861–5863)
5861   Preparing—General
5862   Preparing—Alarm
5863   Remaining in bed

Self-recreation—Sleep (5901–5902)
5901   In bed
5902   Nap/doze

Self-recreation—Relax, rest
(5910–5912)
5910   General
5911   Sit down
5912   Doing nothing

Self-recreation—Thinking
(5921–5923)
5921   Planning present
        day—Whole
5922   Planning—Future
5923   Musing

Self-recreation—TV (5930–5934)
5930   General
5931   News
5932   Soap operas
5933   Specific programs
5934   On/off—Check programs

Self-recreation—Stereo (5940)
5940   Stereo

Self-recreation—Radio (5950)
5950   Radio

Self-recreation—Music and news
(5961–5962)
5961   Music (unknown source)
5962   News (unknown source)

Self-recreation—Read (5970–5974)
5970   General
5971   Book
5972   Magazines
5973   Newspaper
5974   In bed

Self-recreation—Hobby (5981–5984)
5981   Arts, crafts, collections
5982   Music
5983   Puzzles, games
5984   Out of home

Self-recration—Exercise (5990)
5990   Exercise

Care of pets and plants—Pets
(6100–6210)
6100   Whole process
6110   Feed
6120   Water
6130   Walk
6140   Letting out
6150   Bringing in
6160   Play
6170   Clean litter box
6180   Clean cages
6190   Clean pet
6200   Health care
6210   Check pet

Plants (6300–6340)
6300   General care
6310   Specific care
6320   Watering
6330   Potting
6340   Move-straighten

Interaction with others—Helping
nonimmediate family (7100–7110)

7100 General
7110 Chauffeuring

Neighboring (7210–7290)
7210 General favors
7220 Receiving favors
7230 Child care—Formal
7240 Child care—Informal
7250 Borrowing
7260 Driving
7270 Gatherings—
      Meetings/coffees
7280 Chatting/visiting
7290 Walked to neighbors

Written communication (7300)
7300 Written communication with
      nonimmediate family/friends

Talk (7400–7470)
7400 General with unknowns
7410 Specific with unknowns
7420 About past/next day with
      unknowns
7430 With nonimmediate family
7440 With children's friends
7450 With friends
7460 With service people
7470 With business relations

Phone calls (7500–7570)
7500 General
7510 General—Received
7520 General—Made
7530 Nonimmediate family
7540 Friends
7550 Medical
7560 General service/information
7570 Repair/service personnel

Visit (7600–7650)
7600 General
7610 Nonimmediate family
7620 Friends—General
7630 Friends—Leave home
7640 Friends—At home
7650 Nursing home/hospital

Entertaining (7710–7730)

7710 Planning/arranging
7720 Food preparation
7730 Receiving

Answering door (7800)
7800 Answering door

Household papers—Paperwork
(8100)

Finances (8210–8260)
8210 Bills—General
8220 Bills—Organizing
8230 Balancing
8240 Personal payments
8250 Credit
8260 Stocks/taxes

Mail (8310–8370)
8310 Bring in
8320 Open/read
8330 Sort
8340 Put away
8350 Wrap package
8360 Open gifts
8370 Wrap gifts

Get newspaper (8400)
8400 Get newspaper

Going to and from places—Arrive
home (9100)
9100 Arrive home

Left home (9200)
9200 Left home

Driving (9300)
9300 Driving

Biking (9400)
9400 Biking

Walking (9500)
9500 Walking

Movement in house (9600–9630)
9600 General
9610 Upstairs
9620 Downstairs
9630 Into/out of house

Household Activities Sorted by Husbands in Order of Accomplishment

1. Ate breakfast
2. Ate dinner
3. Ate snack
4. Bathed children
5. Called (specify whom)
6. Cleaned kitchen
7. Cleaned up after breakfast
8. Cleared dinner table
9. Combed hair
10. Drank coffee
11. Dressed
12. Dressed children
13. Dried dishes
14. Drove children to school or bus stop
15. Emptied garbage
16. Fed pet
17. Went to bank
18. Went to gas station
19. Got phone call (specify from whom)
20. Did household repair or remodeling
21. Left for work
22. Let pet out or in
23. Loaded dishwasher
24. Made beds
25. Made breakfast
26. Made coffee or tea
27. Made dinner
28. Made part of dinner
29. Made sack lunch
30. Made snack
31. Paid bills/handled finances
32. Played with children
33. Prepared for bed
34. Put away dinner leftovers
35. Put children to bed
36. Put dishes away
37. Put dishes in sink
38. Read book
39. Read magazine
40. Read newspaper
41. Rinsed dishes
42. Ran errand (where?)
43. Served dinner
44. Set table
45. Shaved
46. Showered or bathed
47. Straightened house
48. Talked with children
49. Talked with wife
50. Washed dishes
51. Washed up, brushed teeth

52. Watched TV
53. Went out (visiting, bowling, movies, etc.)
54. Went out for entertainment (other than theater, movie, or concert)
55. Wiped dinner table
56. Wiped stove top or kitchen counters
57. Woke children
58. Woke up
59. Woke wife
60. Did yard work
61. Anything else (specify)
62. Handled banking (checking, savings, and loans)
63. Did household budgeting
64. Planned change in or around the house
65. Planned family activities
66. Prepared household record or paperwork
67. Talked with friends or neighbors
68. Wrote a note or a letter
69. Wrote a greeting or condolence card
70. Went to store
71. Studied (what?)
72. Read brochures, articles, catalogs, etc.
73. Did arithmetic
74. Went to theater, concert, or movies
75. Visited friends or neighbors
76. Friends or neighbors visited
77. Went to governmental or official event or location
78. Wrote a list
79. Copied a document
80. Filed household records or paperwork
81. Helped children with schoolwork

Index